Roosevelt 'Rosey' Grier

with
Dennis Baker

ROSEY

AN AUTOBIOGRAPHY

THE
GENTLE GIANT

A DIVISION OF HARRISON HOUSE

TULSA

ROSEY
AN AUTOBIOGRAPHY
The
Gentle Giant

Copyright © 1986 by Roosevelt Grier
3005 South Grand
Los Angeles, California 90007

ISBN 0-89274-406-5

Honor Books
A Division of Harrison House, Inc.
P. O. Box 35035
Tulsa, Oklahoma 74153

CONTENTS

FOREWORD

by Roosevelt Kennedy Grier

This is the story of my dad's life, and I'm happy and proud to be a part of it. I'm proud of him for making a name for himself as one of the greatest defensive linemen in NFL history. I'm also proud of him for helping to apprehend the armed and dangerous assassin, Sirhan Sirhan. I admire all of the hard work he's put forth to help kids and senior citizens who are less fortunate than we. I think he's also beginning to sing better.

Not many kids get to meet the President of the United States and sleep in the White House. Since my dad is so busy helping people and speaking around the country, the best part about going to the White House was having that time alone with him. I cherish these special times when I do get to travel and be with him.

I love my dad and think he is one of the greatest men in the world. I'm only fourteen, so it's only natural that I think he can be impossible at times (I guess no one can be right all of the time). But, if I didn't feel that way, he'd probably be falling down on the hard-pressing job of being a parent.

But the best part of all this — the thing I'm happiest about and most thankful for — is the fact that, together, we both made the decision to serve Jesus Christ. Jesus made our broken, war-torn family whole again. Nothing could possibly be better than that! Enjoy!

ACKNOWLEDGMENTS

Willie Naulls deserves the credit for nagging long enough to get me started writing this book. Willie's the man when it comes to getting things launched.

Then along came Buddy Harrison, a publisher with a faith that won't let go. He saw the potential of this book when as yet there was none of it.

Next was Keith Provance, Harrison's manager, who proved himself an able workman by taking over where Willie left off. I'm sending Keith a bottle of liniment for his elbow, which should be sore from all the nudges he's had to give me.

To Connie Blackwell belongs immeasurable credit for the long, hard hours she spent assembling my story and giving it its first shape. It was a labor of love done by an expert for whom I am deeply grateful.

Humble and hearty thanks are due to a number of people who helped make the information in this book clear and accurate. First and foremost among them are the librarians at the Camarillo Library, Camarillo, California, who checked details, including the heights and weights of an untold number of athletes, with untiring perseverance and cheerfulness.

Then, in something akin to the chronological sequence of my life, special thanks must go to my sister, Eva Hodges, the family historian; Mrs. Skidmore of the Roselle School District's administration office who was actually willing and able to dig up the records of my years at Abraham Clark High School; Dave Baker, the man with the incredible memory at the Penn State sports information office (and Cynthia who was always able to find Dave); Joe Horrigan, historian at the NFL Hall of Fame who remembers most of it (including the spelling of Guglielmi) and has the rest at his fingertips; and Lillian Arbenz in the Rams' public relations department who dropped everything to help us meet an impossible deadline.

ROSEY

AN AUTOBIOGRAPHY

1

GEORGIA BOY

It was a Saturday night in 1937 and, at five, I was finally getting my first chance to fire the shotgun.

On Saturday nights, if Mama and Poppa were gone, we played the "gun game." We pretended someone was hiding in the barn or skulking around outside and then we'd fire away at them with the old twelve-gauge shotgun.

One of my older brothers would yell, "Who's out there?"

If no one said anything — and no one ever did — we would go to the window, and one of us would fire that big contraption up into the air. I'd watched my brothers do this a lot of times, and I had been nagging them for a chance to try my hand at it for longer than they could stand it. Anyway, this Saturday night, my oldest brother Mose finally said I could.

All I knew about it was that it was exciting and dangerous and loud — and that we'd get a lickin' if our folks found out about it. But I hadn't watched carefully to see how the older ones actually went about doing it. So, when the gun was handed to me, I pointed it out the open window and pulled the trigger: BLAM! The thing exploded and, the next thing I knew, I was picking myself up off the floor while my brothers laughed uproariously. Luckily, I had nestled the butt snugly against my shoulder, so nothing was hurt except my five-year-old dignity.

I was born July 14, 1932, in Cuthbert, Georgia. My parents named me Roosevelt after the man who was running on the Democratic ticket for President that summer. I suspect my folks may have sensed that he would stand for a square deal for black people, but, if not, he was the Democratic standard bearer and, in 1932, the "Solid South" was still very solid. Besides, Mr. Roosevelt had a good name in Georgia because he had established the Georgia Warm Springs Foundation to help poor people with polio to be able to afford to use the springs.

Warm Springs is about eighty miles north of Cuthbert. Cuthbert sits near the Alabama line in Randolph County, about eighty miles north of the Florida line.

My parents, Joseph and Ruthie Bell Grier, were Georgians by birth. My maternal grandfather, Mose Newkirk, had come to this part of Georgia from Wilmington, North Carolina, where his parents had been born in slavery.

Cuthbert is the county seat and the biggest town around. With four thousand people, that's not saying much, but it seemed big to me. The countryside is hilly and used mostly for growing peanuts. The humidity from the Gulf makes the summer heat seem intense. The unbearable heat is one of my most vivid memories.

Poppa was a farmer, and life was hard, but no harder than for many Americans in the thirties. Most black farmers in the South were sharecroppers. A sharecropper grows his crops on another man's land. For the use of the land, buildings, livestock, and equipment (and sometimes seed, fertilizer, insecticide, and cash or credit for family living expenses) the sharecropper paid the landowner at least half and often all the crops he could grow. It was a system that perpetuated many of the patterns that had prevailed during slavery days.

Somehow, my dad and mom had managed to escape that trap. He rented our farm from a white landowner for cash. That meant we raised our own food and made our own deals with anybody who would buy from us. We didn't make a lot of money because we did not have the best land. We rented land through a government program, and it could be pretty rocky soil. We raised our own crops, then hired out to other farmers for cash or in exchange for labor. We worked in cotton, peanuts, watermelon, cane, and soybeans. A lot of pecans and cattle are grown there, also.

At the end of each summer, a big threshing machine made the rounds of the farms to harvest the crops. That was when everybody had to get out into the fields and work hard, and all the neighbors helped each other.

Harvest time is traditionally a glad time for a farmer, but not always so in Georgia in the 1930s, especially among the sharecroppers. That was because it was a time for the reckoning of accounts. All season long a sharecropper was running up a bill for the stuff he bought from the landowner on credit. Once the crop was in and sold, that debt had to be paid off. Whatever was left was the sharecropper's to keep. Many times that net left over amounted to no more than a few dollars. The very best most of them got was fifty dollars, but many times they would find they had just "broke even." And, what made it worse, most of the time the figuring was done by the owner because the sharecropper was deficient in math and reading. Many a sharecropper was left feeling cheated but with no way of proving it.

We were a little better off by renting our land outright. At least, we always had plenty of food. I guess that is where my love of good food started, sitting up to the breakfast table every day with country ham, eggs, grits, biscuits, homemade cane syrup, corn, and, sometimes on Sunday mornings, fried chicken. Things were good enough for us that I was able to attend school. The owners of the big farms would encourage sharecroppers to take their children out of school.

"Look at that great big family you have. You're really fortunate to have so much help. Those children ought to be out working on the farm," landowners would say. "What good is school going to do them?"

Racial suppression was woven deeply into the fabric of life in south Georgia in the thirties. But it was not so deep that my father was robbed of all self-respect. He was supporting us and able to keep his head above water. That means a lot to any man. As a result, I grew up without any particular hostility against white people. Whatever prejudice they felt against my race did not seem to cause me to suffer unduly. To me, people were people and their color had nothing to do with who they were.

What was much more real and threatening to me was death. My first awareness of death came when I was very young. While we lived on the Moyer place near Cuthbert, some kids I used to play and fight with had an uncle — just a teenager — that they talked about with both admiration and apprehension.

"That boy is going to kill somebody someday," they would say.

One Sunday in the churchyard, a group of guys got into a fight and, sure enough, that boy they always talked about took out a knife and stabbed another boy to death. The victim was just a youngster and the horror of the violence and the reality that someone could bleed to death and never come back, gripped me with fear.

The kids at school and church, of course, found out that death frightened me, and they teased me about it.

"Roosevelt," they would say, "you're going to die."

That used to make me cry, which is why they did it. I thought a lot about death, though, of course, I never told my parents or any other adult about it. So well did that fear become nurtured in my heart that it stayed with me for years.

When my brother Mose married and moved a few miles away, I went to visit him just about every Friday night and Saturday so I could listen to the Grand Ole Opry and things like that on his radio. We didn't have a radio. We didn't even have electricity. I walked both ways to Mose's house and had to go through the woods at a place called Culpepper Fork.

People said ghosts hung around there, the ghosts of folks who had been killed in accidents at the bad curve in the road. One of the ghosts was named "Pete." The thought of meeting a dead man's ghost frightened the daylights out of me, so I used to run from the Fork all the way through the woods, a good distance. Any sound would make me run faster. Whenever I approached that curve, my heart started to beat and my adrenalin started to flow as the terror spread through me.

The positive result of this was that I got a lot of experience running. I built both speed and endurance in those days around Culpepper Fork. The faster I ran, it seemed, the lighter I felt.

I guess I need to qualify my fear. It never stopped me from going over to my brother's place. It just made me run faster. If that was the worst it did, it must not have been all that bad.

My dad used to say, "A man can be run home, but if he's run past his home, he has no place else to run to."

He meant by this that if you got in a fight and someone chased you home, that was where you had to make your stand. There could be no escaping from there. So, I learned a common-sense kind of courage that never permitted the fear I felt to take over completely. Other kids might chase me home but, from then on, they were in a fight! I developed my arm throwing rocks. You could bet on one thing: If you missed me, you were going to get hit with a rock. I never tried to hurt anyone, but I learned early how to make a stand and ward off my attackers.

My first taste of serious violence came when I was about nine. My brother, Arthur, and I went into a little wide place in the road called Benevolence (about eight miles north of Cuthbert) one Saturday night. Benevolence boasted two stores, but it was the only place to go on Saturday nights.

A big crowd of people had gathered as usual. Arthur and I were standing around watching the adults. I was standing next to a man who suddenly got into a violent argument with another man just a few feet away. The crowd was so thick, I couldn't have stepped away even if I had had enough sense to. It was scary to hear them yelling, saying horrible things. I didn't want to get involved, so I just kept my head down.

But suddenly it all ended with the loud blast of a pistol. The man I was standing nearest to fell backward to the ground. He never said a word. The bullet had gone right into his head. His face was a horrible sight. I stared down at him. I don't know if he was still alive for a moment, but his right leg bent up at the knee, like he was trying to get back on his feet. I cannot describe the shock and horror I felt in that moment. Deadly violence and bloodshed became loathsome to me in a way that has never left me. I have never understood how people could do such horrible things to each other. My dad said we should "love each other as we loved ourselves."

Another Saturday, Arthur and I were in town, and he got into an argument with a man who took a shot at him. Arthur had to run for his life and he was burning with humiliation when he got home. "I'm going to get even with that sap-sucker!" he told me as he grabbed the shotgun out of the closet.

I was really alarmed and worried for my brother, so I said, "I'll go with you."

We sat up all night in a wooded area outside the man's house laying for him. Happily, he never appeared.

7

I don't know what I would have done if he had. Would I have had the courage to stop my brother from doing something we would have regretted? Or would I have gone along and allowed him to ruin our lives? I choose to think not.

After we sat outside all night, Arthur felt better. He had done something to ease his embarrassment. But, sometimes, things are not so easily solved.

The story of Cy Saul, a black man, was told many times in my hearing. It bespoke the underlying discontent that all black people felt about living in a "Jim Crow" society. Cy Saul was a strong, proud man with a farm and family. He taught his young son to respect himself as well as all other people — black or white.

The boy complained that white kids would drive by him on his way to and from school, hooting at him and calling him names.

"What should I do, Dad?" he asked.

"It's not even worth fighting over," his dad would say.

"But, Dad, the things they say hurt bad!"

"I know it. But just because people call you something doesn't mean that's what you are. When they do that, the Good Book says to turn the other cheek. Only a fool lets other folks know they got him to lose his temper. You just got to let it go by and act like it don't bother you."

"But, remember, son," Cy Saul added. "There does come a time in every man's life when he has to take a stand for what he believes is right."

One day, Cy and his son were in town walking down the street. In the South at that time, if white people were coming down the street, blacks were supposed to get off the sidewalk and let them pass. Cy Saul resignedly stepped off the sidewalk into the street, but he looked up in horror to see that his boy had not come with him. The whites he was challenging on the sidewalk turned out to be a couple of unruly bullies who knocked the boy down for his impertinence.

Cy's son got up, tears in his eyes, and looked at his father, "Dad, is this the time?"

"Just get yourself on home to your mama as fast as your legs can carry you," Cy Saul told his son. Then he walked up onto the sidewalk and confronted the two whites: "You knocked my boy down and I ain't gonna stand for it."

"Oh, yeah, nigger," one of them sneered. "Whatcha gonna do about it?"

Cy Saul, who knew he already had done enough to earn a flogging, if not a lynching, hauled back and smashed a hard right into the man's jaw that sent him sprawling to the sidewalk. The other man started to pull a gun, but Saul grabbed him and took it away from him. Now his fate was sealed: he was a crazy, "uppity" nigger who needed hanging. In the melee that followed, he shot three men, killing one. And he managed to get away and arrive home ahead of his pursuers.

He hugged his wife and son, said goodbye and headed for the swamps.

When the men chasing him got to his house, his wife told them he'd run off but she didn't know where. Their tracking dogs followed him into the swamps where they lost him.

Cy Saul knew the swamps like the back of his hand. He set traps to discourage his trackers and succeeded in hurting a number of them. He continued to elude them so that his case was becoming notorious. The local authorities couldn't afford to allow a black man to escape justice so they went to the state prison and found a man who knew the swamps. They promised him his freedom if he would find Cy Saul and bring him in — dead or alive.

This man "escaped" from prison and was chased into the swamps where, eventually, he met up with Cy Saul. He took time to win Saul's confidence, and then, one night, when Cy's guard was down, the man shot him in his sleep. He brought the body out to prove he had fulfilled his half of the deal, and the townspeople took it and dragged it through the streets in triumph.

Saul's story ended sadly, but it taught me that there comes a time when a man needs to stand up for what he believes to be the truth, even if it costs him his life. Although Cy Saul was a murderer, he was also a symbol to me and to many of the black people in south Georgia. His story showed that no matter how easy-going and happy we might seem to be in the face of racism, it was nevertheless something all of us hated and knew was wrong.

Always I wondered in the back of my mind if I were called on by circumstances to take a stand, what would I do?

One time we came perilously close to a serious racial incident with a neighbor. He was a sheriff and a farmer both, and he raised corn in a fenced-in field. Once one of our cows got through the fence and into his corn. He brought her back, cursing the cow and everything else in his way.

"Look, don't be cussing in front of my family," Poppa said. But the man kept right on.

"You stay right here," my dad told him.

He went into the house, and we had to hold him so he wouldn't get his shotgun and go after that sheriff! My dad would not allow his wife and children to be exposed to that kind of language no matter who was using it! Until I heard that sheriff, I didn't know anything about foul language except that it was a sin. The sheriff thought my dad was crazy and apparently didn't take the incident very seriously — so nothing else happened. In later years, I have thought it was a miracle that my dad was not at least beaten up, a black man talking to a sheriff that way.

There was a little white girl at a store where we went to buy soda crackers and cheese about a mile down the road from us. I used to play with her and her brothers. As we began to get older, her father wanted me to call her "Miss Lady." No longer could I call her by her first name — when he was around! But I just thought he was a little peculiar.

So, throughout my childhood, the violence and ugliness of segregation were always there, just below the surface. They were underlying threads, but not the entire cloth of my growing up years.

2

CHILDHOOD DAYS

My parents were good people, easy to honor. Life was hard, but seldom miserable. We never had luxuries. At times, we only had the barest necessities. But I would not trade my childhood for that of any other person.

I was child number nine in a string of thirteen to whom my mother gave birth, so my parents didn't have time to show each child very much individual attention. But, as the custom was in those days, the older children in the family kind of looked after the younger ones.

Farm life in the country for a boy like me meant working long days in the fields and walking miles to school. But I was never given a curfew like any city kid would be today (and like I give my own son). That Saturday night Arthur and I spent lurking outside the house of the man who'd taken a shot at him was never questioned by my parents as I recall. They probably figured we were out hunting. Besides, life in the country then was not filled with the fear and anxiety that seems to go with big city life today.

Nor did my parents ever say I had to go to school. I went because I wanted to learn. And I worked because we all had to work to live.

One of the best things about growing up in that time and setting was the near absence of peer pressure in the ways we think of it today.

Today youngsters (and all of us) are bombarded by many sorts of images and notions through television. The pressure to conform to mass norms is nearly overwhelming. I don't say that to deny that there were forces at work which shaped me. But the forces that did work on me and the way they worked left a lot more room for healthy individuality.

The back-breaking work of the fields was the big reality of my early life, but I was also free to roam the hills and woods, wade in the creeks and play with the dogs. Some of my earliest memories are of our dogs. On the Moyer place, a fairly rocky farm, we had two dogs, Charlie Brown and Staple. Poppa liked to go hunting with his shotgun and the dogs. The dogs, of course, were supposed to go ahead and chase the game out into the open. But old Charlie Brown had his own idea about how long a hunting expedition should last. Poppa would take them hunting and, about an hour later, Charlie would show up back at the house.

My dad would come home disgustedly muttering, "That dog!"

One time, Poppa started out hunting and the dogs turned around and came back almost as soon as they got out of sight of the house. Poppa got so exasperated that he shot at them, and buckshot went flying all around the yard. That was an exciting day.

On Sundays, we went to church. Sometimes we rode in a wagon pulled by mules. Other times we walked. Everyone went to church and, many times, each family brought food and spread it out on tables under the trees in the churchyard. You could go from one family's table to the next, sampling. The food was good — plain, wholesome home cooking. The grown-ups exchanged the week's news and gossip, and the kids ran around making friends.

We went to the Baptist church which was right next to the Methodist church. Whatever differences kept those two churches separate must not have been very important. Each congregation attended the other's revivals, "singin's," socials, and potlucks.

I liked church. It meant being with other kids and seeing all the people. When the pastor got to preaching good, he would start to talk in a sort of humming or half-singing tone, and the people would begin shouting. It was very emotional, and I always felt good when I went to church. I felt free from all those things that caused me to feel bad during the week, the fears and lonely times.

I was baptized when I was seven, not as a result of any personal conversion or religious experience, but because it was expected of me and everyone else did it. Nevertheless, I felt an inner satisfaction about being baptized. The camaraderie and friendship at church were really important to me, and I wanted to be a part of it in every way I could.

The church was the biggest thing in our world beyond the farm. Magazines and newspapers did not arrive at our mailbox, so the world beyond Randolph County was largely unknown to us. And though I was happy, sometimes I still wondered if what I was experiencing was all there was to life.

I don't know if I thought about it then — I don't imagine I did — but it occurs to me in looking back that I seldom had the undivided or private attention of either of my parents. As I said earlier, that's one of the consequences of living in a big family. I must not have resented it, because I cannot recall ever having wanted one of my older brothers or sisters to leave home. Instead, I remember clearly the feelings of grief that came each time one of them left.

As I said, Mama bore thirteen little Griers. Mose was (and is) the oldest. Then came Robert, whom we called Butler, Eula, James, Eva, Arthur, me, Alice, Willie Bee, Sammy Lee and Rufus Carl, nicknamed Baba (which we pronounced "Bay-bay"). An older brother died at birth and an older sister, Katherine, died with pneumonia when she was five.

All of us were born at home, most with the assistance of a midwife. Doctors and hospitals were out of the reach of most people because of the expense, and I never heard of a hospital around where we lived that would even admit black people.

My mother was a hardy woman. Any woman who wasn't could never have survived under such circumstances. But time took its toll and when she began to give birth to number thirteen, something went wrong. Mama was crying and groaning. I had never heard her carry on like that, and I didn't want her to hurt.

"I never hurt so bad in my life," she finally cried out to my dad.

I sat in the other room and felt awful because I couldn't do anything to help her. Poppa became desperate and went after a doctor. I don't know how he talked that man into coming out to our farm but, when he went in to examine my mother, he became very angry! He yelled at Poppa, "Why didn't you tell me she was just pregnant?"

The doctor was mad, but he helped to ease my mother's pains and Baba arrived safely.

Mama was a neat lady, hardworking and honest. She kept all of us and the house clean. She corrected us, and she comforted us. She was not real heavy and stood only about five-feet-four. In my early memories of her, I see her cooking over a wood stove with a child pulling at her apron or out in the yard washing clothes in a big iron pot with a scrubboard or in the field with a hoe.

Poppa was usually easy-going, not interested in making a lot of rules. But he would whip us if occasion demanded.

I can remember him more than once giving me fair warning: "Roosevelt," Poppa would say, "I'm not going to whip you this time, but if you do it again, I'll whip you twice."

Well, I would always wind up doing it again and getting two whippings at once, because my dad kept his word.

My mom would never whip me. "Boy, you wait till your papa comes home. I'm going to tell him what you did," she would say.

"Mama, I can't stand to wait for Poppa to get home. Please give me my whippin' now. Please!"

"No, Roosevelt, you wait for your papa."

"Mama, why can't you whip me now?"

I never got an answer to that question. She must have known what most sons discover early: a mother's spankings are much lighter affairs than a father's — and a light spanking has little effect on behavior.

My dad's spankings were not light and they taught me to walk in paths of righteousness for my fanny's sake! But he was never mean or abusive. He made us feel like doing the right thing because to do otherwise would cause pain.

He was only about five-feet-eight, and more than one of his sons could look down on him in time. But there was never any doubt about who was in charge in our family.

People often remarked about Joseph Grier's great wisdom. He had no formal education, yet people came frequently to him for advice. They would sit and talk in the kitchen or the front room, and usually the visitor went off feeling better.

I admired his ability to do that, and, more than almost anything, I wanted to be like him in that regard when I grew up. His uncommon good sense was a gift honed by hard experience, not anything he might have learned from a book.

Poppa was also a man of courage and integrity. A lot of black people in the South were so intimidated by whites they wouldn't look one in the eye when they talked. But my dad was never afflicted with that problem — eye contact was always part of his conversation with anybody, black or white.

I bragged, "My dad's not afraid of anybody." He had gone beyond the example of Cy Saul and set a better one for us of how to blend and balance courage and wisdom in a way that allowed life to proceed with a measure of dignity. That is a wonderful gift for any man to bestow on his children.

The whole family used to sit on the porch on warm evenings and sing — usually hymns and spirituals. The neighbors would hear us and come over to the house to listen and join in. We Griers sounded good together. I remember my mother singing around the house and the yard. It seems, thinking back, someone was singing at our house nearly all the time.

As the years passed, the older brothers left the farm — Butler and James followed Mose. That left Arthur and me as the two oldest boys. So, Arthur succeeded to the unenviable job of being the chief hand on the farm. Whether out of dislike for his job or in response to more inner urges, at age 16 Arthur up and left home to marry a girl named Bertha May.

Poppa felt hurt by Arthur's departure, and, after that, he'd sometimes say to me, "Well, I guess you'll be running off to get married, too."

And I would say, "No, Poppa, I'm going to stay with you. I won't leave you, Poppa." I wanted him to feel good again.

I, of course, inherited Arthur's job, but Poppa knew I was still too young to take on the full load of responsibilities. My youthful naiveness was displayed one day when I announced, "Poppa, I'll work a year if you'll just pay me a whole dollar." In those days a dollar seemed like a fortune to me!

It gave me an uncomfortable feeling to be the oldest boy at home. There was so much responsibility. Poppa eventually began to really depend on me. What I wanted most by that time, however, was to go to school. Even back when I was six and seven, I had started getting up early in the morning to work hard in the fields in order to get through with my chores in time for school.

The first school I attended was Pleasant Grove, a one-room affair heated by a wood-burning stove that sat squarely in the middle of the room. Once I went home with a big burn on my arm after being forced up against that stove when all the kids were crowding around trying to get warm.

There were woods on the way to school, and we would scare one another with stories about "haints," or ghosts. It was exciting to run through those woods feeling that something was about to "git" us.

But there was nothing exciting about getting the immunization shots administered by a Randolph County nurse who came out to our school from town. When we saw her coming, we would all scatter like rabbits when a dog barks. We would climb trees in the nearby woods or hide in the weeds. Once when she was sighted on the road, I ran into a big clump of weeds and slid on a snake. It could have bit me, but it didn't. That really scared me, but not enough to make me want to go back and get my shot!

The Moyer place was the first place I lived. That's where I was born. We lived there for several years, but some time in the late thirties we moved to a new place, "Miss Nimm" Crodger's where there was a large barn and a really neat house. The barn had a tin roof. We would climb up into the loft and jump out the door onto big bundles of hay. One day, Arthur and I decided to climb up to the ridgepole and slide down the roof. Sometimes, we would get to sliding so fast that we couldn't stop at the edge. I was a little afraid of that. The ground was awfully hard! But we never broke any bones.

Arthur always wanted to do stuff like that. Sometimes, like a lot of older brothers, he would bully me. Once we got into a fight, and I thought he was going to kill me because he beat my head against the ground. I broke away and ran home, and he chased me all the way. My way of fighting was to get on my back and kick. So when Arthur ran into the house, I was waiting for him with my feet up, and I kicked that boy backwards really hard. It felt good to have some means of defense that worked!

Two of our sisters would take sides in our fights. Eula would take Arthur's, and Eva would take my side. That is how our fights generally ended up, paired off two against two. Sometimes one side would win, sometimes the other.

Arthur liked practical jokes. One of his favorites was to wait until the workers helping out in someone's field took a short nap after lunch. Then he would go over and tie the legs of one of them together. When it was time to go back to work, Arthur would yell out, " 'The Man' is coming," and the guy would jump up and fall when he tried to run.

I thought that was funny, but I never liked the idea of acting one way when "the Man" was there and another way when he wasn't. I thought you had to be who you are at all times. You should not be one way when someone is watching you and another way when you are by yourself. I made up my mind to be the same all the time.

Years later, when I was working in a factory in New Jersey, I went to sleep on a break. When I woke up, the boss was standing there looking at me.

I said, "How you doing?"

He said, "Were you taking a nap?"

"Yeah," I answered.

He said, "Okay," and walked away.

I remembered how workers in the peanut fields used to jump up and act apologetic. Even if I lost my job, I was not going to do that.

I learned a lot of lessons about life through Arthur. I remember one in particular: It started with our two mules. We had a black one and a brown one. The black one was ornery, real "mulish." You would be riding along on him thinking you had it made and all of a sudden find yourself on the ground.

One day he threw me off and almost killed me. I decided I'd had it with that mule. I was not going to ride him anymore. I took him to the barn where I knew I would probably find Arthur because, every day at lunch, I had noticed him going there. And, when I got in the barn, there was Arthur, selling liquor to various folks.

I said, "I'm going to tell Poppa."

He gave me a whole bottle of whiskey not to tell, and I consumed most of that bottle in short order.

I was not quite eleven, and I had heard that drinking liquor and eating watermelon at the same time would kill you. We were working in the watermelon patch that day and, during the afternoon break, they cut some melons. I had to eat some in order not to arouse my dad's suspicion.

Maybe it was the power of suggestion, but, after I ate, I was a sick boy! I spent the whole afternoon laughing and being sick and was the silliest thing at the supper table that night. I tried to get out of eating, but my dad said, "Boy, you have to eat." I thought I was going to die. It was like being in a fog for days. I was laughing, but I was hurting too. This went on for nearly a week, after which I said, "Never again." I'll always be grateful to Arthur for the lesson I learned that summer.

After living at "Miss Nimm's" place for some time, we moved near Pumpkintown, then to the Lonnie Ware farm, the last place we lived in Georgia. Living at the Ware farm also meant a long walk — ten miles! — to school. I went every day I could, but there was a catch. Those were the days after Arthur got married and I became the oldest one at home with more and more responsibilities and chores to take care of. If I got up at four o'clock and worked until seven, my dad would let me go to school. The catch was that if I was late to school, the teacher gave me a whipping. More often than not, thanks to that long walk, I was late — alas.

On the way to school, I had to pass a family of mean boys. They would chase anyone who passed. I and most of the other kids learned to really "truck" passing this house. I wanted to be braver about it and not show my fear by running, but my feet would start running in spite of me.

I must have been serious about school and learning, considering what I had to endure to get there every day.

3

FAMILY TIES

As you can see, my closest associate in my childhood was my brother Arthur. But what of the others? I loved them all, and as I've grown older, I have come to value each member of my family more highly than I did when I was younger. Now I wish that we had all gotten to know each other more intimately in those early years than we did.

My oldest brother Mose is a quiet, easy-going person and peaceful to be around. He and his wife, Ozie Lee, have six children and still live back in my birthplace, Cuthbert, Georgia. He is the only one of us to remain in the South.

What I most enjoyed about my brother Butler in those early years was his great sense of humor. He loved to laugh. He lives today in Linden, New Jersey, with his wife, Edna.

My sister Eula is and always was a very thrifty person. She married young, and her husband was in the armed services. She saved the money he sent home so that when he got out, they had a nice nest egg. I stole some quarters out of her purse one day to buy candy, the only time in my life I remember stealing anything. It left me with a guilty conscience, besides which I had to eat the candy all at once to keep from getting caught. I made up my mind not to ever do that again, and I didn't. I still feel bad about doing it.

When her husband, King Blackwell, came home from the service, his head was all banged up. He didn't get wounded in the war. He got hurt in a Southern town. He and some other black servicemen were returning home, and their car was stopped by the police in this town.

The police said, "I guess you boys have got pictures of a lot of white girls in your wallets."

Unfortunately, one of the guys did have a picture of a white girl from overseas in his billfold, and the police beat them. I mean, they really whipped them. My brother-in-law was hurt badly. I was stunned by the whole thing. That was one of the few times as a kid that I remember being just full of anger. Somehow, however, I didn't realize that this was a general attitude. I thought it was an isolated incident, just a town where the police were mean and looking for excuses to beat up people.

Eula is a widow now and lives in Roselle, New Jersey. She and King had three children: Leonard, Robert and Joyce.

James was a hard worker but different from the rest of us. We called him "the black sheep." He had his own ways. He could work hard, but he didn't want to work steady. But, as far as I was concerned, James was tops because he could be depended on when I was in college to give me pocket money. He also lives in Linden with his wife, Rachel.

Eva was next in line, but I'll discuss her later.

Arthur lives in Irvington, New Jersey, with his wife Lizzie.

Alice and I were close because she was my little sister, very close to me in age. She married Gordie Williams, and they have three children. They live in Somerset, New Jersey. She is a lot like I always wanted to be: smart, strong, and with a good head for business. She helped me when she could, even letting me use her car one year at Penn State when mine was out of commission.

Willie Bee was a good athlete. I liked to watch him play, but we were never really close until recent years. When I had the opportunity to get to know him, I was too busy with my own life and he with his. He married and had a baby, but the marriage didn't work out. Later, he remarried and this time is doing fine. He and his wife Stella and their daughter Keisha live in Roselle.

I probably paid more attention to Sammy Lee as he grew up than I did to any of the others. He was the only one besides me to finish high school. I watched him play ball, and got him a tryout with the New York Giants. Sam did not do too badly but, later on, the Giants cut him. He works at the University of California in Los Angeles and has four children.

Baba has four children now, and a good job. He lives in Linden with his wife Ruby. He has a likable personality and seems to be enjoying life. A traumatic thing happened to him when he was two or three years old. Sammy Lee and Willie Bee were in the house playing while Mama was outside washing clothes in the big iron wash pot over an open fire. They got the shotgun down, and somehow it was pointed at Baba when the trigger got pulled. Four of his toes were almost shot off. Sammy Lee went running out to Mama, yelling that they had shot Baba.

She didn't understand what he was saying at first. When he got her attention, she ran in the house to find Willie Bee trying to tie the toes back on Baba's foot. They were all crying. Mama wrapped a blanket around the foot and stood out in the road until a man came along who would take her to the hospital. The doctor cut the toes the rest of the way off, taped up the foot, and sent him back home.

It took a long time for the family to get over that. Anytime we talked about it, we would all cry. We tried to comfort Baba, but whenever his nearly toe-less foot hurt or whenever he happened to think about it, he would cry loudly.

"Mama," he would say, "they shot my toes off. They shot me, Mama."

My older sister Eva was the one who brought home to me the reality of life and death. One day while we were working in the field together, she asked me the hardest question I had ever been asked.

She said, "Roosevelt, what are you going to do when you grow up?"

Eva tells me that I said, "Well, there's one thing for sure. I'm not going to be carrying peanut bags all my life."

"What are you going to be doing then?"

That seemed an odd question to me, because I planned to always stay with Mama and Poppa. When I told her that, she asked me something that I thought was not just odd, but terrible!

"What will you do when Mama and Poppa die?"

I thought, "What a cruel thing to say!" Of course, I had no answer for her. She had uttered the unthinkable. It disturbed me and made me angry, but I think Eva sensed something about me that made it important for me to face that question and begin thinking about it.

Eva has a tremendous heart for people and, not surprisingly, she chose nursing as a career. She lives in Elizabeth, New Jersey, with her husband Rastus Hodges. They have five children.

Before that day in the field when Eva asked me that awful question, I had never thought about what I wanted to do with my life. I didn't even know what a person was supposed to do with his life. I thought you just lived your life and, whatever came, you went along with it and did it. To have some choice, some authority and control over life, did not seem possible.

That day in the peanut field, I could never have guessed what lay ahead for me. Nothing I had seen or heard by that day pointed beyond anything more than dirt farming in south Georgia. And, yet, Eva somehow knew I needed to start thinking about the future.

It is impossible to see one's self and life objectively or to pick out all the things that shape one's character. But no one could argue that those first eleven years of my life on the farmlands of south Georgia began to form the Rosey Grier of today. I can see in them the roots of a great desire for people to love one another, to be fair and just in their dealings with one another, and an intense dislike of violence. Also, I see the roots of a deep love for this country — nurtured in the rocky soil of south Georgia.

4

A NEW WORLD
IN JERSEY

In 1943, my father made a decision that affected my life in a big way. "Roosevelt," he announced, "I'm going up North. I want you to be the head of the house and take care of the family until I send for you."

My mother's sister, Lulabelle Kegler, lived in New Jersey and had been writing to my dad for some time.

"Bring your family out from down there, boy. Move your family," she kept writing. The war had made a boom town out of the entire industrial north; jobs were plentiful and there was room for us in Aunt Lulabelle's house as soon as Poppa found a job.

My older brothers and sisters, except Mose and Eula, had already made the move and located either in New Jersey or Pennsylvania. So my dad got on the train that historic day, leaving Mama and me with instructions to sell the furniture and farm equipment.

At eleven years of age, the job of being the man of the house fell on my shoulders as a painful burden. I had no choice but to make the best of it, but I didn't like it very much. In one day I was robbed of my boyhood freedoms and saddled with the responsibility of looking after a household of seven people (Eula was living with us while her husband, King Blackwell, was away in the army). I had never before felt tied down like that. It was so unpleasant that I developed a dread of ever letting it happen to me again — and that was something which would affect my relationships with people for many years to come.

After Poppa left, I did a lot of fishing, but it was not for recreation. I had to find food for Mama to prepare so we could eat. One time, I hauled in an eel, the first time I ever caught one. We liked eel. Another time, I killed more than a dozen birds roosting on the ground with one blast of buckshot from the shotgun. That was great. We ate birds for days.

But I recalled more carefree days with longing. Like the time my friend John Arthur Wilson and I got the shotgun out of my house, loaded it, and went looking for something to shoot. We saw this pig out in the barnyard and shot at it. We hit it, but we also managed to set the barn on fire at the same time.

What a commotion that caused! The alarm was raised and out came Butler, James, Eva, Arthur, and Eula, running to put out the fire. I got a whipping when my dad got home from the fields, and John Arthur got two. He got one at my house and another one when he got home. That's the way it worked then. If you had been visiting and got a whipping, your folks gave you another one when you got home for having to be spanked in the first place.

(By the way, the pig died, and we feasted on pork roasts and bacon for some weeks after that.)

Now, in the autumn of 1943, Poppa and my big brothers were gone. There was no one to put out the fires but me. That realization was much more painful than any number of whippings.

Another thing added to the distaste for responsibility I was acquiring so rapidly in those days. And that was that I had already decided hunting was not one of my favorite pastimes. It probably started one afternoon several years before when I had taken the shotgun and gone looking for something to shoot. I kept walking through the woods hoping to spot a rabbit, but they all kept out of sight. Finally, I saw a fair-sized bird sitting up in a tree. And I shot it. But the moment I saw its feathers flying and its shattered body falling to the ground, I felt remorse. "Roosevelt," I scolded myself, "you wasted that bird."

Even snakes, as much as they frightened me, were exempt. I didn't want to kill one of them unless it was necessary. Once Arthur and I were riding through the peanut field in Arthur's wagon which was loaded with poles, and we spotted a snake sunning itself on the ground.

My brother said, "Let's kill it!"

"Why?" I protested. "He ain't bothering us."

But he got down off the wagon and started beating it with one of the poles. The snake coiled to try to protect itself, but Arthur kept whacking it until its head was crushed. Then he threw it into the woods. I stayed on the wagon and watched. I wasn't going to put my foot on the ground with a snake in sight. Besides, it hadn't been bothering us, so I thought we ought to leave it alone.

When I first was allowed to go hunting, I felt really grown-up. I was filled with excitement as we started out — Poppa and James and Arthur and I. We were going after 'possum. But the excitement wore off quickly. It was cold and wet, and it seemed mosquitoes were out hunting too — and we were the game! We were out all night long walking and I didn't bag a single 'possum. I got home dead tired and disappointed. It had been a useless trip for me, no fun after all. I went a couple more times, but each time I gained more sympathy for our dog Charlie Brown who didn't much like hunting, either. I would do it if I had to, but not for recreation.

I loved eating the 'possum, though. People don't eat it much anymore. But, man, it was good. A 'possum has to be skinned and cleaned just like a turkey. You also have to be sure to get the musk glands from the small of the back and under the front legs. Rinse it off well, then rub it inside and out with salt, pepper, and sage, or red pepper and whatever spices you like. Then you put it in a pan and pour boiling water over it. After it simmers awhile, covered over a low flame, you pull it out and surround it with sweet potatoes, peeled and dotted with butter. Cook until it's tender, and take the cover off to let it brown. That's good eating!

After several weeks, my ordeal was over. Poppa's letter arrived at last, telling us to get on the train — he was ready for us to travel north. We had finished selling everything and were packed and ready to leave as soon as we heard from him. So there was nothing left to do but to notify friends and kin, and go down to the depot to purchase our tickets and board the train. We Griers were bound for the Promised Land! There was Mama, Eula, me, and the four younger ones, Alice, Willie Bee, Sammy Lee, and Baba. When we got on the train to leave, all of our friends were at the station to see us off. We waved goodbye, feeling like royalty.

I had some definite expectations about what we would find up there. My cousins from Pennsylvania had come to visit us dressed so nicely, and they had such different ideas than we had in the South. I figured they had money trees and that as soon as we got there we could relax in the lap of luxury. I fully intended to shake some trees for some of those dollars!

In a more sober retrospective I can see we were doing a momentous thing. We sold our furniture, the cows and mules, the pigs, and the tools without — so far as I could tell — giving it a second thought. We were leaving behind our farm, where we had a roof over our heads with meat, vegetables, food for the animals, syrup for sweetening. We even grew corn for cornmeal. And there was plenty of wood to fuel the fires. And a hand pump kept us in fresh water year-round. We didn't have a lot of fancy clothes or a big automobile, but our basic needs were met.

Where we were going we would need cash to pay for all the things we took for granted in Georgia. I think my dad had weighed these considerations as much as he could, and had decided that the advantages outweighed the disadvantages. In retrospect I can see he made a choice that would cost him his life, but which brought his family to a place of new possibilities. He made a great sacrifice for us. For me, personally, New Jersey was to mean more freedom to attend school and less hard work (and, eventually, such things as I never dreamed of).

We rode that train about three days and nights. What a ride! I had fun walking up and down through the cars, looking out the windows at all the different scenes. I got off once in some town because I had been amazed to see an automobile perched aloft in some big trees. I went out to take a closer look, but I didn't venture far because I was afraid the train might leave without me. Every time I have gone South since then I have tried to find that car. I tried to imagine how it got up there, and the best theory I came up with was that high flood water had floated it up there. To me, at eleven, it was the oddest thing I had ever seen.

As the train kept pushing northward, I watched the fields rushing by and was so happy because I would never have to pick cotton or peanuts again! The clackety-clack of the train wheels seemed to be saying, "Headed for the Promised Land, headed for the Promised Land."

Even the restrooms contained unheard-of marvels: running water and flush toilets.

When I got hungry, I would go back to where my mother and the others were and get some fried chicken. Mother and Eula had prepared a big stock of food to bring along on the trip — boxes and boxes of fried chicken and cake and other good things.

I didn't know it then, but we were part of a great migration of blacks out of the South, which was, in turn, part of the great rural-to-urban migration that went on from the 30s to the 70s in this country. Everyone seemed to take along boxes of fried chicken to eat. In those years, that was the mainstay of "Sunday dinner" for the poor and middle-class — black or white. In fact, by the late 50s, that north-bound train we rode was nicknamed "the Chickenbone Express," because by the time it arrived in New York City, its coaches were full of boxes of chicken bones. All I knew in 1943 was that I was having the most fun I had ever had, and that it was terrific to have all that food to eat on the way, lots and lots of it.

We arrived in Roselle, New Jersey, early one morning. It was unlike anything we had seen before: the houses were built close to one another and the noise of traffic and people was a constant hum. We felt we were entering another world. We found our house, 1200 Warren Street, and moved in. My aunt lived upstairs and a lot of cousins were there to meet us. We had a big celebration.

This was the most excitement I had ever felt. I was living in a new house and beginning a new school in new surroundings. I didn't have any friends or know anything about living in a city, so I was also a little uneasy. My heavy Southern accent drew howls of laughter from the other kids that first day I went to school. I was embarrassed and befuddled because I could not figure out what was so funny. In the entrance physical examinations, the nurse found that I had a vision problem. That occasioned my first visit to an optometrist and my first pair of glasses.

The second day at school, I was walking down the hall feeling very grown-up when a group of boys surrounded me. They said I was going to be initiated. They frightened me because they were so different and I didn't know what "initiated" meant. I had never been around kids with so much education, so many abilities, and such a way of talking. That afternoon, they took me away from the school building into a field with a small pond. They told me that if I let them throw me in the pond, I could be a member of their club.

"I'm not going to let you throw me into that pond with my good clothes on!" I protested.

I was far from puny by that age and so, although I was scared, I was also mad and stubborn. If I didn't let them, they couldn't do it. They tried to push me into the water anyway. That's when I pulled the knife I had long been in the habit of carrying with me. That had the desired effect at first — nobody tried to shove me anymore. But it also brought a response that struck terror in me: "He's got a knife! He's got a knife," they said. "Tomorrow, everyone bring a knife."

I didn't say anything that night to any of my family. I didn't want to involve anyone else. But I worried about it all night long. Wanting to be prepared, the next morning I wore two pairs of pants with a knife in every pocket. At school, I kept waiting for someone to say something, but no one ever mentioned being initiated again or talked about what had happened at the pond. As time went on, I became accepted and began to blend into the crowd at Lincoln Elementary School on Warren Street in the conventional ways.

I was placed in my right grade, the fifth, which pleased me. Usually when students came in from the South, they had to be put back a grade or two. But I had really studied during the time I was able to attend school in Georgia, and now it was paying off for me.

Two years later, in the seventh grade, I went to Abraham Clark High School, a combination of junior and senior high school. My seventh grade marks were not that good — C's and B's. That began to worry me and get me to thinking. There was an Italian boy in my class named John Grossi. He used to get all A's.

"John," I asked, "how did you get all A's?"

"I'm smart," he said.

Then I asked, "How can I get all A's?"

He said, "Well, you're not as smart as I am, so you're going to have to study."

I realized he was right and I began to study harder. I never got all A's, but I did make the merit roll all the way through high school.

Ironically and sadly, John Grossi dropped out of school, and I never saw him again. I'll always owe him because he made me realize that discipline and determination can be more important than a high IQ.

Once I was in the seventh grade, I found others like myself who enjoyed singing: Clyde and Cleo Robinson, Bill Land, Thaddeus Brantley, and I formed a singing group which stayed together all through our high school years. I was also involved in a choir and, later, I sang in a lot of quartets and ensembles.

By the time I was ready for the ninth grade, my height and weight had begun to achieve unusual proportions. I had little background in regular competitive sports, however. So, I didn't make the connection between my bulk and football. But the school's football coach did. He came up to me one day after school while I was watching the guys on the field and asked why I didn't try out.

"I don't know anything about football," I said. I had played in the schoolyard in junior high but never really understood the game. We just threw the ball in the air, and the one that caught it got pounced on.

"Do you want to get in there?" he replied, almost as if he hadn't heard me.

"Okay," I said. It was flattering to be asked, but I decided not to push my luck. I put my glasses and books down on the grass and went into the locker room to put on the equipment. A few minutes later, the players ran up the field and trampled all over my things.

"What's the matter with you guys?" I yelled at them as I picked up my smashed eyeglasses.

"This is a football field," somebody said. "Learn to put your glasses in a locker."

That's how much I knew about football. But I was a fast learner with an aptitude for the game. I made the team and, thanks to my size and speed, I soon found myself playing on the varsity squad. The other guys on the team began to look up to me (they had to, I was the tallest member) and talk to me. That felt good and, before long, I found myself hanging around with the popular kids and being invited to their parties — heady stuff for any adolescent, let alone a Georgia farm boy.

One day, as if on cue, the principal, Albert S. Peeling, called me in for a special talk. "Roosevelt, you are going to be a big fellow and a good athlete. A lot of students already admire you. You have a decision to make: whether to be a good example or a bad example to them. Only you can make that decision, but you know which one I hope you'll make."

"Thank you, Mr. Peeling," I replied, "I want to set a good example." I was a little awe-struck by the personal attention which I suppose is what he intended. But I meant it. I wanted to be good.

It will probably come as no surprise to you that I was not, however, a perfect angel — either before or after my talk with the principal. One Halloween night about the time I was in the ninth grade, a group of fellows I ran around with were throwing eggs at passing cars. I didn't throw any, but I was with them when the police came by in a plain car. When they pelted it, a big, black cop jumped out and started chasing us.

Back home in Georgia, all anyone had to say to start my friend John Arthur Wilson and me running for home was to yell, "The cops are coming." We had no curiosity about what would happen if we fell into their hands.

"Trouble is easy to get into but hard to get out of," Poppa used to say.

So, that Halloween when I saw that policeman come out of that car, I turned and ran for my life. Being fast, I got down the street and around the corner ahead of the pack. I stopped there in front of my house and turned in. Then the other guys came running past. When the cops got to my house, one of them asked, "Did you see any of those guys who threw eggs at us?"

Trying not to sound out of breath, I said, "No, sir!"

John Arthur was with us that night, too. When we were friends in Georgia, he and his sister were living with their grandmother. His father was already working in New Jersey. After we moved North, John Arthur came to live with his father. That meant he lived right down the street from me so that our friendship continued to grow. We have remained lifelong friends.

One night, I went with some guys to steal fruit out of a man's yard. I played "chicken" or lookout for them while they went in and picked the fruit. Then we ran. Another night, they decided to go into the school and get a ball to play with, so I was the lookout again. The guys got into the school through some kind of trapdoor on the roof, came out with the ball, bounced it around for a while and ended up throwing it into someone's yard. That was the extent of my criminal activities.

I never got into a real fight, although boys from the two neighboring towns, Roselle and Linden, were fighting constantly as rivals. The town border was the middle of a street. Certain gangs fought regularly back and forth over that line. One night, the guys I ran around with went out and had a big fight with a group of boys from Linden. I was not with them. I did not go out much at night because I had made up my mind to study.

The day after the street battle, I went to the corner store, and some of the Linden guys were there. Out on the sidewalk, they threatened me with broken bottles to get me to tell who had attacked them the night before. I backed into a corner as far as I could go. I was being forced to make up my mind quickly to fight or run. But it never came to that because my dad came upon the scene and everybody scattered. I was never more glad to see him!

So, on the whole, I tried to keep my nose clean and live up to the challenge Mr. Peeling had given me. Eva's challenge was the one the jury hadn't come in on yet. I still didn't know what I was going to do with my life, but somehow I had the sense not to throw it away for nothing.

5

ATHLETE IN
THE MAKING

During my high school days I was a shy loner, especially when it came to girls. There were only two in whom I took much of an interest. One was nice, but I never knew quite what to say to her. I had an unusual rapport with the other — felt comfortable with her. But she was white and that was a "no-no," even in the North. However, I was still mostly oblivious to things like that so I pursued the relationship. Her parents invited me over to their house. I think they understood the friendship was genuine and that I wasn't bucking the "racial code" out of some kind of social consciousness.

My junior and senior high school years were a happy time for me. I made All-Union County and All-State football lineman and All-American in track. I had a great time and knew a lot of guys. I can't say, however, that I was ever really close to any of them. Perhaps it was because I was pretty serious about trying to set a good example. Sometimes, I was a downright pain in the neck about it.

For example, if I was hanging out with some guys who went into a store to shoplift, I wouldn't let them out the door.

I would stand at the door and say, "Did you pay for your stuff?"

If anybody said, "No," then I would say, "Well, you can't come out. Go back and pay for it." I wouldn't do it any differently today, but it may explain why I found it hard to experience closeness with some of my friends.

Another reason for my failure to develop close relationships with my high school chums may have been that I got preoccupied with problems at home. My dad had been working at a chemical plant and came down sick as a result of chemical poisoning. It was horrible to watch: he would grit his teeth to bear the pain in his stomach. Other times I saw him doubled over, but he hardly ever cried out or complained. I wanted so much to be able to help him, but there was nothing I could do.

He had to quit working, and after a while, his disability payments ran out. Our newfound affluence disappeared overnight and soon we were scraping bottom. My mother started taking domestic jobs to bring in cash, and I had to cook for my younger brothers and sister. The menu never varied much. I used to cook pork and beans and corn, or pork and beans and hot dogs every day. The pattern persisted for as long as I was in high school.

One day, Alice protested that she was not going to eat pork and beans anymore, and we got into a big fight. I didn't like having to eat such a monotonous diet any better than she did. But what choice did we have?

But the most painful part of that era was what was happening between Mama and Poppa. The pattern of my parents' arguments was established back on the farms in Georgia. The pressures brought on by my dad's illness increased the frequency and intensity of their battles many times. Each night as the family bedded down, I would listen to them start to talk. After a little while the talk would become an argument. When that happened, Mama found it impossible to let go. I felt sorry for Poppa and I was upset at Mama. I couldn't understand her desperation, and my stomach knotted as I listened in the dark.

"Why don't you just hush, Mama? He's sick," I would think at her as hard as I could, trying to will her to keep quiet.

Sometimes I would sit up in bed and listen. I was afraid for Mama, afraid Poppa would lose his temper and hurt her. But he never did. One day, however, Poppa came home drunk. That was very unusual. Joseph Grier was not a drinker. He had a gun in his hand and was muttering angrily and incoherently. The gun and the drinking were expressions of his frustration at being sick and out of work.

To keep anything from happening, I wrapped my long arms around him from behind and immobilized him. My size came in handy. Alice, in the meantime, was trying to pry the pistol out of Poppa's hand. She got so involved with her task that she failed to notice the muzzle was aimed right at her face.

I knew the trigger might be sensitive, and tried to tell her, "Don't point the gun at your face."

But this was no time to engage in elaborate explanations. I got my hand on the gun and took it away from Poppa.

"Give me that gun back!" he snapped.

But I wouldn't do it. I took it and destroyed it. I had seen what bullets could do to flesh and bone. I broke that pistol so that no one would ever use it again. Then I threw it away in the trash.

Eva's words — "But Roosevelt, what will you do when Mama and Poppa are gone?" — rang in my ears that day. I was still clinging to my dream to have the family always be together, but now my family was being torn apart at its center.

The torturing pain that now threatened to overwhelm me had gotten its start as a small ache back in Georgia when I was little. Once in those early years I had felt a comfort and security with my gathered family that was like a warm blanket — new and whole. But with each departure of one of my siblings that blanket was eaten a little bit by moths around the edges. My security was diminished and I felt a measure of the pain of grief. But now my blanket was being eaten right at its center. There would be nothing left of it after this. What was I going to do?

I tried to roll up inside myself to get away from things, as if that would stop them from happening. I didn't know I was looking for love. We loved one another deeply in our family, but we generally held back in the ways we allowed ourselves to show it. And so I ached with loneliness for the hugs and kisses I wanted so badly and yet was unable myself to give to those I loved.

Maybe it was a partial attempt to answer Eva's question — maybe it was my only acceptable avenue of escape from the pain of what was happening to my family. But, for whatever reason, I became deeply absorbed in high school athletics. I played varsity football and basketball and excelled in track. Coach Ralph Arminio helped me a lot. But I learned the javelin, discus, and shot put on my own because we didn't have coaches for those events. I learned by watching other people throw in competition at the meets we participated in.

But in the midst of my successes I suffered my first serious injury. It happened when a guy I tackled fell on my back during practice. My back became stiff, and I could hardly move. The coach sent me to a doctor who gave me a shot of novocaine so I could keep on playing, and nothing was done to treat the injury itself. My back has hurt me ever since. The sort of neglect I suffered then, back in the forties, is part of the reason for the explosion of litigation in our country today. People are no longer willing to put up with that sort of thing. And rightly so. High school athletes need and deserve first-class medical and therapeutic treatment for the injuries they suffer on the playing field. Anything less is criminal.

I know that now, but I didn't then. I was big and tough, and I could endure a lot of punishment. At least it seemed so then. Anyway, I was having a great time. My athletic year started at the end of each summer with football practice. Then I spent the fall in the weekly gridiron contests against the other high schools in our vicinity — Roselle Park, Cranford, Union, Hillside, Neptune, Rahway, Westfield, Plainfield, Scotch Plains. My size always got me put on the line where the play was roughest. I didn't mind the roughness. Sometimes I even enjoyed it, but it was never my goal to hurt another player. Early on, in fact, I learned to play the ball. That meant I kept my attention — no matter what position I was playing — primarily on the ball and what was happening to it. My objective was always to get the ball away from our opponents, or, failing that, to bring down their ball carrier — preferably behind the line of scrimmage. Combining that singlemindedness with my size and speed gave me a certain reputation among Union County's high school quarterbacks, a role I loved.

Once the football season was over, it was time to go indoors for the winter and play basketball. At six-five, I was one of the tallest players in Union County and my speed was good enough to keep up with the best of them. I usually played center. Basketball is an exhausting game, in some ways more physically demanding than football. Abraham Clark's team went to the playoffs during both my junior and senior years, but we never made it to the state finals.

After basketball season, it was back outdoors for track. I ran on the relay teams, but I enjoyed the field events more. The javelin, discus, and shot put often get eclipsed in high school competition. If it weren't for the Olympics I sometimes wonder if they might not disappear entirely. Anyway, those of us who competed in these events in the late 1940s in that part of New Jersey were a fraternity of young men proud to do our part to keep the flame burning.

During the summers, I worked. Life in Georgia had accustomed me to hard work, and it never seemed odd to me that I paid my share of the groceries and bought my own clothes. I was always able to get a job, and I usually learned something valuable from each one I held. Once, for example, I worked at a used car lot cleaning the vehicles.

One day, I was cleaning a car that had white-walled tires and long skirts. In order to finish scrubbing those whitewalls, I needed someone to move the car because I was still too young to have a driver's license. But I looked like I was old enough, and one of the salesmen, seeing my dilemma, suggested that I move the car myself.

That was all the excuse I needed. I reached in, turned the key and then slipped the automatic shift lever into drive, thinking it would edge forward slowly and I would drop it back out of gear. But the car took off and left me standing there. I yelled to a man in its path and he jumped out of the way just before the car crashed into the side of another vehicle.

I was almost as startled as I had been that first time I fired off the shotgun and got set on my behind. It all happened in a flash, and I had hardly had time to think about it before I heard the manager's voice roaring obscenities as he came running toward me.

"You _____ !!!! What the _____ are you doing starting that car?! Look at that dent, will you? Do you have any _____ idea how much that will cost to fix?"

He didn't seem to know how to stop. The filth kept pouring out of his mouth as if from a bottomless pit of abusiveness. I started feeling angry. I was willing to accept the responsibility for what I had done, but I didn't deserve this sort of treatment. I remembered my dad's example and lifted my head to engage my boss's eyes. That seemed to help him stop, and then I spoke. "I'm sorry and I promise to take care of whatever I've done. But I need you to stop cussing at me." I said it firmly and quietly.

With that, he wheeled around and stomped away without saying another word. I waited for the other shoe to drop, figuring I might get a slip of paper telling me I was fired.

After a little while, I left the lot and got one of my brothers, James, as best I can recall, to talk to the boss. James told me that he repeated what I said about paying for the damages and added that he himself would back me in that with his own money if need be. Then he said the boss told him he'd let us know after he'd had time to think about it.

But neither James nor I, nor any other Grier ever heard another word about it. I was not fired, nor was I required to pay for the repairs. I never found out why. It could be the salesman who'd suggested I move the car felt responsible and offered to pay. Or maybe the boss just decided to forgive me.

What I learned was that I had apparently done the right thing by confronting my boss and politely demanding an end to the abuse while at the same time being willing to accept whatever consequences my foolishness deserved. I also saw that my family was willing to stand by me in the face of trouble. That felt good.

Another summer I worked at a garbage dump boxing metal and selling it to a scrap dealer. Sometimes I made as much as twenty-five dollars a week doing that (remember, this was in the 1940s). After high school graduation in 1951, I went to work for a refining company in the gold-smelting section. The man who had the job before me was caught trying to smuggle out some gold. I don't know how he did it. To get into the smelting area, you had to go into a locker room, take off all your clothes and put on special work clothes. When you left, the process had to be done in reverse — usually while a supervisor was around.

Going to work in a regular factory every day was another great new experience for me. I felt really grown-up. I worked the midnight-to-eight shift, and every morning as I went home, I would pick up a box of corn flakes, a quart of milk, and about a dozen bananas. Then I would sit down before I went to bed and eat it all. One day I did this and got sick. I had never been that sick in all my life. So I stopped eating bananas.

Going overboard with things I liked to eat was an old habit of mine from childhood days in Georgia. I used, for example, to go to town on Saturdays and stuff myself with soda crackers and cheese.

I remember once on the farm that sugar-cane juice was my downfall. We were making syrup one morning, and I went out early and drank a lot of cane juice. It was my favorite. This was a Saturday, and I was going to town with Poppa on the wagon. I had on a gray outfit suitable for such a trip. Well, drinking all that cane juice so early and then being jostled around on the wagon made my stomach just curl up. On the way to town, I had to go to the bathroom, and there's nowhere to go on a wagon. Also, we were in open fields where there was no place to go.

So, I "had an accident" on the wagon and arrived in town wrapped in a blanket. My dad bought me a new outfit and, as we were walking around, I had another accident. This happened three times that day. I wound up going back home in a blanket. But at least I had gained a wardrobe!

The family tells about another time when I was quite small. We were accustomed to eating cornbread and biscuits, but did not have a lot of store-bought bread. We called it "light bread" or "loaf bread" and regarded it as something special. When we went to town, I usually got some sort of treat to eat and, one time, it was an entire loaf of bread. It was fresh-baked and smelled just wonderful to me. I started eating it and couldn't stop. And I was so absorbed in what I was doing that I absent mindedly kept walking in circles around a pole until I had consumed the whole thing. Evidently I attracted the amused attention of a number of the local street loungers because I was kidded about it both in town and by family members for years after that.

Shortly after graduation from high school, I received more than twenty invitations to visit colleges, some of which were offering me athletic scholarships for full tuition, fees, room and board. I didn't know what to think. I was the first in my immediate family to have finished high school. And, all along, that had been my ultimate academic goal. Going to college was unimaginable, out of reach. Besides, I had a regular industrial job — a real sign of manhood. Did I want to give that up?

But when the letters came and I read them, I felt excited. Of course, it was important to act as if it didn't matter to me at all. Inside, however, it seemed like the night sky was lit by a hundred skyrockets above a huge sign that proclaimed: "Roosevelt Grier, we think you're good and we want you!" Can you imagine how that made me feel? It surpassed some of my wildest adolescent fantasies.

As preposterous as it seemed, I decided it wouldn't cost me anything to at least go take a look. So I accepted some of the invitations. The trip I remember especially was Virginia State University down in Petersburg. It was a public co-ed school that must have conducted beauty contests as part of its entrance exams for female students. I had never seen so many good-looking women in one place at one time (Could that have been part of their recruitment strategy for prospective athletes? — if so, it was a good one!). Most of the girls I met that weekend were black, one of whom I remember especially because she had blue eyes, something I had never seen before.

Pennsylvania State University, however, held more appeal for me. For one thing, I knew it had greater academic prestige than Virginia State. Assistant track coach Norm Gordon actually came to our house and left an invitation for me to visit their campus up in State College. My dad told me about the invitation when I got home from work.

I said, "I don't have money to go up to that school."

The next day, Mr. Gordon came back to the house and told my dad the school would pay my way. They were offering me a track scholarship, and he told Poppa that he wanted me to consider it seriously. So I agreed to visit them.

I wanted my dad to tell me what I ought to do. But he had the good sense to compel me to make up my own mind. Although he let me know how he felt about the choice between staying at the factory and going to college. "Boy," he said, "now you have a chance to make something of yourself."

State College, Pennsylvania, sits astride the Alleghenies out in the middle of nowhere almost smack-dab in the middle of the state, equally remote from Philadelphia and Pittsburgh. Being back in the countryside after seven years of urban living felt good. When I got there I liked the campus, and I liked the way they treated me. They didn't try to sell me on what they were going to do for me. They talked to me about education and about what a good school it was. The kids who showed me around did not try to high-pressure me into coming there. I fell in love with Penn State. I did not know whether I could make it, but I decided the least I could do was give it a try. I filled in the papers and shook hands with the administrator in charge of scholarships. The scholarship was for track, but I knew good and well I would go out for football, too. It would all start the coming autumn of 1951.

6

WALKING IN
TALL GRASS

"How did he get here, that guy?"

I kept asking myself that in those words my first year at Penn State. Here I was, enrolled in this prestigious institution of higher learning whose president was no less than Milton Eisenhower, brother of the man who had only recently led all the Allies to victory in Europe. It was all so far beyond the scope of my imagination that it seemed unreal — which is probably why I used the "he" to refer to myself. My roots were so deep in the rocky soil of south Georgia that the passage of eight years of my short life in New Jersey and its public schools had only just barely prepared me for this. I had some doubts about my ability to meet the academic standards of the university, but they were tiny compared to my doubts about my ability to make the emotional adjustment this new setting was requiring of me.

The one place I felt at home, of course, was on the playing fields. Even though my way was being paid by a track scholarship, I had no intention of waiting around for spring track season before I got out on those fields. I was a football player. After four years of it in high school, it was in my blood.

Tryouts for the Penn State team were held several weeks before the beginning of classes, so I quit my job at the gold smeltery early

41

and headed for State College to be there in time. That job had paid well enough for me to buy the clothes I needed, so I arrived with a respectable wardrobe.

Penn State's football tryouts were an assembly of the biggest men on campus — literally. But the two who stood tallest were Jesse Arnelle and I. Jesse was a freshman from New York and both of us measured in at 6'5." Jesse was first and foremost a basketball player, so his weight did not quite match my 230 pounds. Throughout my high school career I had always been the biggest person on the field, but from the first day of those tryouts at Penn State I realized my size was no longer going to give me the overwhelming advantage it once had. I was going to be playing against my peers and I would have to show that I knew how to play the game with the best of them if I were going to make the team.

Rip Engle was the head coach. At forty-five, he had just finished his first year of coaching at Penn State. Before that he had been head coach at Brown from 1944 through 1949. There he had introduced the winged T formation, and, in 1949, he compiled a record of eight wins with only one loss (to Princeton). All of us — about fifty men — gathered around to listen to his welcoming speech. After he introduced himself and the other coaches (among them was Joe Paterno who had come with Rip from Brown), he got down to business: "You guys may think you're in shape, but you're not. Don't get worried, though, because the program you're starting today will put you in top shape. But," he added with a meaningful pause, "every one of you who makes this team is going to be in better than top shape.

"I expect anyone who makes this team to run the mile in under six minutes. Football games are won by people who can run fast and who can keep running fast for two hours. In scrimmage, we expect you to be as aggressive as in a real game."

Some of the assistant coaches at Penn State, I began to see in the days that followed, relied on the same psychology my high school coaches had used. They reasoned that football was a game which required extraordinary energy and aggression. And they figured the way to produce that aggression in us players was to stir us up and make us mad by screaming and yelling at us. That may have worked for some of the players, but not for me.

I had begun to realize in high school that my size and strength required that I keep myself under control. Otherwise, I would inflict serious injuries during scrimmage or play, and that was something I could not tolerate. Don't get me wrong, I enjoyed the roughness of the game, but I drew a line when it came to brutality. So, especially in scrimmages, instead of driving into my own guys, I pulled them down by tackling them.

I didn't think I needed to get mad to enjoy the game or to be a good athlete. It used to amuse me when they'd try to make me angry. I remember once, however, in college, when I did get mad. During practice, one of the guys tore up my chin. I mean, tore it up! There was no blood, but I was dizzy, and they took me off the field for a minute. For a brief second, I saw red and was ready to kill. I never sorted those feelings out in my mind at the time, but neither did I let them take control. No matter what happened, I did not want to go out on the field angry. Athletics should be fun, not a war.

My attitude brought me into tension with coaches who found it difficult to understand my quiet ways and sometimes accused me of being poorly motivated. Today I can look back and see what was going on then, but, at the time, it was hard for me. I was not a rebel and I didn't enjoy conflict with authority figures. On the contrary, I wanted to please them, although not at the cost of my integrity.

Had someone used a different motivational technique, perhaps I would have played a different style of game. But they didn't and the resultant tension kept me from achieving my athletic potential — something I regret, but which was the source of important lessons for me in growing up.

Penn State's football team does not belong to a particular athletic conference. Like Notre Dame, Army, Navy, Pittsburgh, Tulane, South Carolina, and some others, it is an independent team. Consequently, our schedule varied from year to year with one exception: Pittsburgh. The game against Pitt was the last game of each season, the big cross-state rivalry.

The 1951 season opened with a home game on September 29 against Boston University which we won 40-34. I was a second-string defensive tackle and it hurt me to sit on the bench and see Boston pile up so many points. I was churning to get in there and help stop them, but I was, after all, an untried freshman with more of a reputation for track than for football.

My second-string freshman status kept me out of the next two games which were played away from Penn State's campus (transportation was limited to the proven veterans). The first was against Villanova, which we lost 20-14, and the second was against Nebraska, which we won 15-7.

The team returned home to drop another game, 32-21, to Michigan State. It was the week after that when I made first string. I acted cool about the accomplishment, but it felt pretty good to be a freshman and a member of that elect group. The next Saturday afternoon we played at home again and beat Virginia, 13-7.

The next week, a train carried us to West Lafayette, Indiana, where we humbled Purdue, 28-0. Do I need to report that those of us on the defensive squad felt a little smug that Saturday evening?

Our last game at home that season was against Syracuse on November 10, which we won 32-13. The next Saturday took us close to my home when we played Rutgers in New Brunswick, New Jersey. I hoped to see some of my family in the stands, but they were not there because I had not written anyone in the family to tell them about it. I was too proud, I guess. We won, 13-7.

The season ended sadly when we lost to Pitt, 13-7, the following Saturday, November 24. We comforted ourselves that we had finished the season 6 and 3, which was pretty respectable. And I was honored to be chosen first team, All-East defense that year.

Meanwhile, back in the classroom, I was not enjoying the same degree of success. When I enrolled for classes, I had put down music as my major. It had seemed a natural choice. Next to sports, I loved singing. At Abraham Clark I had been part of every singing group on campus. But I learned something important that fall semester of 1951: Loving music and studying it are two different things. Music's closest cousin in the academic world is mathematics, and to major in either of those disciplines is an incredibly demanding task.

In addition to the theory classes, I was also required to learn how to play an instrument. It was in that setting that I was introduced to the cello. Anyone who has seen the size of my fingers can quickly imagine the difficulty I encountered trying to play the cello. I can recall no other time in my life when I have felt so frustrated — that cello refused to yield to my best efforts.

As the end of the semester approached, it was clear that I was flunking out. It was a terribly difficult time for me. At Abraham Clark I had enjoyed academic success simply as a result of hard work, but, at college, that formula was not getting me the same results. I had worked hard and I was still falling short of the mark. Maybe I had been right at the beginning of the semester. I didn't belong here. The whole thing had been a fantasy.

About three weeks after the close of the football season, I was back in Roselle for the Christmas holidays. It felt good to be back with my family — comforting in the face of my academic difficulties that cast such an ominous shadow on my future. My father's health was failing fast, a fact that made me think even more seriously about just giving up on college. After all, with Poppa so sick, what would make more sense, but for me to come home, get my job at the smeltery back, and help support Mama?

I thought of little else that Christmas vacation. The ideal of staying in school was there, and it was reinforced by the thought that, if I could somehow make it academically, I could keep playing football. But how was I going to make it academically? Who was I trying to kid? I might as well face the fact that I wasn't hacking it at college and throw in the towel.

Poppa's words — "Now you have a chance to make something of yourself" — rang in my ears. But my chance was gone, wasn't it? Confused and depressed, I went out for a walk one evening. It was chilly and bleak that night. No snow softened the scenes of the streets. As I walked, though, my eyes began to open to what I was seeing — the grim lot of those who had given up and thrown in the towel. Some of them lay drunken in the gutters that night, but many more were living quiet grey lives in drab little row houses. Every morning, those men got up and went to the factories. Every night they came home. One day they would die and what would their lives have meant? A deep shiver went through me as I contemplated joining them in their quiet desperation.

After that walk on the sidewalks of Roselle that night, I knew I had to go back and give it a second effort. I went back to Penn State and spent hours cramming for the finals that would be held around the end of January.

In the meantime, the indoor track season got underway just as soon as I returned to campus. We went to the Washington Star Games (a meet that is no longer held) on January 12, 1952, and participated in four or five dual meets, one of which took us up to West Point to compete with the cadets. During that season I managed to break the Penn State record for putting the shot, but I can't remember the precise statistics and Penn State's records from that era are incomplete.

In the midst of that season I sat down to my first round of semester final exams in college. It was a harrowing and humiliating experience — the expression on the face of the examiner who had to hear me play the cello was a mixture of pain and unbelief. My determination to make that second effort by cramming managed only to pull my grades out of the gutter and halfway up onto the curb. I could see that I was going to have to choose between athletics and music. There was not enough time in a day for me to succeed in both at Penn State.

A guidance counselor and one of the coaches helped me think the question through. Before the start of the new semester, I had a plan: I would change my major to physical education where the conflict between athletics and academics would be least. In that setting, my capacity for hard work would have a chance to produce results in the limited time available. And, I told myself, with a degree in phys ed, I could become a teacher and coach in any of a number of good-sized high schools.

Because my grade-point average fell below the acceptable minimum at the end of that first semester, I was not allowed to participate in outdoor track during the spring semester. That gave me time to study, settle down, and get on the right track in academics. But another crisis arose at Easter time which threatened to derail me once again.

When I returned home to Roselle for the Easter recess, my father was in the hospital. I had seen it coming when I'd been home at semester break — he had looked really bad. But I had refused to face what that meant. None of us in the family talked about it. A grim shadow was clouding our horizon and we felt powerless in the face of it — and it was too awful to talk about.

The next morning I went to the hospital in Elizabeth. Poppa was in an oxygen tent, coughing a lot. That strong man who had plowed the fields and administered my whippings with a firm and purposeful arm now lay before me — gaunt and weak. He had always been there when I had needed him, even down to that day I was facing the toughs from Linden who were brandishing their broken bottles at me. Seeing him like this made me feel afraid. I had not the foggiest idea what I should do or say. And Eva's question — would I have to answer it so soon?

"Hey, Poppa," I said flippantly, "how'd you get in here? They don't allow no colored folks in these places. You sneak in the back door?"

He smiled faintly at my little joke. We were men and this was no time for sentimentality and soft expressions of love. How I ache now that I made none — that I didn't pull up a chair, take hold of his hand and speak softly in his ear: "Poppa, I love you and I'm going to miss you. Thank you for being a wonderful father to me. I've always admired you and thought you were the finest man there ever was." Then, as I was about to leave, I would have pulled aside that tent and kissed him on the cheek. But I was too young and scared. I just tried to act loose and carefree — to close out and deny the pain I felt and that I am sure he felt.

Back at home, I learned how rough things were for my mother. She had been forced to apply for welfare to keep groceries on the table for my younger brothers and Alice. Mama hated having to take charity, but she was a sensible woman who knew better than to let pride rob her of what she needed so desperately. She had done the best she could.

A couple of mornings later — it was the Saturday between Good Friday and Easter, the phone rang. I tensed with dread. Then I heard Eula's husband, King Blackwell, answer it. He spoke too quietly for me to make out his words, then he hung up.

"Roosevelt?" he called to me upstairs.

"Yeah?" I replied.

"Get dressed," he said. "We've got to go get your mother. Your father just died."

I lay there on the upstairs couch, looking at the newspaper. I felt no response to his words — nothing. I chastised myself, "You cold fish, what's the matter with you? Your father just died and you don't feel anything."

I got up and went into the bathroom to wash my face. Then, with my face covered with soap, it suddenly erupted. A deep sobbing came from down inside me — someplace I had never known existed. I felt as if I were coming apart at the seams. Grief, regret, guilt, anger, and a dozen other emotions flooded through me in a torrent.

After a little bit, I pulled myself together and went downstairs. A lot of things had to be done — calling, sending telegrams. The preacher came over and helped us with the plans for the funeral. Then there was the mortician to deal with — and the florist.

The funeral took place the following Saturday at the Bethlehem Baptist Church of Roselle. Reverend Bullock officiated, and King's sister-in-law, Fredie Mae Blackwell, sang Poppa's favorite hymn, "The Days Have Passed and Gone." Poppa had been a deacon in the church and was remembered by the pastor as Deacon Grier that day. The thing I remember most, however, is that the sanctuary was filled to capacity. In addition to those who lived in the immediate vicinity, my father's friends and relatives came from California, Georgia, Florida, Pennsylvania, and North Carolina to pay their last respects. Many who were there that afternoon wanted to say a word to express their feelings about Joseph Grier, so the service continued for well over an hour. Poppa was only fifty-one when he died, a fact that made his passing doubly sad.

After the funeral, I was trying to decide whether to go back to college or stay home and help my family. I had already missed a week of classes, and the temptation to drop out was again strong, almost as strong as it had been at the end of the first semester, about three months earlier. Word of my thinking must have gotten back to the school, because the mayor of nearby Rahway, New Jersey, who was a Penn State alumnus, came over to the house and talked to me.

"You'll be able to help your family a lot more by getting an education than by staying at home," he told me.

Poppa had a life insurance policy of which my mother was the main beneficiary. (It was amazing to see how various people tried, mostly in vain, to get that money away from Mama after the check arrived from the insurance company.) She received enough to buy a home in Linden and to provide income so that she would no longer have to receive welfare.

Mama had told us about the insurance during the week before the funeral. So, the knowledge that she would be taken care of helped me to take the mayor's advice to return and finish the semester.

I took my share of Poppa's life insurance benefit and bought a used Chevrolet in which I drove back to State College. Having an automobile made a lot of friends for me. Everyone didn't take a car to college with them in those days. A lot of guys would borrow mine, especially my teammates, to take out their girls.

My second semester at Penn State ended much more satisfactorily than my first. Penn State's curriculum for physical education majors was not a cinch, but, unlike music, it did yield to hard work and diligent study. My grades changed dramatically. By June, I was out of the woods and on course. And I felt good about myself in a way I had never experienced before.

Over the summer I got another job and lived with Mama, Alice, and my brothers in the house in Linden. Mama was adjusting well to Poppa's absence. The two years that he was sick gave her time to make some of that adjustment ahead of time. We were all thankful for an uneventful season in our lives.

Events got underway for me very quickly in the fall, however, with the opening of the 1952 football season. This time I had the position of defensive tackle sewed up from the start, and I managed to land a place on the offensive line, as well. We had a ten-game season facing us, so we got started a week early by playing our first game at home against Temple University, a Philadelphia school, on September 20. Penn State's football stadium is located on the northwest corner of the campus. Since 1952, the stadium has been remodeled, but it still sits only about a quarter of a mile from Old Main, the center of the campus. So, when we played at home, we were really at home.

Temple succumbed to us, 20-13, and then we tied Purdue at twenty points the following week. We had still not played away from home when we defeated William and Mary the following week, 35-23. October 11, however, found us down in Morgantown in a contest with West Virginia which we won, 35-21.

We held the Cornhuskers scoreless the following Saturday at University Park (Penn State's campus has its own post office by that name, a branch of the main office in the city of State College) in a strong defensive match in which we accumulated only ten points.

On October 25 we traveled to East Lansing to play Michigan State. On the first offensive play of the game, we got the ball and ran a trick play. Our tight end, Donald Malinak, was wide open and went in for a touchdown. That was the only time we scored. They beat us 34 to 7! But we came back the next week in Philadelphia to beat the University of Pennsylvania, 14-7.

On November 8 we rode to upstate New York to drop one to Syracuse, 25-7. Our last home game was a close win over Rutgers, 7-6, followed by a decisive trouncing of Pitt, 17-0, on their turf on November 22. We ended the season 7-2-1. Rip Engle was pleased and so were we. Holding Pitt scoreless after they had beat us the previous year was the crowning event of the season.

Being a first-string football player and having a car of my own made me a highly eligible campus bachelor. I was dating more frequently — getting over some of my high school shyness — but I didn't make a steady habit out of anyone in particular. I was attracted by several young women, but every time a relationship started to develop, I would begin to feel tied down. It was much the same feeling I had when Poppa left me in charge in Georgia while he went up to New Jersey to look for a job. That sense that someone was depending on me or had a claim on me inevitably muddied those relationships and made it impossible for me to enjoy them. When a relationship started to grow, I found myself worrying about the girl or jealous of her, or feeling resentful because she was jealous of me.

But my distaste for relationships grew dramatically as a result of one I became involved in over the Christmas holidays in 1952. I met Doris while I was home for those holidays and things moved with exciting speed. (Did the thought that it would be over right after the holidays make it more attractive to me?) Anyway, our romance progressed rapidly and recklessly beyond the kissing stage, and we spent a lot of time together. Then, at the end of the holidays, I kissed Doris goodbye and hit the road for State College.

Some weeks later, I got a phone call. It was Doris and she announced, "Rosey, I'm going to have your baby, and I'm calling to tell you not to leave me holding the bag."

I swallowed hard and promised I'd get back to her, and then I went looking for advice. A few people suggested abortion. Others told me to let Doris wing it on her own. Still others said I had to marry her. Nothing I heard seemed to fit the situation. Abortion was out of the question and I could not ignore something I knew I was responsible for. But neither was I ready to get married, especially since I was not in love with Doris.

After a few days, I called Doris back and told her that all I could promise was financial support. Marriage was out of the question. That was hard and I was glad for the school schedule and the distance between us which helped me to keep the problem at arm's distance for a few months, at least. Summer would be a time of reckoning, but I tried not to think about that.

After that, I got through my second round of finals since changing my major to phys ed. The results were satisfactory and I was feeling more and more like I belonged in this setting.

Spring arrived shortly and, with it, the outdoor regular track season. At last I could get to work on earning the scholarship money that had been sustaining me through the previous three semesters. Although I had participated in indoor track during my freshman year, I had been ineligible for outdoor track because of my grades.

True to the expectations of the coaches who had recruited me from high school, Chick Werner and Norm Gordon, I won the shot put and the discus in most of our five dual meets. My coaches knew how to help me. Chick got mad sometimes, but mostly he worked on techniques. I learned from him that you lead by your performance. He also taught me that my attitude in competition and the ability to stick to my goals and commitments are more important than winning. But I still liked winning better than losing.

Chick and Norm knew track and field events well and were able to teach them. And they were unwilling to let any of us try to slide by in academics by keeping only the barest minimum grade requirements. Instead, they worked seriously with us to see that we were doing our best in the classroom.

Overall, the track team had a dismal season, winning only one of its five regular meets. The records show that I placed fourth in the shot put at the big IC4A (Inter-Collegiate Amateur Athletic Association of America) meet that culminated each season, and that I bettered the unspecified school record I had set for the shot put the previous year during indoor track.

People familiar with collegiate track meets in more recent times may want to understand that, during the years I was at Penn State (and for some years after that), track meets were conceived of as team events. They were reported in terms of the overall scores accumulated by the two teams, much as if they had been football games. We may have gathered for a meet against Navy, for example, in which yet a third school may have participated. But the statistical records show only that Penn State accumulated so many points, Navy so many, and the other school so many. The team with the most points won the meet, while the other two lost.

In the years since then the schools have recognized increasingly that track is a group of individual efforts, distinct from the team sports. Consequently, scores are no longer maintained in the same ways they were when I was an undergraduate.

The reality of this individual aspect of track was always there, of course. And, since football is the most team-oriented of all the team sports, track afforded me a counterbalancing opportunity to develop and express my individuality. And that was important to me — a need I felt so strongly that I took a lot of speech classes. I had first taken them when they became available to me as high school electives because I wanted to rid myself of my Southern accent. They also served to reinforce my language skills which helped my performance in English classes where I struggled harder for good grades than in most of my other classes.

I continued to take speech classes at Penn State, and how many times I remember the teacher asking for someone to give an extemporaneous talk, and me raising my hand. But when I found myself actually standing in front of the class, my mind went blank. I forgot my name, along with anything else I had planned to say. It was enormously discouraging, but something inside me made me continue to go for it.

I do not pretend to understand fully what that something was, but I do have some thoughts on the matter. During nearly all the time I was at Penn State, I continued to experience that odd feeling of duality about myself I had discovered earlier. I felt I was two people, and one of us was standing on the outside, watching me and saying, "How are you going to do all those things?"

It was a way I had of challenging myself to keep moving and not to give up — to become the person I was supposed to be: able to weather trials, and to remain true to myself, not bending just because others did.

At the same time it seemed my life was simply happening. As I kept walking forward, doors kept opening before me. That reinforced something which helped me more than anything else in my struggles — the belief that God was on my side. I didn't go to church any longer (I had stopped during my freshman year because the first couple of times I went the preacher seemed so dull and campus chapel services at the university proved unbearably dry). Yet, somehow I still believed God cared about me. I was well aware that my life did not measure up to the moral precepts of the Bible, but I also vaguely understood that though my sins would find me out (as, indeed, they had), they did not diminish God's essential love for me. It had something to do with mercy and grace.

My faith, of course, stemmed from my childhood — from the songs we used to sing in church and out on our front porch. I took a large record collection of gospel songs to college and when things got tough, as when my dad died, I would play those songs and cry. Listening to them gave me fresh determination to keep going, even though I felt, most of the time, like I was walking in tall grass, not knowing where the next step would lead — or what snake might be lurking underfoot. Yet I was going forward, knowing that somehow I would arrive safely on the other side.

I'm grateful for that faith because the doggedness it gave me was paying off. In spite of my halting performance in speech class, my grade average attained a gentlemanly respectability after finals that spring.

But, back in Roselle for the summer, there was anything but gentlemanly respectability for me. As soon as I got home, my mother said, "Roosevelt, the Linden police called here and said they wanted to talk to you when you got home."

"But what for?" I demanded.

"I don't know, but it sounded serious."

In spite of my apprehension about policemen, I went down to the station. After I identified myself to the desk sergeant, he said, "Mr. Grier, you're under arrest for bastardy."

I stood there in stunned disbelief. What had I done? I didn't want to look foolish by asking him what bastardy was. To me, it was a horrible obscenity with a "y" on the end.

I was booked on this bewildering charge, fingerprints and all. I decided it must not be too serious because I was not placed in a cell. But I did have to spend the day at the station until Mama could come down and post bail for me. She was not too shy to ask what the charge meant and the sergeant explained that Doris's mother had filed a complaint about her pregnancy. Mama got the bail money back not long after that. When the judge learned that both Doris and I were over eighteen, he dismissed the charge.

I had imagined as a child that being arrested meant the police would put a strap around your chest and pull it tight. The real experience was less fearsome. I had spent my day in jail roaming the aisles outside the cells, talking with various prisoners. But it was still enough to show me that being in prison is indeed like having a strap around your chest. Nothing had ever felt so hateful. I made up my mind never to do anything again that would put me in that kind of situation.

Word of the situation with Doris spread widely in the circle of my family and acquaintances. It was painfully embarrassing. I felt ashamed and vaguely guilty.

That vague guilt came clearly into focus when Doris bore our daughter on August 14, 1953. I went to see the baby in the hospital and felt like a creep because I was still unwilling to marry her mother. After that, there was a real person, a baby named Sheryl, whom I saw I was neglecting by my refusal to give her my last name.

I have carried the load of that guilt ever since. At the time of this writing, Sheryl is a mature woman, and she has graciously forgiven me for my failure. I feel and appreciate that forgiveness. But it cannot erase the consequences of my failure, especially in terms of the deprivation I inflicted on Sheryl throughout her childhood by my absence.

Nor are those consequences erased to the extent that I can be entitled to the name of father in the full sense of that word. But I love Sheryl and her former husband, Eddie, and their children, Keith and Kimberly, my grandchildren. And I am grateful that we have kept in touch and that a friendship has grown between us.

On July 14, 1953, my twenty-first birthday passed largely unnoticed. Mostly, I was looking forward to getting out of town for football practice and to the reopening of school in the fall.

7

OUT OF THE TALL GRASS

It was good to be back at University Park after the sobering events of the summer. I need to be thankful for those events, however. They brought me back onto campus with a new resolve to finish what I had started by coming to Penn State in the first place.

In addition to the situation with Doris, the summer had given me further cause for reflection. That had happened when I looked up some old high school chums. Seeing them and the course their lives were following made me feel doubly thankful for the opportunity that had been handed me by Penn State. My athletic gifts had made a place for me, and now I was reaching out for something. I did not know what that something was, nor how I was going to attain it. Except that I did know I needed more than ever to commit myself to athletic and academic achievement. That in itself seemed so formidable that I hardly gave thought to what might lie beyond it. I only remember that I kept telling myself, "God will help me." I didn't know much about God, but I knew enough to trust Him.

The football season opened on September 26 in Madison, with a game against the University of Wisconsin. There I first encountered someone I was going to see a lot more of in my life, Alan "The Horse" Ameche. I had watched him run, and he ran straight-up. That posture made him look unusually vulnerable to me. I figured we ought to be able to tear up anyone who ran that high. Penn State was so good, there was no way he would be able to run through us.

But we had no idea how good the Wisconsin Badgers were. Ameche played great football and was anything but vulnerable. The Badgers gave us a nasty setback for our season opener, 20-0. It took us a long time to come out of that. We thought we were off and running, and we were — but we weren't running that far!

And we hardly felt any better when we lost to Penn, 13-7, the following Saturday in Philadelphia. But the third time around, we finally got it right and beat Boston University, 35-13, in Boston.

The homecoming game was against Syracuse whom we were glad to defeat, 20-14, after having lost to them in 1952. All the remaining games of the season were played at Beaver Stadium as well, except the last one against Pitt. Of those, we lost only one, a close one, to West Virginia, 20-19. The rest of the time we spent beating Texas Christian, Fordham, and Rutgers. And the season ended on a much better note than the one on which it had begun when we again humbled Pitt, 17-0. That brought the season to a respectable tally of six wins and three losses.

Freshman Lenny Moore was our star player, demonstrating every Saturday afternoon the ball-carrying skills that would carry him through a spectacular eleven-year career with the Baltimore Colts and on into the NFL Hall of Fame. But the Penn State football team boasted a number of fine players in the 1953 season: Jesse Arnelle was notable as an All-American basketball player and a great tight end on the football squad, but even more as an excellent student with strong leadership qualities. He was the first black to become student body president at Penn State. Our quarterback was Don Bailey who performed steadily and admirably in that capacity. Charlie Blockson was a big angular kid who was almost as good as Lenny. Today Charlie is a great black historian.

Danny (Dante was his given name) DeFalco stood the defensive line with me, an aggressive player and classmate who earned my admiration. Jim Garrity was another good offensive player who ran and kicked for us. Don Balthaser, another strong defensive player, and Garrity would become co-captains of the team during my senior year. Others I remember were Sam Green (defense), Sam Valentine (defense), and Milt Plum (offense). Sam Green lettered in '52 and '53 and is today a deputy sheriff in Pottstown, Pennsylvania. Valentine was a guard who made All-American the season after my last at Penn State. He died in 1984. Milt Plum played in the '54, '55, and '56 seasons and went on to play for the Lions and the Browns as a quarterback. He once led the NFL by having the fewest interceptions in one season.

All of the above were great athletes. With their help, Penn State was beginning to build a national reputation in athletics. Our games began to be broadcast over the radio fairly often. One of them was even televised that season. We had guys who made All-American and All-East, and I had a great year — actually gaining a little reputation as a good college athlete by making first-team All-East and various teams. Then, in addition, I received the accolades that go with being touted as a potential All-American: those included newspaper stories that dubbed me Penn State's "Iron Curtain" and "The Mountain" — and some feelers from NFL teams (which I ignored). But what was even more pleasing for me, my sister Eva and my cousin Thelma came to a game to see me play that season. Sadly, it was the one we dropped in Philadelphia, though that hardly diminished my joy in having them there.

As the first semester of my junior year neared its end, I realized I would not be ready to graduate with my classmates in June of 1955. That was because I had fallen behind in grade points and credits during that first semester I had spent majoring in music. Everything since then had been fine, but I had not used summer sessions in an effort to catch up, partly because the university assisted me financially by helping to arrange summer jobs for me.

Of course, that was not the only reason I wasn't playing catch up on the academic front. As one old fraternity song says, "For it's not for knowledge that we came to college, but to have fun while we're here." Having fun may not have been my primary goal, but neither was I an all work and no play student. My chief form of recreation was found with a little ensemble of singers. We called ourselves "The Midnight Cavaliers" and roamed around at night serenading the girls in the dorms (they still resided in separate dorms in those days). At first, they called us the "mysterious singers," but later they found out who we were. The college paper occasionally reported on our activities and once said that our appearance on a wintry night was eagerly anticipated in the dorms. We loved the publicity, but most of all, we were having fun.

The ensemble was comprised of Earl Mundell (one of the fullbacks), Sam Green, Seth Brown, and me. The next year, after Earl and Sam finished school, James Chester and Carl Henson joined Brown and me, with Harry Mitchell acting as our manager and agent (things got a little more structured with time). Lenny Moore wanted in on the fun, but he couldn't sing a note. So, we told him he could come along on one condition, that he promise not to sing! He agreed, and when he joined us in our serenades, he opened his mouth and only pretended to sing.

One Friday after classes, Lenny Moore, Jesse Arnelle, Sam Green, Charlie Blockson, and I took off in my car. Jesse and I were both from out of state, but the other three were Pennsylvanians and we spent the entire weekend visiting their homes: Norristown (Charlie), Reading (Lenny), and Pottstown (Sam) — all towns in the southeastern part of the state on the outskirts of Philadelphia. We were joy riding through the Alleghenies on our way back to campus and I got to feeling reckless. So, after descending a long grade, we were barreling along at a good clip. Then, up ahead in a small town, there was a traffic light which turned red shortly before I arrived at it. Feeling my oats, I disregarded it and went through it without slowing down even a little. Everybody laughed, but, after a few moments, I was stricken with pangs of conscience over what I'd done. In a horrible instant, the headline flashed before my eyes: "Five State Gridders Killed in Collision."

I have castigated myself for that bit of recklessness for so long that I almost lost sight of the fact we were spared and for that I am thankful.

During my freshman and sophomore years, I spent most of my free time with a young lady named Sarah. During my junior and senior years it was Delores Washington and Joyce Mitchell.

It was also during my junior year in the summer that I developed a friendship with a white coed named Joan whose family lived near campus. Her parents seemed to take no offense at our relationship which was, in fact, low-key and non-romantic. I was always welcomed warmly into their home which I visited frequently.

Early one Sunday after I had been keeping company with this girl for about five weeks, I got a phone call. It was one of my coaches who said, "What's this I hear about you having a white girl in the bushes?"

"That's not true!" I protested.

"Well, people are talking," he said, "and I thought you oughta know. Just watch your step, Rosey."

I was really burned at him for having made himself a conduit for racism. Until that moment, my exposure to racism had been second-hand, except for some minor stuff that had not affected me in any important way. Until that moment. . . .

But I responded very calmly. I was determined not to show that I was hurt. Nor did I respond to the intimidation by breaking off my friendship. In fact, I never mentioned to her or her parents what had been said. And, I'm glad to say, our friendship continued throughout the remaining time I was at the university.

Track season arrived once again, first indoor and then outdoor. And I was there for both. The team redeemed itself from its poor showing the previous year by taking all four of its dual meets. In our meet against Navy on May 1, I put the shot 55 feet, 8¼ inches. That set a new record for Penn State, and, at the end of the season, it turned out to be the second best in college competition throughout the United States. At the Penn Relays, I took third in the shot put and fifth in the discus, and, at the IC4A championships (May 28-29) in New York, in which the Penn State team took overall first place, I took first in the shot put and second in the discus. In June, I went to the NCAA finals in Ann Arbor, Michigan, and placed fifth in the shot put with what was, for me, a mediocre distance of 52 feet, 11 inches.

At the end of my junior year, I was elected co-captain of the track team with Roy A. Brunjes. Roy was an engineering student from Long Island and a fine hurdler. Co-captain — it wasn't bad. I had come a long way and now I was standing on the brink of my senior year. The goal was in sight.

My summer passed uneventfully and Penn State's 1954 football season opened in Champaign against Illinois, a Big Ten powerhouse with an unbeatable offensive backfield. They figured to send us limping back to Pennsylvania, but they only partly succeeded. In a hard-fought contest, Jesse Arnelle and then Lenny Moore each scored a touchdown during the first half. We went to the lockers, leading 14-6. In the second half, the Illini made a strong effort that netted them another touchdown but, again, failed to gain the extra point. At that moment, our defensive squad went into full gear against the much-touted Illini offensive machine (which had made the school co-champion of the Big Ten the previous year) and rendered it ineffective for the rest of the game.

Having gone into the game as 17-point underdogs, we had scored the upset (14-12) and collected a choice laurel for ourselves in front of a record opening-game crowd of 54,094. But that aggressive defense of the second half had cost me personally. In the final quarter with a few minutes remaining in the game, I hurt my knee making a tackle. It was my first injury in college play.

We whooped it up on the train ride back to State College where we got a booming reception from the student body. But I was troubled. The pain in my knee told me this was no light bruise that would disappear overnight. The doc looked at it but could only tell me to take it easy the rest of the week (sports medicine was still in its infancy). I was heartsick as I contemplated how this would probably affect my chances for making All-American.

The following Saturday, we were scheduled to travel two-hundred miles north to play Syracuse. The game would be personally momentous for me because it would be the first of a long series of encounters I would have with one of football's all-time great offensive players, Jim Brown. Like me, Jim was a Georgian by birth, from St. Simon's Island. He was four years my junior, so this was only his first year with the Syracuse team. Already, however, it was plain, he was the man to stop. As I sat in a darkened classroom one afternoon that week, watching film clips of the Syracuse team, I was impressed by what I saw. And I was discouraged by the ache in my knee. Still, there was nothing to do but stop the young stallion and his teammates — to let them know what a real defense could do.

It did not matter that I was injured and not at my peak. I had to play that game — even though my mobility was restricted to a straight-ahead attack. We had spent three seasons growing together, and that experience made me more useful in the game than an uninjured, but less-experienced player would have been. In addition, I had a reputation which affected our opponents. And that made it doubly important for me to come on the field — without limping.

Jim Brown was excellent and I got so absorbed in the hard work of stopping him that I nearly forgot about my knee. I was finding out something about myself in those days: I could only play my best when I was up against the best. Well, Lenny got us on the board late in the first quarter with a 22-yard scamper off tackle, but our offense was having on off-day, lots of fumbles and a faltering pass attack. We didn't score again until the third period. The final score was Penn State 13, Syracuse 0.

We came home to play Virginia the following Saturday, October 9. It was a lopsided contest and we swamped them 34-7. The next Saturday drew a record crowd (32,221) for the season's official homecoming game which would see us in a rematch against West Virginia's Mountaineers who had beat us in 1953.

After West Virginia put the first score on the board, Moore and Bailey paced a downfield attack that ended with Ron Younker snagging a ten-yard pass from Bailey for the touchdown. A little while later, Lenny scored from the eight. Both times Jim Garrity connected for the extra points, and we went off the field at halftime, leading 14-6.

But the second half saw our offense stagger, unable to put any more points on the board. Still, we stood firm against the West Virginia offense and held onto the lead. Everything was going well in the fourth quarter when, suddenly, the Mountaineers came alive. In the space of three minutes they put two touchdowns and an extra point on the board. The score was 19-14 against us. We only needed a touchdown to regain the lead. Bailey and Moore set out in a determined effort to make that touchdown, but a fumble on the West Virginia 40 in the last few minutes of the game ended our hopes.

The next Saturday marked another first for me: my first trip west of the Mississippi as we rode to Fort Worth to play Texas Christian. We had beaten them in State College in 1953, and now it was our turn to visit them. They scored two quick touchdowns in the opening quarter. Then we got down to business and kept them away from their end zone until the final quarter when they got across its line once more to bring the score to a humiliating 20-0. At last, we rallied and drove sixty-five yards in four plays. In the last of those four, Lenny Moore made a spectacular diving catch of a Bailey pass in the end zone in the final forty-seven seconds of the game. Final score: 20-7.

The next game was special because it was telecast as the game of the week on whatever network was doing that in 1954. To play it we traveled downstate to Philadelphia, eager to avenge our previous year's loss to the University of Pennsylvania. Lenny Moore carried the ball for touchdowns three times that afternoon, and a sophomore named Billy Kane ran in two others. The vengeance was sweet, 35-13.

That left us with a 4-2 record as we headed into the last three games of the season. The first two would be at Penn State's Beaver Field against Holy Cross and Rutgers; the last against Pittsburgh in their huge oval stadium.

Holy Cross was no match for us that year. We rolled over them 39-7 in a game that was notable because it was the occasion on which Lenny Moore broke Penn State's rushing record. The next Saturday's victory over Rutgers, 37-14, was attributed, I was proud to read later, to "superior line play and a bruising ground and aerial attack. . . ."

Pittsburgh had a cornerback named Henry "Model-T" Ford. He was a defensive back, and, since I was playing on both our offensive and defensive lines, I had a lot of collisions with the Model-T. The game ended, a hard-fought victory for Penn State, 13-0. It was our third win in as many years in the traditional season finale — the perfect finish, especially for us who were seniors. And to have held two tough teams, Syracuse and Pitt, scoreless was a particular plum for us on the defensive platoon.

When the season was tallied, we had won seven and lost two, the best record for the team in the four years I played with it. Our scores totalled 211 points, while we had held our opponents to 87. We were the runner-up for the Lambert Trophy for the top team of the East Coast. Lenny Moore was first-team All-American and I made third-team All-American, and first-team All-East.

It was my senior year and I had done well enough, in spite of that injury in the Wisconsin game, to qualify for some of the post-season games. That would be fun and I was looking forward to it. And, sure enough, Coach Engle asked me to meet him in his office near the end of the season.

"Rosey," he began, his face unusually somber, "you've helped put Penn State on the map ever since you got here, and this season has only confirmed your place as one of the finest football players to have ever attended this school."

"Thanks, coach," I replied, feeling slightly bewildered. The remarks were great, but their tone strangely foreboding.

"You've earned the right to participate in at least one of the post-season games, but I have to tell you you're not going to get an invitation to any of them."

"How come?"

"Rosey, it's a shame on college football, but the powers that be have ordained a quota system. Only a certain percentage of the students selected for the special games can be colored. The rest have to be white," he said and cast his eyes downward.

I stiffened. This was ten times more hateful than the call I'd gotten about a white girl in the bushes. But I kept a poker face and acted as if it were a matter of indifference to me.

"Rosey, I'm truly sorry. If there were anything I could do to change it, I'd have done it long ago. But the system is fixed — this year at least. You deserve to play in one of those games, and you deserve even more to know why that right is being denied you."

I knew about the quota system. Every black athlete knew about it. In some ways, we were proud about it because it meant that any black athlete who made it did so because he was significantly superior to a white athlete in the same position. But that didn't lessen my pain or the pain of any deserving black athlete who was excluded because of it. Prejudice was hitting me hard, right where I lived. And there was nothing I could do about it, which was the most maddening thing of all.

I did have a source of comfort, however. Several NFL teams had written me letters during the season: the Pittsburgh Steelers, the Los Angeles Rams, the Baltimore Colts, the Philadelphia Eagles, and others. I had replied to each of those letters by writing back that the only team I wanted to play with was the New York Giants. I suppose this shows my naivete either about business negotiation or the NFL draft system. Happily for me, the coaches and managers in the NFL were used to that sort of thing from the young athletes and usually found ways to accommodate them. In my case, I was drafted on the third round by the Los Angeles Rams and then traded to the Giants. By Christmastime I had what every college senior wants: a job awaiting after graduation. It gave me a wonderfully secure feeling which made it a lot easier to bear the pain inflicted on me by the quota system.

With my last college football season behind me, it was time to turn my attention to track once again. It was more poignant to be starting my last season of track since it would, most likely, be my very last. After all, it was a track scholarship that had carried me through Penn State, and it was the track team that had elected me its co-captain. And it was the shot put which had already given me All-American status. Football had not been quite as rewarding — although it was offering to put the groceries on my table, and there was a lot to be said for that!

The 1955 regular outdoor season opened in Annapolis, Maryland, in a meet against Navy and Penn on April 16. Penn State rolled up more points than both of the other teams combined.

The next week we went to the Ohio State Relays, and I came up against a big fellow named Tom Jones. The evening before the meet, he and I were practicing and checking each other out. We were throwing that shot a country mile trying to outdo each other and wearing ourselves out in the process. It felt so good we kept at it for a long time. I could just feel that record falling into my hands. He and I had earlier put the shot 59 feet and 60 feet, respectively, in separate practice sessions — the week before the Ohio relays got some attention in the newspapers. Olympic champion Perry O'Brien of California had established an Olympic record of 57 feet, 1½ inches in Helsinki in 1952. In 1955, he held the world record at 58 feet, 11 inches. Both Tom and I were after that record.

As a result of our over-exertion, the next day we had a hard time qualifying for the finals. Tom came in third, while I managed to place second.

The following week, on April 29-30, we went to the annual Penn Relays in Philadelphia, where I took first in the shot put with a throw of 54 feet, 8 inches.

Our next meet was at home on May 7 with Michigan and Navy. We took second place (although, in the manner of keeping records that prevailed then, it was counted as a loss).

The next Saturday, May 14, we hosted Boston University for a meet we won, 104-26. For me it was memorable because I put the shot 56 feet, 3½ inches. That established a Penn State record which stood for fourteen years until Mike Reid put it 57 feet, 5 1/2 inches in 1969. Our fourth and final regular meet was with Pitt four days later, on May 18, a Wednesday. We won it.

The following Saturday, I was in Los Angeles (my first visit there) for an invitational meet, the Coliseum Relays. It was fun to make the trip, but my performance was lackluster. I took fourth in the discus and fifth in the shot put with a put of 53 feet, ¼ inch. In fact, that week in practice I put the shot 60 feet, 3 inches. The newspapers played that up big. The morning of the meet Perry O'Brien came over to me and said simply, "We'll see. We'll see." O'Brien took first with 58 feet. I did throw one over 59 feet, but it was disqualified because I fouled.

The next weekend found me and my teammates at the IC4A championships in New York, where something very special happened to me. The shot put had long been my forte rather than the discus. So, naturally, I thirsted the more earnestly for success when it came to discus competition. And that thirst had long been heightened by an athlete named Al Thompson, who had beaten me in discus all through high school. Our paths had continued to cross at various meets during my college years and the pattern had continued.

Now, at this IC4A meet, I would get my last chance to better Al in the discus. So, after the shot put, which I won, I went over to the discus event where he was, as usual, the leading thrower. My teammate, Charlie Blockson, was third. I don't know what happened to me, but I knew I was up against it when I stepped into that ring. I made the most faultless spin of my career and sent that baby sailing as I had never done before. When the measurement came in, I could hardly believe my ears: 170 feet, 6 inches — the farthest I had ever hurled a discus. Nor was it shabby by other standards. The Olympic record then stood at 168 feet, 8½ inches. Few things in life have made me as happy as I felt at that moment.

Thompson already had a throw of 160 feet. He came back for another turn (in these events, each competitor is entitled to four preliminary throws and the six top qualifiers get three additional throws). He huffed, and he puffed, but he couldn't make it. He was flabbergasted to see that I had finally, after all those years, whipped him. It also turned out that my mark established a Penn State record that, like my shot put record, stood for fourteen years, until it was broken by an additional five inches in 1969 by Fred Kingston.

To put these records in contemporary perspective, the world shot put record in 1984 stood at 72 feet, 10¾ inches (held by Udo Beyer of East Germany), and the discus record stood at 235 feet, 9 inches (by Yuriy Dumchev of the Soviet Union). We were the forerunners of new and better training techniques, weight rooms and other aids.

I never did bring myself to smear my cheek with resin. Perry O'Brien and Tom Jones smeared their cheeks with it because it helped reduce the slippage that occurs because of facial perspiration. It was a practice I first witnessed during my high school years, and I have always wondered how much farther I might have put the shot if I had been able to overcome my reluctance to put that gooey stuff on my skin.

I possessed the requisite strength and agility to turn in a great performance, but they are only the raw materials. Today I look back on myself with a bit of disgust for the things — like my inhibition about resin — which showed I lacked the attitude and maturity it took. I find it as hard to forgive myself for that as I do for my mistake with Doris. How nice it would have been to be as strong and wise as I looked. But, like most young men emerging from their teens, I found myself losing the struggle to bring myself and my body into submission, either on the playing field or in the dating game. From where I stand today, I need to be philosophical about that, but I also have to acknowledge that it kept me from achieving my fullest potential as an athlete and as a person.

My college days were over, except that I didn't graduate that June. I still needed some more credits to complete my Bachelor of Science in Physical Education. I arranged with Penn State to get those credits by returning to classes in the second semester, February-June, 1956, which would follow immediately on my rookie season with the New York Giants. What that rookie year would involve, however, was now the biggest question mark in my mind.

8

MY ROOKIE
YEAR WITH
THE GIANTS

In the spring of 1955, shortly before the end of the semester, I was selected by the pro scouts to play in the 22nd Annual All-Star Football Game. This was an event, sponsored by the Chicago Tribune Charities, that had gotten started in 1934 as a result of the efforts of Arch Ward, the *Chicago Tribune* sports editor. The idea was to assemble a team of college All-Star rookies and to pit them against the previous season's NFL championship team. It may sound a bit bizarre by today's standards, but it is important to recall that college football enjoyed greater popularity in those years than did pro ball. So, it made perfect sense to spark interest in the professional game by linking it closely with the college game in this way.

I was the only player from Penn State chosen to be on that All-Star team. It was a great honor which I was pleased to receive. I got a lot of attention in the *Daily Collegian*, Penn State's college newspaper, which made it all the more fun, if a little bit embarrassing.

The All-Star game was scheduled for Friday, August 12, and would be played at its regular site, Soldier's Field in Chicago. Our opponents would be the Cleveland Browns, but we would also get to scrimmage "The Monsters of the Midway," the Chicago Bears. It promised to be an unparalleled introduction to the pro game and the people who played it. I could hardly wait.

But wait I did. I went home to Linden and touched bases with friends and relatives. I wanted especially to see my older brother James who had appreciated and enjoyed my athletic achievements in a way that gave me a lot of encouragement. I always called on him when I was home from college. He hung out in an unsavory section of Newark called "The Neck" — perhaps because anyone who went in there was risking his neck. But it was safe for me to go there because of my connection with James.

The grapevine in The Neck was fast and reliable. Whenever I went to see James — usually to hit him up for a little money — I would go first to a certain area where people congregated and put the word out to one or two of those who were standing around that I was looking for my brother, James Grier. Not long after that, the message would reach him wherever in the district he happened to be: "Your brother that plays ball for Penn State is looking for you."

He would appear awhile after that, and he always had a few dollars for me. Maybe ten or fifteen, which was enough to carry me a long time at school in those days. I didn't have much to spend money on, just a hot dog once in a while or taking a girl to a movie.

Now, of course, school was over and I had a job. I wanted to see James to thank him again for the kindness he had shown me over the last four years.

"Hey, kid," he laughed, "it's okay. Just remember, I'm here if you need me, and I'll be rootin' for you when you start playing for the Giants. When do you leave for training camp?"

"I'm supposed to report right after the All-Star game on August 12," I replied.

"You gonna be in the All-Star game? Hey, that's great, man. Wait'll I tell 'em back at the place that my kid brother'll be in that! Roosevelt, you're doin' good. I'm proud of you."

"Thanks, that means a lot," I grinned a little sheepishly.

"Here," he said, stuffing a ten-spot in my hand, "just one more for old times' sake. Don't tell me you can't use it, either. Hey, it's gettin' on dinner time. C'mon, I'll buy ya a steak for getting on that All-Star team."

When I got to the All-Star camp in Chicago in the early part of August, I met someone with whom I had a lot in common. His name was Mel Triplett. Mel was my age and had been born in Indianola, Mississippi. His father had been a farmer and his siblings had numbered sixteen. And he knew what it was to plow a field with a team of mules. His family had moved to Ohio after tornadoes had ruined the cotton crop one year. He was already married and had two kids when he was offered a scholarship to play for Toledo University. He was a fine running back who had helped Toledo assemble a respectable record the last few years. Now, like me, he was headed for the Giants' training camp in Salem, Oregon, as soon as the All-Star game was over.

I was also glad to see a familiar face in Tom Jones from Miami University of Ohio. This is the same Tom Jones with whom I practiced putting the shot that evening back in late April before the Ohio Relays. Jones was big, an inch taller than I at 6-feet-6, and he was not skinny. Some of the other All-Stars whose names I recall were Alan Ameche ("The Horse" from the Penn State-Wisconsin game in 1953), Frank Eidom, Hank Bullough (who coaches the Buffalo Bills today), Ralph Guglielmi, Tad Weed, Joe Heap (a Giants' rookie back), Bobby Watkins, Rex Boggan (a Mississippian like Triplett, a tackle like me, and a Giants' rookie like both of us) and Frank Varrichione, a fellow lineman. The entire team numbered about fifty.

During the practices in the days before the game I got a little lesson in the value of publicity. One of the players on our All-Star team quickly demonstrated an appalling mediocrity in his ability to play football. It was so noticeable that someone finally asked him how he had managed to make All-American, the status which had apparently earned him a place on this team.

I heard him reply, "I can tell you why I'm All-American. I have a good public relations firm."

Oh well.

Our coach for the contest with the Browns was Curly Lambeau (then the former Packers' coach), who was assisted by Hunk Anderson, Steve Owen (the Giants' coach 1931-53), and Hampton Poole. The Browns, of course, had their regular coach, Paul Brown, at the helm. Their quarterback that day was the famous Otto Graham, who was about to begin his last season in professional football. Seventy-five thousand fans showed up at Soldier's Field that Friday night to watch us play.

I played defensive tackle during the game. In the first quarter, the Browns' fullback, Maurice Bassett, fumbled and I made the recovery.

That helped set up the first of several field goals kicked that night by Tad Weed.

The man I faced off against in that contest was already a legend in the NFL, Lou Groza, the Browns' offensive tackle and kicker. His kicking exploits had earned him the nickname "The Toe" and — at six-three and 250 pounds — he provided me with some serious competition. Lou was a veteran. He had signed on with the Browns when they were organized in 1946 under the old AAFC, right after he'd gotten out of the army in which he had fought as an infantryman in the Far East during the Second World War.

I was so fired up during the game that Lou finally said to me, "Rosey, the play is over, man!" — to get me to lay off after the ref had blown the whistle. I had developed a technique of sticking my hand in my opponent's face, and it was working so beautifully, I didn't want to stop. All that enthusiasm and vigor earned me the distinction of being runner-up to Tad Weed as outstanding player of that game.

But I'm getting ahead of myself. In the last quarter the game was tied at 27. Tad Weed kicked yet another field goal at the last minute and we All-Stars won it, amazingly, 30-27.

The night after the game, I reported to the Giants' camp, along with Joe Heap, Rex Boggan and Mel Triplett. We were a week late, and already they had played an exhibition game against the Green Bay Packers.

Early that first morning, Coach Jim Lee Howell got the three of us All-Star players out on the practice field for publicity photographs. That, it turned out, was the most pleasant experience I would have during the next few weeks. When the other players joined us, Coach Howell got down to business.

"Today," he announced angrily, "we're going to learn how to tackle on a kick-off. And I mean tackle the ball carrier and the football!"

The week before, during that exhibition game against Green Bay, the Giants had allowed one of the Packers to run a kick-off of more than a hundred yards upfield from the point of reception. So, my first day with the Giants was an eye-opener. Ben Agajanian kicked the ball off, and all of us had to run down the field in waves as fast as we could and tag the ball carrier, under game conditions. We had blockers to deal with. It was like running through a maze.

That practice meant we were doing 130-yard sprints over and over — chasing the running back who was carrying the ball. If we didn't tag him, we had to run all the way back up the field until we did tag him. He didn't stand still and wait for us to find him either! If Coach Howell saw a player taking it easy, he would add laps around the field in addition to practice. I was among those so honored, and after a while, I had never been so tired in my whole life.

"Mel, do you think we are going to make it?" I asked breathlessly.

"They can't kill us, Rosey," Triplett replied. "They can't kill us."

By the end of the day, however, we were not so sure. I went to bed as soon as practice was over. College practice had been a lot harder than high school, and I had thought playing pro ball would be more of the same. But nothing I had ever done even came close to what I experienced in those first weeks of training with the Giants. I didn't mind hard work but, up until then, work was work, and football was play. I wasn't sure I liked the change.

That first day out in the hot sun, with my heart pounding and my legs aching, with what felt like my life's blood running down my face and bruised body, was an unpleasant surprise. The thought of the money I was making for all that hard work crossed my mind, but I wondered if it was worth it. It was much the same feeling I had felt that day in the peanut field when I resolved, at the age of five, that I did not want to make a career of picking peanuts.

I was not sure what to expect from this group of men. My racial consciousness had been raised, especially by my experience with the post-season college games. How were these men going to regard and treat me as a Negro (the term we used in 1955)?

Several significant members of the organization were Southerners. Head coach Jim Lee Howell was from Arkansas, quarterback Charlie Conerly was from Mississippi, running back Kyle Rote was from Texas, and middle linebacker Ray Beck was from Georgia. It seemed to me that I might encounter prejudice from men with such backgrounds. But I didn't.

Jim Lee Howell had replaced the venerable Steve Owen as head coach in 1953. I quickly found him to be an absolutely fair and impartial man. He never played favorites. He would get on veteran Charlie Conerly or star pass receiver and runner Frank Gifford as readily as on any rookie. He got on whoever needed it without regard to status or seniority. He imposed a fine on anyone who was late to practice, no matter who it was. He once fined Tom Landry fifty dollars for being late. (But, believe me, no one laughed about it!)

After mentioning Tom Landry's name, I realize I need to explain that, as incredible as it may sound from the perspective of these waning years of the twentieth century, the two most remembered assistant coaches on the Giants' staff when I arrived in 1955 were Vince Lombardi and Tom Landry. Their names, of course, have since eclipsed that of Jim Lee Howell and those of many other superb head coaches of the 1950s. But none of us knew that was going to happen then. We just knew we had a fine coaching staff. However, readers today will have little trouble understanding how the New York Giants rose to national prominence in those days.

Now, back to 1955. Coach Howell stood six-four and weighed 220 pounds. An Arkansas farmer, he had been a captain in the Marines during the war and, as a coach, delegated his authority with an ease that showed he never felt threatened. He trusted his players and coaches and knew how to get the most out of them. He didn't try to prove what a great man he was. He tried, instead, to prove how great his players were. I felt he was a true friend, someone around whom I could put my arm.

Tom Landry began his professional football career in 1949 — after a stint at the University of Texas which bracketed his service in a B-17 bomber — with a short-lived team, the New York Yankees. When the Yankees folded a year later, he was scooped up by the Giants as a defensive back. He took over as defensive coach in 1954 while continuing to play. His name was still on the roster of players in 1955.

Landry didn't (and doesn't) talk a lot, as I suppose nearly everyone knows. He told the players what he expected of them, but he didn't stay after them by yelling and screaming. If a player didn't do as he was told, Landry took him out of the game to sit on the bench and contemplate the error of his ways. It was simple and effective.

Vince Lombardi had been hired by Jim Lee Howell in 1953. He had been assistant coach at West Point under the legendary Red Blaik — in the days of the infamous cribbing scandals. He had played college ball for Fordham where he had been one of the "Seven Blocks of Granite." He was our offensive coach and a great teacher. But he was a screamer who yelled and cursed at the players — something I couldn't abide and which made me glad I was a defensive player.

Coach Howell always said of Landry and Lombardi that he had the two smartest assistant coaches in football. He recognized Vince as an emotional person who screamed, ranted, and jumped up and down, but who knew how far he could go. Landry's contrasting imperturbability made them a remarkable pair. And he supervised the two of them according to their temperaments — Lombardi's leash was shorter. The other coaches were Ed Coleman and Ken Cavanaugh.

In addition to the four rookies — Triplett, Boggan, Heap, and me — there were three new faces in camp that August who were not rookies: Jim Patton and Alex Webster, who were both backs, and Harland Svare, a defensive linebacker. Alex had been playing pro ball in Canada very successfully for two seasons before the Giants signed him for this season.

Coach Howell scheduled two practices a day, and it was murder. I only went three places: to bed, to meetings, and to practice. It took two or three weeks to get our legs, then they cut down practice and began the exhibition games. The exhibition season consisted of six games, usually played on Saturdays. But we still had a practice game during the week. So there were only two hard days once the exhibition season started.

Pro football was still young in those days. Most of us were making modest salaries and thought nothing of it. We probably would have played for nothing if they had asked us. The fact that they gave us money to play was icing on the cake. The team spirit was marvelous: we all helped each other to make the team the best it could be, without much regard for our personal interests. I saw that right away when Ray Collins, the Giants' defensive tackle, took me under wing and taught me all he knew about playing that position. He did such a good job that his name does not even appear on the 1955 roster of the team. He helped me take his job away.

So it was that as a rookie still in training camp, I made the starting defensive team. Back then the front line of the defense still consisted of six players, two guards in the middle, two tackles on their outsides, and two ends. The day of the "front four" — a Landry invention — had not yet arrived.

First-team defensive tackle — I can't deny it, I was proud of that title, and I hung on to it for the entire twelve years of my professional football career.

The first time I played was in the Giants' second preseason game, an exhibition match against the San Francisco 49ers, in Seattle. Their offensive tackle on my side was Bobby Sinclair. I was an eager young rookie feeling my oats and having a good time, and I began to get on his nerves. After a while, I pulled my little technique on Bobby — I stuck my hand in his face. That was it! Without further ado, he let me have it right in the jaw, hard! It hurt so bad that I went to the sidelines.

"What happened, Rosey?" some of my teammates inquired when I arrived, rubbing my chin.

"That Sinclair guy is playing dirty," I complained. "He socked me one right in the jaw!"

They smiled and said, "Rosey, you can't let that guy beat you up on the football field like that."

So I went back out there and stuck my hand in his face, and he popped me again. I went to the sidelines again, but, this time, I went straight to Jim Lee Howell.

"Coach," I protested, "their tackle is playing dirty."

Howell's face remained placid, "Play ball, Rosey."

"But, Coach. . . ."

"Rosey," he said, "if you don't learn to take care of yourself, they'll beat you up every time you walk out on the field."

I got the message. I went back out there, and instead of sticking my hand in Bobby's face, I stuck my elbow in his face and hit him twice. The referee stepped in and stopped the fight, thank goodness.

After that, Sinclair said, "Let's play ball, Rosey," and we shook hands.

I had no more trouble again like that in my entire rookie year. It was a baptism of sorts, and, after that, Coach Landry turned me loose to rush the passer for a sack (we didn't call it that then, but that's what it was). It was something I liked to do and I did it well.

But I was still a rookie. I had to get used to longer quarters and a longer season. Our regular season opener came on a Saturday afternoon in Philadelphia against the Eagles. The World Series was about to begin in New York between the Yankees and the Dodgers, so we played in relative obscurity. But you couldn't have told that by me. I was going like a house afire, and I became exhausted near the end of the half. I went over to the sidelines, completely out of breath, and trainer Sid Morrett doused me with a bucket of cold water. I passed out in the midst of telling him I was going to kill him. After that, I learned how to pace myself and conserve my strength.

We lost that opener to the Eagles, 27-17. And the next week we dropped our second to the Bears in Chicago, 28-17. The next weekend we went to Pittsburgh to try our stuff against the Steelers. But we lost again, 30-23.

So, we came back to New York, 0-3, to play in a heavy rainstorm at the Polo Grounds. Amazingly, 12,000 fans showed up in spite of the weather. The mud was thick and the going hard, perfect conditions for an effective defense — which is exactly what happened. We won our first game of the season, 10-0.

After that, we dropped a second game to the Steelers, and beat the Redskins the following week at the Polo Grounds. The seventh game of our twelve-game season was against the league leaders, the Cleveland Browns, on their turf. We lost a brutal contest that saw Alex Webster carried off the field on a stretcher and one of the Browns' defensive players took a swing at our quarterback, Charlie Conerly. Browns' quarterback Otto Graham had to be helped off the field; he accused us on the defensive line of playing "dirty football."

With a pitiful record of two wins and five losses, we were back at the Polo Grounds the following Sunday afternoon to face the Baltimore Colts. They had signed Alan Ameche — whom I knew from Penn State's loss to Wisconsin and, second, from the college All-Star game. Even though a rookie, Alan was already leading the league in total rushing yards. Also, the Colts' defense was anchored by a clever fellow named Don Shula. Six thousand optimistic fans from Baltimore — waving their Confederate flags — were sitting alongside 24,000 New Yorkers that day.

But that turned out to be the day the New York Giants came alive and started playing the kind of football we would soon be famous for.

We held Ameche to forty yards that day — well below half his average — and we beat the Colts, 17-7.

That left us 3-5 with four games to play. The next week, the Philadelphia Eagles came to the Polo Grounds. They were the leading offensive team in the league, but Tom Landry prepared us well. We intercepted six Philadelphia passes and forced another six fumbles. Until that game they had averaged 310 yards a game, but we held them to 155. We trampled them, 31-7.

Then came the rematch with the Browns, and everyone in the press was asking what it might be like in light of the brutality of the first match in Cleveland. The pre-game hoopla attracted the season's largest crowd, 45,699, and they saw a memorable game.

Don Heinrich led the attack in the first two quarters while Charlie Conerly watched from the bench. Coach Howell explained that the strategy behind this arrangement was to allow Charlie to size up our opponents before entering the game. Charlie never said much about that, but any player knows the worst seat in the house is the bench.

In any event, Heinrich did a fine job in two drives that netted us fourteen points. Otto Graham and the Browns came back with a relentless pass attack that narrowed the score to 14-7 at halftime. In the third quarter Graham kept doing the same thing until the Browns led, 21-14. But our offensive end, Bob Schnelker, recovered a fumble in the end zone to tie the score just at the end of the quarter.

In the fourth quarter, a touchdown for each side brought the tie score to 28. Then the Browns intercepted a pass from Charlie Conerly and ran with it for a touchdown, 35-28. With only minutes left, Charlie and the offensive squad started an eighty-five-yard drive amidst a din of screaming fans such as I had never heard. With three minutes left in the game, Frank Gifford took a twenty-three-yard pass from Charlie and scored with it. Ben Agajanian, our toeless kicker, got the extra point and the game was tied again, at 35 points.

Now it was my turn to get back on the field and help keep Graham from getting the ball into field goal range for Lou Groza and his mighty toe. But, in four plays, they were at the fourteen, knocking at our door. Twenty-five seconds remained on the clock when Lou Groza came on to kick from the twenty-one.

The ball was snapped and the scramble was on. I pushed with all my might, but it was not enough. Groza's toe connected with the pigskin and up it went. Then, suddenly, one of our ends, Pat Knight, leaped high into the air with his hands outstretched. Groza's ball hit Pat's hands and tumbled pitifully to the grass below. Every fan in the stadium was on his feet roaring with pleasure as the gun sounded the end of the game — a thirty-five-point tie.

That was the last time the Giants ever played at the Polo Grounds and it made a fitting end to their long association with that site. The final two games of our season would be played on the road against the Washington Redskins and, in turn, the Detroit Lions. Neither one of those games would be a pushover, but we won them both. The score of the Washington game was 27-20, and we bearded the Lions, 24-19. It was the first New York victory against Detroit since 1945.

At the end of the season, our record was a pallid 6-5-1, but we knew that we had not lost a single one of our last five games. The tide had turned for us in mid-season. Nineteen-fifty-six would tell a different story. We would play our home games at Yankee Stadium from now on, and we would receive some powerful reinforcements.

As for me, I had a great time and learned a lot. And when we got back from Detroit, I went home to spend Christmas and January with my mother in Linden. I got over to "The Neck" and saw James a couple of times, too. At the end of January, I packed my bags and drove the familiar route between Linden and College Station, Pennsylvania. The time had come for me to collect the final credits I needed to finish my degree at Penn State.

9

BECOMING
A PRO

Being back at Penn State was anticlimactic. It was spring, and I was a pro. No more amateur sports for me. I hit the books and attended those last classes I needed to finish my degree. And, as soon as finals were over, I headed home. Graduation ceremonies seemed a little beside the point since I wouldn't be in the company of my classmates. I asked the university to send me my diploma in the mail.

I spent June and July in Linden. That gave me an opportunity to spend a little time with Sheryl by taking her out on occasional outings. She was approaching her third birthday and was scampering around, beautiful to watch. It was good to get a chance to see how she was doing. I was keeping my pledge to Doris to help her take care of Sheryl.

Nineteen-fifty-six was the year that Queen Elizabeth welcomed Marilyn Monroe at Buckingham Palace. The newsreels of the two of them standing and talking to each other caused a lot of humor in my circle of friends. We couldn't tell if the odd expression on the queen's face was curiosity or jealousy.

Hula hoops were all the rage. I was terrible at it, as I recall. Elvis Presley made his movie debut in *Love Me Tender*. I liked Elvis' music. But, mostly, I liked to play football. Training camp and the new season couldn't start too soon for me. This year, the team would train in Winooski, Vermont.

It was nice not to be a rookie at camp that August — being the new kid on the block is never fun. This time, instead, I was being reunited with men I was already beginning to care a great deal for — Charlie Conerly, Rosey Brown, Kyle Rote, Mel Triplett, and the others.

I remember how my friendship with Kyle Rote first developed. Pre-game jitters are a part of every ball player's life — they hit me in the form of nausea — and each of us had various ways of dealing with them. A lot of players controlled their jitters with grim determination — which showed on their faces. But not Kyle Rote and me. He and I got in the habit, shortly before a game, of retreating to some corner to tell jokes and recall funny anecdotes. Kyle was a good storyteller, and I was a good listener because I always laughed heartily at his jokes. Laughing helped me to stave off that nausea.

Kyle's granddaddy was the man who escaped from the Alamo in 1836 to carry the message, "God and Texas, victory or death!" So he was a Texan all the way. It had been another famous moment in 1949 when Rote was a junior at Southern Methodist and went into the game against Notre Dame to replace an injured back. SMU was trailing 13-0, but in an incredible performance, Kyle ran the ball 115 yards in twenty-four carries and scored all three of SMU's touchdowns. Notre Dame won, but only narrowly, because of Kyle.

The Giants signed him in 1951 right after he graduated, but knee injuries had plagued him. It had been Tom Landry's idea in 1954 to make Kyle an end rather than a back. That took a lot of the pressure off those knees and made him a much more effective player.

It was at that summer camp in 1956 that I met some new people, too, men with whom I was going to be playing a lot more closely than with Kyle because, of course, he was on the offensive squad. Those men were Sam Huff, Andy Robustelli, Jim Katcavage, Dick Modzelewski, and Don Chandler. Andy, Jim, and Dick would join me on the front defensive line to form what sportswriters called the team's backbone.

Andy came to us on a trade from the Rams for whom he had played for several years since graduating from college. But he was no stranger to Winooski, Vermont, because that is where his alma mater,

Arnold College, was located. He got the returning hero treatment from all the local folks that August.

Jim Katcavage, from Philadelphia, was a rookie out of Dayton College. Like most of us, he was superstitious, but his superstition was unusual. Jim always had to be first in whatever we did, first on the bus, first to get taped, whatever it was. It wasn't an ego trip, just old-fashioned athletic superstition. Once, in Cleveland, we all left for the game in the bus, but, when we got to the stadium, we realized Jim wasn't with us. So, back to the hotel we went to get him. Nobody was going to get off that bus ahead of Jim. It might have cost us the game!

Dick Modzelewski was the shortest of the four of us, standing six-feet-one. Thus his nickname, "Little Mo." Born in West Natrona, Pennsylvania, he had played ball for the University of Maryland and had been there in 1951 when they upset Tennessee, 28-13, in the Sugar Bowl. An All-American, he was awarded the Knute Rockne trophy in 1952. He arrived that summer of 1956 in the Giants' training camp after having played three seasons of NFL football, first for the Redskins and then for the Steelers.

Tom Landry dropped out of the defensive backfield in 1956 to take up coaching exclusively. He was replaced by a newcomer named Ed Hughes.

Our season opened with three games on the road: San Francisco, Chicago, and Cleveland. We won the first and lost the second. Then came the Browns who were without Otto Graham. Lacking his veteran quarterback, coach Paul Brown decided to equip his three new quarterbacks with tiny radio receivers in their helmets so he could talk to them directly. Well, it was a good idea, but it didn't work quite the way the coach had figured. The Cleveland crowd was rooting so loudly for their team that their quarterbacks could not hear their coach on the headsets. But a rookie receiver from Michigan named Bob Topp was sitting on our bench with a radio receiver that had a bigger speaker than those mounted in the Cleveland helmets. He heard every word Paul Brown uttered into his microphone that day, and, as soon as he heard the next play, he'd give it to Tom Landry who would yell it out to us on the defense, loud and clear. We won easily, 21-9.

That brought us to Yankee Stadium on October 21, 1956, to play before the largest opening-day crowd that had ever watched the Giants play football, 48,108. The locker rooms in Yankee Stadium were a lot nicer than the ones at the Polo Grounds. The toilets even flushed. When we saw that, we knew we'd hit the big time.

It didn't hurt, either, that we were now going to be closely associated in the minds of our New York fans with the winning Yankees baseball club. The last game played in the Stadium before our arrival had been the famous perfect game of the World Series pitched by Don Larsen. When we went into the lockers, there were their names: Mickey Mantle, Billy Martin, all the rest. Charlie Conerly took Mantle's locker.

On the Sunday afternoon of the game, the fans watched us play a near-perfect football game in which we demolished the Steelers, 38-10. That brought our season record to 3-1. The Chicago Cardinals led the league with a record of 4 and 0. (That's right, I said "Chicago." They didn't move to St. Louis until 1960.)

The next Sunday we entertained the Eagles. That was the game in which Sam Huff became a regular member of the defensive squad. Sam had been on those West Virginia teams that had beaten Penn State in '53 and '54 (recalling, of course, that Penn State won the contest in 1952). The son of a coal miner, Sam, like me, had sharpened his defensive skills in those college years by stopping Jim Brown when it was West Virginia's turn to play Syracuse. Now we would have the opportunity to try our hands together at stopping Jimmy during the next few years.

But, at that moment, our object was to stop the Eagles, which we did handily, as the score, 20-3, shows. Our twenty points reflected a new Lombardi strategy called "the sweep" which had produced a spectacular 37-yard run by Gifford. Happily, while we were beating the Eagles, the Cards were losing their first game to the Redskins. That put us into a tie with the Cards for first place; each of us with a 4-1 record. Each team won the following Sunday, bringing the tying records to 5-1.

And who were we set to play after that? Who else? The Cards themselves — who had beaten us back in the second game of the season. Neither the Redskins nor any other team in the league would help us take first place this weekend. We would have to beat them ourselves.

The Cards' leading rusher, Ollie Matson, was also the Eastern Conference's leading rusher. (The NFL was then comprised of twelve teams, six in the Eastern Conference and six in the Western. The teams in each conference with the best record of wins at the end of the season played each other for the championship of the entire NFL.) Yankee Stadium was crowded with the largest number of fans to watch a Giants' football game since 1928 when Red Grange had been the draw, 62,410.

They gave us all injections of B vitamins before we went on the field, which I thought was a little silly. But all the pre-game nervousness and odds setting meant little once the game got going. We held Ollie Matson to 43 yards and beat the Cards, 23-10. At last, we were at the front of the pack in the East with a 6-1 record.

The next week, however, the Washington Redskins halted our winning streak, but the Cards also lost which left us still in the lead, 6-2 against their 5-3. Our next opponents would be the team in first place in the Western Conference with a 7-1 record, the Chicago Bears.

The Bears were leading the entire league in rushing and passing. It was going to be another test of our defensive mettle, and it was going to be the occasion of Emlen Tunnell's 100th consecutive game as a Giant. Em was the first black man ever hired by the Giants when he walked into their offices in 1948 and asked for a job. He was the senior member of the defensive squad, famous for his record of interception, kick, and punt returns. In 1952, the yardage he accumulated on his returns was greater than that of the league's leading rusher, Deacon Dan Towler.

The Bears brought out the best in us defenders. We held their league-leading rusher to 13 yards. And, because we threw so many of their ball carriers for minus yardage, their total of yards against us was only 12. In the fourth quarter we were leading 17-3, but, in those last minutes, we let two long passes get away, and the game ended in a tie.

That put the Redskins into contention for the title because their schedule gave them their final game a week later than ours. After the Sunday of our tie with the Bears, when we stood 6-2-1 and the Cards 6-3, the Redskins were 5-3. We were scheduled to play them in the Stadium the following Sunday. If they could beat us, they had a good chance at the conference title because the last three games of their season were against the three teams with the greatest records of losses, the Eagles, the Steelers, and the Colts.

Frank Gifford was the star of that game. He made three of the four touchdowns we scored against the 'Skins and he made the pass that brought in the fourth. Frank was our movie star from Southern

California, a handsome and classy guy who had joined the Giants out of college in 1952. When he played ball at USC he had accumulated an impressive record, leading the Trojans in an upset of California which ended its long domination of the Pacific Coast Conference. He had also appeared in two movies while he was an undergraduate. It was this 1956 season, however, which made him an NFL hero. During it, he led the NFL in total yardage, and he led the Giants in rushing and receiving. We voted him the most valuable player on the team that season.

We beat the Redskins, 28-14. The next Sunday would bring us up against the Cleveland Browns. A victory against them would clinch the title for us, but we never did things the easy way. On a snowy and rainy afternoon in the Bronx, the Browns trampled us, 24-7. That left us with seven wins, three losses, and a tie, which meant the Redskins, with 6-4, were still in contention if we dropped our final game against Philadelphia, and they won both of their final games.

But we didn't drop our final; we won it, 21-7. The next morning in New York, we got the news: we would play the Chicago Bears for the world championship on December 30 in Yankee Stadium. It was the first chance the Giants had had at the big title since 1946, when the contest had also been with the Bears. The same two teams had clashed in 1933 in the league's first championship game. These championships were the prototypes for the Super Bowls which began in 1967.

In 1956, the press started calling the forthcoming championship game between the Giants and the Bears a perfect match. The Bears were the finest offensive players in the league and we were the finest defensive players; the oddsmakers were calling it a close one, especially in light of our tie game with the Bears in mid-season. The Bears were a bunch of roughnecks — the reputation has persisted, deservedly, through the years — who frequently led the league in penalties. I, for one, was eager for the opportunity to prove we were the better team.

It was while we were getting ready for the big game that the ballots were cast for the NFL's twenty-two-man All-Star team — eleven defensemen and eleven offensemen. Andy Robustelli, Em Tunnell, and I were named to the first group, while Rosey Brown and Frank Gifford made it on the offensive lineup. That five of the twenty-two NFL All-Stars were Giants made everybody on the team feel good.

The weather turned frigid that week before the game. The winds howled down out of Canada and everybody went indoors — except us. But, as we worked out on our practice field, the turf clattered beneath our cleats; the ground was as hard as concrete. We stumbled and slipped every time we tried anything the least bit fancy in terms of maneuvers. "What are we gonna do, coach?" we complained.

The answer to that came not from Coach Howell, but from the team's owner, Wellington Mara, whose father, Tim, had founded the team in 1925. Early that week he met us in the dressing room. "Boys," he announced, "back in '34 we played the Bears for the championship in weather just as bad as this, and we nearly lost. The team went into the lockers at halftime, trailing 13-3. Then one of the players remembered playing successfully on frozen turf in Montana by wearing sneakers instead of football shoes.

"Anything was worth a try, but where were we going to get twelve pairs of sneakers on a Sunday afternoon? The answer came from a friend of my father's named Abe Cohen. Abe was a tailor who helped in the basketball locker room down at Manhattan College. He and some friends went down there, broke into the lockers and got back to the Polo Grounds with the sneakers just as the halftime was ending. Our boys scored twenty-seven points in that second half, and we were the world champions for the first time.

"This year we are going to do the same thing, except that we don't have to steal the sneakers."

Mara turned to my fellow lineman, "Andy, you own a sporting goods store. Can you fill an order for a good pair of sneakers for every man on the team by the end of the week?"

"You betcha, Mr. Mara," Robustelli replied.

The morning of the game came with the wind gusting nastily. The ground was as hard as ever, and Coach Howell sent Ed Hughes and Gene Filipski out to test the ground with their sneakers on before the game. They came back and reported that they had tried some sharp cuts and hard running, but had not fallen. The coach told us to put our sneakers on. We also had a defensive surprise for them. Modzelewski and I switched positions. Stan Jones of the Bears was a high blocker, and they gave him to me. The other guard was a cutter (a term we applied to linemen who specialized in cross-body blocking) and Mo loved handling cutters.

We were feeling our oats. The sneakers gave us grist for a lot of wisecracks and jokes. The locker room was noisy with laughter — nervous pre-game laughter. I don't think Coach Howell approved. He told an assistant, "In my time, people were pretty quiet before a big game." Kyle Rote and I were enjoying our usual exchange — but I got a little self-conscious thinking how silly I would look in those sneakers when the fans saw us.

But I forgot about that when we went out onto the field and those fans — more than 58,000 of them — were on their feet, cheering wildly. That gave me chills, over and above what the wind was giving me. This was the Giants' starting lineup printed in the programs that day:

Offense			Defense		
(44)	Rote, SMU	L.E.	(78)	Yowarsky, Ky.	L.E.
(79)	Brown, Morgan St.	L.T.	(77)	Modzelewski, Md.	L.T.
(60)	Austin, Oregon St.	L.G.	(70)	Huff, W. Va.	M.G.
(25)	Wietecha, N'western	C.	(76)	Grier, Penn St.	R.T.
(66)	Stroud, Tenn.	R.G.	(81)	Robustelli, Arnold	R.E.
(72)	Yelvington, Ga.	R.T.	(30)	Svoboda, Tulane	L.LB.
(80)	MacAfee, Ala.	R.E.	(84)	Svare, Wash. St.	R.LB.
(11)	Heinrich, Wash.	Q.B.	(48)	Hughes, Tulsa	L.H.
(16)	Gifford, S. Cal.	L.H.	(25)	Nolan, Md.	R.H.
(29)	Webster, N. Car. St.	R.H.	(45)	Tunnell, Iowa	L.S.
(33)	Triplett, Toledo	F.B.	(20)	Patton, Miss.	R.S.

We won the flip and elected to receive, so I took a seat on the bench to watch the opening play. Gene Filipski ran it back 53 yards to the Bears' thirty-eight. Apparently that little bit of practice on the frozen ground gave him an edge, because the Bears were wearing sneakers, too. Four plays later, Mel Triplett ran seventeen yards for a touchdown.

Fired up, I went out onto the field to help get the ball back as quickly as possible. Speaking of fires, though, I remember looking up into the stands and seeing that some of the fans had actually built little fires in the bleachers in an attempt to keep warm. On the field, we kept warm with vigorous play. On the Bears' second play, we popped Rick Cesares so hard that he dropped the ball. Handily, we recovered. I went back to the bench and wrapped myself in a heavy blanket, until they sent Agajanian out to kick a field goal. I helped keep the Bears away from Ben and his kick made it between the uprights. After that,

Jimmy Patton intercepted a pass by Ed Brown which Agajanian again converted into points, this time in a 43-yard attempt. At the end of the first quarter, we led 13-0.

The Bears finally got on the scoreboard in the second quarter, but not until after Webster had carried the ball into the end zone, 20-7. Charlie Conerly took over from Heinrich and picked up fifty yards on one pass play that connected with Alex Webster. Shortly after that, Webster scored from the one, and it was our turn to get our hands on the Bears' offensive squad once more. We came on hard and stalled them short of a first down. Then their punt was blocked by Ray Beck, and Henry Moore, one of our defensive backs, fell on the loose ball in the end zone to score a fourth touchdown.

As we went into the locker rooms at halftime, we could see that a number of the fans were leaving the stadium. We didn't blame them. The outcome was hardly in doubt, and, besides, they could watch the rest of the game on television in the comfort of their living rooms. Just that season, the NFL had signed its first contract with CBS, granting the network the right to televise any NFL game to any audience except within a 150-mile radius of the city in which the game was being played. However, the 150-mile rule had been waived for the championship game, so that our fans could, for the first time in the season, watch us play a home game on their sets. Chris Schenkel and Johnny Lujack were the announcer-commentators.

That second half saw nothing change except the Giants' half of the scoreboard. Charlie sent Kyle Rote in for one touchdown, and Frank Gifford in for a second. The final score was 47-7. We were the world champion football players! For playing in and winning the game, each of us got a check for $3,779.19, a lot of money to us then.

Only two players from that championship game were chosen unanimously for first-team All-Pro, Harlon Hill, an end for the Chicago Bears, and me. I was also invited, along with Em Tunnell, Charlie Conerly, Frank Gifford, Kyle Rote, and Andy Robustelli, to play in the Pro Bowl. That was an honor, but also something about which many players were ambivalent because it was another opportunity to be injured in a game in which neither the stakes nor the pay were particularly high. After all, the championship was determined in another way. The Pro Bowl served mostly to exhibit the talents of the NFL's most talented. The NFL made a wise decision when it came up with the Super Bowl, combining the championship contest with the bowl concept which had been so popularized by college football. (The Pro Bowl has continued, of course, made more attractive to the players by its relocation to Honolulu and by more suitable game fees.)

Before I left for that game, my draft board in New Jersey sent me notice that my friends and neighbors had called me to serve them in the army. Wow!

10

IN THE ARMY

To have done so well during my second year in the NFL and then to be called out of the game and into the service at a time when our country was engaged in no war upset me. But I was characteristically stoic about it within a few minutes after I opened that unwelcome letter. Then and there I made up my mind not to fight it, but to get it over with as quickly as possible. I made arrangements to report within a few days after the Pro Bowl game.

The Pro Bowl was played in Los Angeles at the Memorial Coliseum that year, so a bunch of us got on a plane at La Guardia shortly after New Year's Day and headed for the West Coast. The game would pit a team of some of the top players from the Eastern Conference (New York, Chicago Cards, Washington, Cleveland, Pittsburgh, and Philadelphia) against a similar team from the Western Conference (Chicago Bears, Detroit, San Francisco, Baltimore, Green Bay, and Los Angeles).

Chuck Bednarik, an Eagle linebacker and center, Ernie Stautner, a Steeler tackle, and two backs from the Cards, Ollie Matson and Dick "Night Train" Lane, were some of the notables who would be joining us six Giants on the Eastern Conference team. Our Western Conference opponents would include Joe Schmidt (LB), Bobby Layne (QB), and Yale Lary (B) from Detroit; Gino Marchetti (E), Artie Donovan (T), and Alan Ameche (B) from Baltimore; Billy Howton (E) of the Packers and Leo Nomellini (T) of the 49ers.

Playing on a team with a strange coaching staff and comprised of a group of players who are not used to playing together is a novel and fun thing to do, in my opinion. It can be a break from regular team play. But, of course, it has its drawbacks. The plays we used had to be pretty basic, nothing fancy. But that was something that bothered the quarterbacks, receivers, and rushers more than it did us linemen. Things seldom got fancy on the front line.

However, in this particular Pro Bowl game, something a little fancy happened on the front line. I was playing nose to nose with the best offensive guards in the Western Conference of the NFL, among them, Stan Jones of the Chicago Bears. As usual, playing against the best brought out the best in me, and getting past Stan to try to bring down quarterback Bobby Layne was such a challenging task that it put my ingenuity to work overtime.

The result was that I learned to head slap Stan rather than stick my hand in his face. I played on the right side of my line, so, in order to rush to the inside of Stan (toward the center of the line and to my left — which was usually the shorter route to the quarterback), I would fake a fast step to the outside with my right foot, then slap him with my left hand on the right side of his helmet. That usually stunned him enough to make it possible to get a one-step advantage to his inside. Once I got there, he could no longer stop me, and I had a clear shot at the quarterback. If I was lucky, the quarterback would be looking hard enough for a pass receiver that he would fail to see me coming until it was too late.

In the end, our Eastern Conference team lost. The final score was West 19, East 10. But that hardly dampened the excitement I felt about my new head-slapping technique. I cannot say absolutely that I was the first lineman ever to do that, but I do not recall seeing it in any of the games I had played in up to that time.

My excitement started flagging, however, on the flight back to New York where my next stop would be an army induction center. I wouldn't get to try the head slap on a pro lineman for the next eighteen months.

When I heard the one-liner that said, "I left home to join the army with thirteen other guys — me and thirteen MPs!" — I loved it because that is how reluctant I felt. I had had a student deferment at Penn State where I had elected to drop out of ROTC after the completion of my compulsory two years. Had I stayed in the program for four years, I would have been commissioned as a second lieutenant in the reserves, and, most likely, called into active service within three months after graduation.

I had postponed the inevitable as long as possible by dropping out of ROTC and by delaying my graduation until 1956 (although that had not been a deliberate act, it just happened that way). Once the word got out that an All-Pro member of the world champion Giants was being drafted, I started getting telephone calls from curious reporters. I had always comforted myself in times of trouble by singing, so I remember singing to myself a lot in those days — especially when I was going to answer the phone.

I had no objections to our system of national defense and I believed I had my duty to perform as a citizen of a nation I love. But my noble beliefs did nothing to keep me from feeling cheated. I had just gotten to the point where I could renegotiate my contract with the Giants for a little fatter pay. Now I was going to be on Uncle Sam's payroll. Later, I was helped to feel not quite so sorry for myself when I saw how many other professional athletes were inducted about the same time I was. Alvin Clinkscale, Sherman Plunkett, Cy Hugo Green, Sandy Koufax, and Don Drysdale were among them.

I reported to the appointed place at the appointed time and soon found myself being introduced to the life of a G.I. draftee at Fort Dix out in the pine flats of central New Jersey. I was not given any special treatment, negative or positive, so far as I could tell.

I did have a little fun right at the beginning when the quartermaster was unable to find a uniform in stock that was big enough to fit me. Consequently, I stayed in civilian clothing a bit longer than the other inductees I was with.

The rigors of military life — getting up at five o'clock in the morning, getting lots of exercise, learning to make a bed the army way, getting all those shots, learning how to take care of a rifle — were not disagreeable to me. Besides, I liked the plentiful food.

The vigorous life helped me shake off the last vestiges of my depression. I decided to give it a good shot as long as I had to be there.

Pretty shortly, I was appointed acting platoon sergeant. I found that if my platoon kept its barracks clean, marched sharply, kept shoes and brass polished, and rifles clean, it would be rewarded with soft duty and weekend leaves. That was simple enough. I just demanded the best from myself and my men, and life was a lot more pleasant for us all.

During basic training I made friends with a G.I. named Wally Choice. Wally and I shared a love of athletics. He was a great basketball player from Indiana whose chances to make a professional career had been blocked by racial prejudice. Wally and I used to go on leaves and passes together. We took both of our cars on trips. If one car broke down, we could get back to camp in the other.

I love to explore and find new routes when I'm traveling in a car, so I managed to get us lost many times. Wally and I would be driving along, and I would see some way we had not traveled before and be eager to try it — to see where it would lead. Once I drove out to Wally's home on Long Island. On the way back to New Jersey from Long Island, I spied 125th Street. I thought, "Well, heck, I'll just take this street and wind up at 125th and Eighth Avenue in Harlem." Never happened. Sometimes, my detours cost us an hour or two of extra driving. But gas was still less than thirty cents a gallon in those days.

My friendship with Wally has persisted and grown over the years since then (in spite of my quixotic driving habits). So, one time, years later, I had a part in an episode of "Kojak." Wally was also hired to serve as my double. We were shooting in New York and one of the scenes called for me to drive out of the scene.

Wally asked the director, "Is there anyone down the street to stop him? If not, he's going to get lost."

There wasn't, and I did.

Army life in the fifties was boring — there wasn't much to do, especially after basic training was over. Happily, I did get a chance to play football with an excellent group of athletes at Fort Dix. The team rolled up an undefeated record which brought us, at the end of the season, to an inter-service bowl game which was held at Cocoa Beach, Florida, in December, 1957. But, once we got to Cocoa Beach, it was all downhill from there.

The morning of the game, a lot of the men on the team went swimming after having partied all night. They were unconcerned about winning, so we lost. After the game, some of us tried to go to a movie, but we were not allowed in because we were black.

That cooled me to the idea of staying any longer in Cocoa Beach, and I decided to go home for Christmas in New Jersey. But, again, I ran into racial obstacles. The bus driver wouldn't let me on until he was sure there was a seat at the back where Negroes "belonged." I was in the company of some of my white friends, but I was not permitted to sit with them. And, so, I got a little taste of segregation's medicine. I didn't care for the flavor.

On top of all that, a white man sitting in the seat in front of me let his seat recline so that it rested against my knees and shins. I felt like I had been crammed into a small box, but, for two days, I endured it patiently while we remained south of the Mason-Dixon line.

But, the minute we were halfway across the bridge that crosses the Delaware River from Delaware to New Jersey, I pushed the seat up and said, "Get that seat off my legs!"

"Oh, I'm sorry," he replied in a surprised, but polite tone of voice.

I felt foolish for having been so gruff. It was my own fault for being so intimidated by my encounters with "Jim Crow." I should have asked him to move the seat long before, rather than letting myself get so steamed at him.

With a six-month early release, I was only in the army eighteen months. The very day I was mustered out, I high-tailed it up to the Giants' training camp in Bear Mountain, New York. They had spent the summer at Willamette University in Salem, Oregon. Now they were almost ready for the new season.

My teammates were glad to see me, at first. But my welcome got a little cooler when they found out what I was going to do with my new electric guitar and amplifier. While in the army, I learned to play an acoustic guitar and then graduated to electric. Once in camp, I started getting up about five-forty-five in the morning to practice.

Charlie Conerly was across the hall, and Frank Gifford and Kyle Rote were close to my room. After a morning or two of awakening them with the sounds of my guitar, I returned to my room in the afternoon to find my instrument missing. I had to hunt a long time to find it, but I succeeded at last so that I didn't have to miss my practice time the next morning. The next day, I had to go hunting for both the guitar and the amplifier. And it turned out they had been put in two entirely different spots. It was a puzzler.

I tried out all my songs and arrangements on my teammates. They were actually pretty good-natured about it, and, in spite of the razzing I got, they also encouraged me. One day, in fact, Kyle said, "When we get back to New York, I'm going to introduce you to a friend of mine, Michael Stewart."

Michael Stewart, a manager-agent for a lot of well-known entertainers and who later became president of United Records, listened to me and told me I ought to take voice training from Carlos Menotti. I was impatient with the training at first. But I stayed with Menotti, and my singing ability did improve. As time went on, reporters began to write about my singing as well as my football career. I got to sing in Carnegie Hall and, in the off-season, I began to go on the road with rhythm and blues singers.

When I arrived at Bear Mountain, my fellow defensive linemen, Dick Modzelewski, Jim Katcavage, and Andy Robustelli told me that Tom Landry had come up with still another new idea for the defense. I say new because he had already, during my rookie year, installed the revolutionary four-man front. Prior to that, the defensive front line had consisted of six players backed by an umbrella of five more.

But this new change, which Dick and the others said was called the "inside-outside-four-three," was something else again. It meant that I had to play from a four-point stance — the customary stance of a lineman was three point, that is, two feet and one hand on the ground with one arm held ready near the waist. The four-point stance required me to place both hands on the turf, the idea being that this would give me greater flexibility to push off either to the right or to the left.

In addition, Landry's plan called for me to have certain inside or outside responsibilities instead of just taking off on my own. Being a stubborn person, I didn't like the changes. No one needed to tell me how to play football, and especially not how to take my stance on the line.

Landry's defensive system did not consist just of those changes, however. The position of middle linebacker came out of it, too. And that was another new-fangled idea I did not have much use for. Coach

Landry — remember, at this time he was an assistant coach, not a legend — would have to show me that his plan was better than mine. The opportunity for that came very soon.

We were holding a scrimmage — a game in which the Giants' defense played against the Giants' offense — and I made what I thought was a sensational play.

I came off the field feeling smug about that. Landry was waiting for me, his face expressionless as usual. Then, in his quiet tone, he said, "If you hadn't made that play, the linebacker would have. The defense was designed for him to make it."

I may have been stubborn, but I didn't argue. Harland Svare was the right linebacker, behind me. Sam Huff was middle linebacker and Cliff Livingston was outside linebacker. I went back into the game, and, when the ball was snapped, I could have made the same play, bringing down the rusher in dramatic fashion. But I let it go. I was going to test Tom and see if he was right. So I let the guy go, and Harland just tore him up. He made a great hit. That was all I needed to become a believer. Don't get me wrong. This new plan didn't put me out of work. A defensive tackle has lots to think about and do. Landry's plan just relieved me of one aspect so that I could give closer attention to the others.

Tom Landry was always thinking about football and how to play it better to win games. His insistence on the four-point stance of his defensive linemen shows that no detail was too small or insignificant to escape his attention.

In time I saw that this stance, which seemed so awkward to me at first, allowed us to perform more sophisticated maneuvers, things like the "switch" or "twist" in which the entire defensive line would literally twist in response to certain offensive plays. Things like that revolutionized the defensive play of the NFL. And, besides, I could still use my head-slap technique when I needed to. It didn't rule that out.

Tom was not a man to leave things to chance. His concept created a plan that specified exactly what each of us would do when the ball was snapped. The four-point stance allowed us to balance on hands and feet, ready to step to the inside or the outside, whichever the defensive captain called. After fulfilling his initial defensive responsibility, each player could play as he felt best until the whistle blew.

Before Landry's new defensive strategy, players had certain responsibilities, of course, but nothing so detailed and carefully thought out as what Coach Landry had conceived.

When Landry watched the films of the other teams, he watched more intently than most of us did. His analytical mind spotted patterns and tendencies in the play of those teams. Even as a player, he had started looking for the "keys" — the stances, gestures, or other indications that members of opposing teams gave unconsciously and which accurately predicted what sort of play they were about to launch against us.

Landry was forging the Giant defense into an even more formidable tool than it had been in 1956. He took the lessons of 1957, in which the defense had fallen behind its 1956 accomplishments, and used them to make us the team to beat in 1958 in the NFL. That season, one of the most memorable of my football career, now lay before us.

11

THE BIG
SEASON OF 1958

My first game when I got back from the service was the Giants' 1958 regular season opener against the Chicago Cardinals. Both their field and ours were still in use for the baseball season, so we had to meet them in Buffalo.

It was good to be back with the "front four" — that's what they called Dick Modzelewski, Andy Robustelli, Jim Katcavage and me because we shared the duty in that hazardous and exciting area on the front line of the defense. It is sometimes called "the pit" and the Baltimore Colts' famous pass receiver, Raymond Berry, once commented about it, "I wandered into 'the pit' three times in my career, chasing tipped passes, and all three times they carried me off, unconscious." The hardships we endured together there built a closeness among us. Katcavage once called it "a manly type of love."

"The man to stop in this game," Coach Landry told us, "is their running back, Ollie Matson. He's fast and he's good. If he gets the ball and starts to run, you'll have to work hard to catch him."

I knew about Ollie. He was probably one of the greatest backs to have ever played in the NFL. So, our attention shifted somewhat from sacking the quarterback to taking out Matson.

Rushing the backfield was my specialty, anyway. I loved to push through that opposing line and get my hands on whoever had the ball. And I really laid hands on them because, in those days, the rules about what a defensive lineman could do with his hands were not so detailed and stringent as they are today. I never wanted to hurt anybody, but, then, nobody ever accused me of not doing my job right.

It was probably during the second quarter that the quarterback again handed the ball to Matson. In a moment, I was through the line and on him! I tackled him with my left arm outstretched so I could give him a good shot with my right.

But at that precise moment one of my teammates — it might have been Sam Huff, one of our linebackers, I can't recall for sure — arrived at exactly the same spot, coming in from the left. My huge frame had already displaced Matson's enough that I caught the brunt of my teammate's attack.

And it was some attack. After the game, I found out the ligaments in my left arm were torn as a result of that collision. At the moment it happened, I just knew I had been hurt and that my left arm wasn't going to be very dangerous to anyone for a while. Still, I decided to keep playing. It would take something more serious than this to make me leave my teammates. Besides, hovering just below three hundred pounds, I was still about the biggest thing between the goal posts — that and my reputation kept Chicago from running as many plays at my position as they might have otherwise.

Our offense did well that Sunday afternoon so that we rolled up a 37-7 victory over the Cards. We on the defensive squad were always a little smug because the Giants were getting a reputation as a defensive team that was hard to beat. And, when we held our opponents to a low score, as we had done this day, that reinforced the reputation and heightened our pleasure all the more.

Our real competition that fall in the Eastern Conference of the NFL was the Cleveland Browns. Their coach's name was Paul Brown and they had a rusher named Jim Brown. Trying to keep all the Browns straight was sometimes a subject for humor, but there was nothing funny about the way Jimmy Brown could chew up yardage on a football field. He was the terror of many a defensive lineman in the NFL in those years — and he always brought out the best in me. But the point of mentioning the Browns here is to explain why we always had one eye fixed on them, no matter whom we were playing that autumn.

Our next game was against the Eagles in Philadelphia. I went into it with my left arm wrapped in a big rubber pad. That, I quickly discovered, was a mistake because my opposite, the offensive guard, could tell exactly where I was hurt. The first time I rushed him, he reached out and gave me a hard shot on that arm. The pain was intense enough to knock me writhing to the ground.

After that, my effectiveness against Philadelphia quarterback Norm Van Brocklin was diminished. I had to do all my tackling with my right arm. He passed for 238 yards and two touchdowns, and we lost the game. But I was a wiser man. Next time I would wrap both arms so offensive linemen would be unable to tell which one was really in trouble.

The following Sunday found us in Washington, D.C., pitted against the Redskins. There I had the satisfaction of visiting my share of terror on quarterback Norm Snead. My teammates and I held them to fourteen points, while Coach Lombardi's offensive squad rolled up twenty-one.

It was a sweet victory, but afterwards my arm was in worse shape than ever. Much to my disappointment, the trainers and the doc told me I was going to have to rest it during our next game. That would be a re-match against the Chicago Cardinals and our first game of the season at home in Yankee Stadium. The New York fans are a special bunch, and it was in the fifties that we first heard them shouting in unison, "DEE-fense! DEE-fense!" — urging us on to still another sack of the quarterback. That, of course, was music to our ears.

An important member of the offensive squad, guard Jack Stroud, was also out of the game with asthma, and scout-publicist Jack Lavelle warned the Giants not to be over-confident after our lopsided victory against the Cards during that season opener. It was a warning that went unheeded: we lost in a 23-6 upset that left Frank Gifford, our leading scorer, in the hospital with injuries.

At the end of the first four games of the season, we had won two and lost two. The Cleveland Browns, however, had won all four of their contests. Things looked grim — even grimmer because our quarterback, Charlie Conerly, had performed so poorly in that second game against the Cards that the usually supportive New York fans had booed him to the sidelines.

But the next week we came back and beat the Pittsburgh Steelers, 17-6. Now we were 3-2 for the season, but the Browns' winning streak remained unbroken and they emerged from the weekend 5-0. In the next, the sixth game of the season, we would no longer have to take sidelong glances in Cleveland's direction. Instead, we would look at them head-on in Cleveland and try our best to break their winning streak.

Coach Landry assigned Sam Huff to "key" on Jim Brown, the Cleveland runner. The coach had watched Cleveland's play carefully and had discovered that the way Jim Brown lined up for a play was a sure predictor of how the down was going to go. Sam and the rest of us would note Jim's position — "key" on him — and have a good idea what to expect in the coming moments.

Brown dominated the attack we were assigned to stop. He carried the ball in fifty-four percent of Cleveland's rushing plays. During the first five games of this '58 season he had already scored fourteen touchdowns, having rushed an average of 163 yards per game. He was more than four hundred yards ahead of the second-best rusher in the league; and the fewest yards he had rushed in one game was 125.

But if any defensive squad was a match for Jimmy and the rest of the Browns, it was us Giants. Behind the four of us on the front line stood a formidable array of linebackers and backs. Beside Sam Huff were the two other linebackers, Harland Svare and Bill Svoboda. The backs were Lindon Crow and Ed Hughes on the outside and Jim Patton and Em Tunnell on the inside. Tunnell was the veteran who seemed to be able to get his hands on the ball more often than anyone else on defense. I was proud to be numbered among these men and I admired the way each of them played football.

We were ready for Jim Brown. And we proved it the first play out of scrimmage by throwing him back for a two-yard loss. He kept coming back, however, and, before the game was over, he'd racked up 113 yards against us. But Mel Triplett, our fullback, tallied 116 yards. Besides that, quarterback Charlie Conerly redeemed himself by throwing three touchdown passes. And we didn't feel so bad about Brown's 113 yards when we realized it was fifty yards below his average. Best of all, we won!

That win helped narrow the score: we were 4-2, the Browns 5-1. But in the coming week we had to face a team from the Western

Conference of the league whose season record (6-0) was better than any other's. That team was the Baltimore Colts. Under quarterback Johnny Unitas they had averaged thirty-nine points a game thus far in the season, while yielding an average of only fifteen to their opponents.

Happily for us, Unitas had cracked three ribs in the previous week's game against Green Bay. His replacement would be George Shaw who had been the team's number one quarterback prior to Unitas' arrival.

The day of the game, Yankee Stadium filled up with nearly 72,000 fans. That included 5,000 who had come up from Baltimore, and it was the largest crowd yet in New York football history.

The opening play of the game was an option pitchout from Conerly to Gifford who passed, in turn, downfield to Schnelker for a sixty-three-yard gain. The play was one of Lombardi's brain children and it had the fans on their feet.

In spite of that shining moment, we were down 14-7 by the third period. At a critical point, Conerly was hit by two linemen but managed a pitchout before he went down that netted us a first down. We were twenty seconds into the last three minutes of the game and the score was tied at 21. The coaches sent in Pat Summerall, one of our kickers who is today more well-known as a CBS broadcaster, to attempt a twenty-eight-yard field goal. Pat told one of the halfbacks, "The pressure's killing me," but he didn't buckle and the ball sailed cleanly between the uprights. We won the game, 24-21. Meanwhile and much to our delight, Cleveland was being upset by Detroit, a team that had only one other victory to its credit that season. That meant we were tied with the Browns in the conference, 5-2.

The next week we slipped a game behind Cleveland by dropping one to Pittsburgh, 31-10, while the Browns beat the Redskins. The week after that found us in Yankee Stadium facing the Redskins whom we held scoreless while our offense scored thirty points. The Browns also won that weekend and the contest stood at six wins and three losses for us against their seven wins and two losses.

The annual college draft was coming up around that time, and the Giants' owner, Wellington Mara, was busy looking for a new quarterback. At thirty-seven, our present quarterback, Charlie Conerly, was one of the oldest men still playing in the NFL. His kidneys were so bruised by this point in the season that he couldn't even bend over to tie his shoes.

Knowing that Charlie was in such tough shape must have sparked us on the defensive squad. In our next game, against the Eagles in Yankee Stadium, we dominated the game by intercepting three of Norm Van Brocklin's passes, recovering three fumbles, and blocking a field goal attempt. The final score was New York 24, and Philadelphia 10.

After that tenth game of the season, we got word in the locker room that the Browns had won theirs, too. So, we still trailed 7-3 to their 8-2. Meanwhile, the Baltimore Colts had already sewed up the Western Conference title.

That week was the college draft. Mara picked up his first choice for quarterback, a player from Utah named Lee Grosscup, as well as an end, Buddy Dial, and a halfback named Joe Morrison. When Charlie Conerly heard about it, he just shrugged and said, "I can't play forever." Our other quarterback, Don Heinrich, wasn't so philosophical.

The following Sunday found us in Detroit playing the Lions. From our point of view on the defense, it started out really great when Jim Katcavage brought down their ball carrier in their end zone during the first quarter of the game. That doesn't happen often. It's called a safety when it does and it's worth two points on the scoreboard. Charlie Conerly connected with a receiver later for a touchdown. The extra point from that, together with a Pat Summerall field goal, gave us twelve points. But near the end of the game, we were behind, 17-12. If we lost this one, we'd be out of the running.

Our job of defense was to dig in and make sure the gap didn't widen any farther. And we did. The Lions were on their own forty-four with a fourth down, needing twenty-one yards to get the first. So, it was no surprise when their punter, Yale Lary, came on the field. When the ball was snapped, we moved in fast to try to block his punt. But he didn't drop the ball to his shoe. Somebody yelled, "Grab him! He's gonna run with it!" It was a nifty little surprise, but they should never have tried it on us. We dropped him just beyond the line of scrimmage and our offense took over on the Lions' forty-five while the Detroit crowd booed their coach's decision.

Conerly connected with Bob Schnelker for a thirty-four-yard pick-up after that to put us nice and close to their end zone. Fourth play came, though, and we still hadn't gone over the line. With only a yard and a half needed, the coach decided to risk the run. Frank Gifford took the ball from Charlie — and made it! We were ahead, 19-17.

But there was still time left in the quarter, and the Lions' offensive squad came back on the field fired up to get that lead back. They pushed us down to the eighteen where a field goal would win the game for them. We huddled briefly. Only eight seconds remained in the game. Robustelli and Svare were covering from the right, Modzelewski and I from the left. Robustelli urged Svare to "drive my man outside so I can sneak through." But Svare said, "No, I got a better angle. Let me sneak through." Svare won the argument — and the game. Andy pushed his man outside for him and Harland managed to block the kick.

The game was over, but the fuss about that faked punt went on for several days. A lot of Detroit fans had money on that game and were asking why any team would do that from midfield when it was leading late in a game? A lot of them hollered that the game must have been fixed — enough of them so that Commissioner Bert Bell had to ask the FBI to check it out. They did and their report showed no unusual patterns in the betting, nor any evidence that any of the players or coaches had been bribed.

That took care of that, and we got ready to meet the Browns the next Sunday at the Stadium in New York. They were 9-2, we were 8-3, and this was the last game of the regular season. We had to win to force a playoff for the Conference title. If we didn't, the season would be over and the Browns would play the Colts for the league championship (there was no Super Bowl in those days).

The sportswriters were dubious about our chances that week because Pat Summerall was out with a nasty charley horse. All week our punter, Don Chandler, was practicing place-kicks. But, come the day of the game, Pat showed up and told Coach Howell he was well enough to play.

It was snowing that Sunday morning, and the forecasters said there would be no clearing for the afternoon. Jim Brown got away from us in that snow right in the first quarter and scored on a sixty-five-yard run. In the second quarter, their kicker, Lou Groza, and ours, Pat Summerall, each scored field goals: Groza from the twenty-three, Pat from the forty-six. We went into the lockers at half-time trailing them 10-3. Tom Landry didn't have much to say. He knew that we knew.

With the odds against us, our defensive line got down to business and held the Browns scoreless for the rest of the game. Summerall's field goal in the first half had come on the heels of a fumble we recovered. The Browns hardly ever fumbled the ball, so we had little reason to hope for a second, even in a snowstorm.

The fourth quarter began with the score unchanged. Suddenly, though, the break we needed came. The Browns flubbed a hand-off and the ball was on the ground. We all dived for it at once, determined to give our offensive boys one more go at it. When the refs got us all off the pile, there was the ball, safely snuggled in Andy Robustelli's bosom. We had it near enough to our goal line to make it hard for their defense to stop us. Too hard, as it turned out, because Gifford connected with Schnelker and the game was tied, 10-10.

We went onto the field after the next kickoff fired up for a victory. We had to get it back for the offense one more time because a tie would leave the Browns with the conference title. So, we got it back. The offense moved the ball down to field goal range and Summerall went in. But his kick went wide and he came back to the bench looking mighty discouraged. We weren't discouraged. "We'll get it back for ya, Pat!" we announced as we went back out there.

We were like a wall of stone to them for the next three downs. They came up short and had to punt. We put a lot of pressure on that punter and the ball landed in midfield. Alex Webster went out for a long pass and was in the clear near the end zone. Charlie sailed the ball to him perfectly — and it went right through his hands to the snowy slush below. At the end of the third down, our guys were still in midfield, in need of a miracle.

Coach Howell sent in Pat Summerall. I couldn't believe it. Nobody could believe it. No kicker could make a field goal from that distance — especially not in the snow! But Jim Lee Howell was the coach and his decision was made.

Ray Wietecha snapped the ball to Charlie Conerly. Ray was so good at being center that he didn't have to look between his legs when he hiked. He was the only "heads-up" center in the league. Charlie placed the ball down, laces to the front as always, in position for Pat's kick. From where I was sitting, the ball was placed on the far side of the fifty-yard line from the end zone — by about two yards, I'd guess. Then Pat hauled off and gave it a hefty shot. Right away we could see it would probably be long enough to make it. But would it make it between the uprights?

Up and up it went, reaching its high point somewhere over the twenty. From where we were sitting, it was impossible to tell if it was on track. Pat said afterward that it was drifting, as best he could see through the falling snow, slightly toward the outside. But, just over the ten, it started breaking back to the inside, sailing easily through the uprights and into the arms of some guy who was standing behind the end zone. That put us in the lead, 13-10, and there was hardly enough time left in the quarter to worry about. We had won, once again in the last possible moment, and forced a playoff game between us and the Browns to see who would play the Colts for the championship.

Excitement ran high that week in New York. We had won the toss, which meant the game was going to be played on our turf again. More than 60,000 tickets went on sale and the fans lined up at Columbus Circle to buy them all.

More than one observer of that playoff game called it the finest clutch defense effort in the history of the NFL. It was our third face-off against the Cleveland team that season. The pressure and the practice must have worked together, because we held Jim Brown to the poorest single performance of his career. His net against us that day was only eight yards in seven carries. The Browns got off only forty offensive plays as opposed to the eighty our boys got to run or pass or kick. We were so tough that day that the Browns never once got the ball into the end zone. We were also so tough that I managed to get my knee banged up — enough to slow me down and take me out of much of the second half of the game.

Meanwhile, our only touchdown of the game was made in the first quarter by Charlie Conerly himself after he took the ball on a lateral from Gifford. In the second quarter, Pat Summerall sent one between the posts from twenty-six yards out. After that, the score remained 10-0. The score and the game symbolized the importance of a tough defense to the success of a professional (or non-professional) football team. The New York Giants topped their conference that year because their defensive squad could and did stop the best offenses in the league. One statistic alone shows how true that was: the total number of points we scored that season, 246, were the fewest in the entire league of twelve teams, except for four others — the Eagles and Redskins, and the 49ers and the Packers.

In those years we beat the Cleveland Browns six games straight, holding Jim Brown to two touchdowns and an average gain in yards of only 66.5 per game. Against the other clubs in the conference, Jim usually managed better than a touchdown per game and always better than a hundred yards. Jim and the rest of the Browns team were our toughest competition year after year, and they always brought out the best in us defensive linemen.

That is how we came to the championship game against the Baltimore Colts three days after Christmas in 1958. We had beaten them in November, but their quarterback, Johnny Unitas, had been out of that contest with injuries. Now was our chance to see first-hand just how good this upstart from the minors (Unitas had been playing for the Bloomfield Rams just three years before this wintry afternoon) really was.

As usual, Coach Landry was a man of few words in the locker room before the game. Coach Howell gave his standard pre-game talk to all of us, but, over on the other side of the Stadium in the Colts' locker room, Coach Ewbank was giving his men a memorable going over. They were favored to win by three points and he wanted to make sure they didn't get too relaxed, I guess. The point of his speech, according to reports after the game, was that the whole team and each member of it had something to prove. They were a rag-tag lot, many of them survivors from the defunct New York Yanks and Dallas Texans. He went through the roster name-by-name and reminded each man from whence he had come and why he had to win today in order to live down his past.

We were the underdogs that day, but that was nothing new to us. Coming from behind at the last possible moment was the way we played each game and the entire season.

We won the toss and elected to receive. Heinrich was quarterbacking, as usual at the opening of play, and failed to get a first down. Chandler punted and it was defense's turn to take the field with the ball on the Colts' thirty. My knee injury was still nagging me and the Baltimore coaching staff knew it and apparently wanted to capitalize on it if they could. First play they sent Lenny Moore (a teammate of mine from Penn State) left and we dropped him for a three-yard loss.

Then their fullback, Alan "The Horse" Ameche, came plowing through the middle to pick up seven. With a third and six, Unitas looked for receivers, found none, and ran for it. Sam Huff caught him three yards past the line of scrimmage and hit him hard enough to pop the ball loose. Jim Patton pounced on it. The crowd roared its delight — we had done our job again.

But we only got to rest for two plays before Heinrich took a turn at dropping the ball and Marchetti of the Colts recovered. Back to work. Unitas and his team pushed us back five yards in two plays. He passed on the third down and our cornerback, Carl Karilivacz, intercepted and ran back to our forty-five. Back to the bench for a rest, but, in spite of a good try by Frank Gifford, we had to punt on the fourth.

We rejoined the Colts' offense at their fifteen. Those linemen knew how to protect Unitas and he got off a long pass to Lenny Moore who caught it in spite of near-perfect coverage by Lindon Crow. That brought them sixty yards to our twenty-five where we stopped them cold. Steve Myrha got two shots at a field goal because one of our men was offside, but, on the second try, Sam Huff came through a hole we opened for him and blocked the kick. Jim Katcavage downed the ball at the twenty-two.

The crowd roared its approval, but the roar grew even louder as we got back to the bench because Charlie Conerly was walking onto the field. The fans really loved old Charlie. On the third down he connected with Gifford while Kyle Rote took out Roosevelt Brown, a gain of thirty-eight yards. Then, when Alex Webster missed a pass that would have been a sure touchdown, the coach sent Pat Summerall to kick from the thirty-six. Pat's kick was good and the scoreboard lit up for the first time, 3-0.

We wouldn't let the Colts go anywhere on their next possession which forced the punt and ended the quarter. But a Gifford fumble near the Colts' twenty had us quickly back in the play where Unitas started punching my sector with running plays. They picked up a first and then sent Lenny Moore around left end — all the way down the field to the two before Jim Patton could get his ankles. We dug in to hold the fort. I was staring into Jim Parker's face as usual when the ball was snapped and he came on me like a tiger. I outweighed him by twenty pounds, but my leg just didn't have the staying power I needed to stop him. He pushed me back into the end zone and Ameche came right behind him with the ball held tightly under his arm. After the conversion, we trailed 7-3.

That play by Jim Parker convinced both Coach Landry and me that I needed to drop out of the game. After that, an interception and another fumble put the ball back in Unitas' hands on his own fourteen. That was the start of the first sustained offensive drive of the game. It ended when Unitas found Raymond Berry in the end zone and scored another touchdown. We went into the locker room for halftime, trailing 14-3.

In the third quarter they moved the ball all the way to our three before we could stop them, but stop them we did and Charlie Conerly got another chance. On his third down he completed a pass to Kyle Rote who made it sixty-two yards to the Colt twenty-five before he fumbled. But Alex Webster recovered for the Giants and carried it to the one. Mel Triplett made it from there and the score was narrowed, 14-10.

In the fourth quarter, Frank Gifford caught a toss from Conerly and went in for a second touchdown, and we were ahead, 17-14.

The Colts managed to move the ball all the way to our twenty-five before Robustelli and Modzelewski started breaking through and sacking Unitas. In the best tradition of our defense, they pushed the Colts back to midfield from where they were forced to punt. Our offense got a first down on our thirty-four. Only two minutes remained in the game; we had it pretty well sewed up. We kept plugging away and came up with a third down and just four to go for a first. Gifford got the ball and headed for the forty-four yard line. From where I sat, it looked like he had made it with room to spare when he was brought down by Gino Marchetti.

Just at that moment, "Big Daddy" Lipscomb (who, at 290, was one of the few men in the league who could match my size and weight) came plowing into the middle of the picture and managed to break Marchetti's leg just above the ankle with a sickening crack.

Marchetti was yelling for Lipscomb to get off him and there was a lot of confusion. Frank claims the official who was supposed to place the ball got distracted and set it down short of where he'd picked it up. The referee called time so they could carry Marchetti off the field and then held up his hands to indicate that we were short of the first down by about six inches.

Coach Howell was faced with a tough choice. A first down would give us possession long enough to eat up the clock and win the game. A lot of us on the team wanted him to do that. The odds were better than usual with Marchetti out of the game. But six inches cannot be guaranteed, even by the most ferocious offensive unit, in a single play. Besides, our punter, Don Chandler, was second in the league. He could almost guarantee that the Colts would have to go a long way in less than two minutes to make a score. And then it would be up to his defensive unit to block their path.

Jim Lee sent Chandler in and the Colts took possession on their fourteen. Their third down found them still sitting on the fourteen after two incomplete passes by Unitas. Only a minute and sixteen seconds remained, and he still had to cover eighty-six yards. The roar of the crowd was almost deafening. Lenny Moore caught the next throw for an eleven-yard gain — first down. Four more plays displayed Raymond Berry's catching talents to their fullest. Their offensive unit rushed hard and cut down our defensive backs. Meanwhile, Berry would run down about ten or fifteen yards, and cut back in for a perfect catch. He pulled down three like that and the Colts were sitting on our thirteen. I looked up: twenty seconds left to play.

Then their field goal kicker, Myrha, came on. He'd already missed one in this game. Could we hope for another miss? I hoped so. But Sam was too late to block it and it went right between the posts. The game was tied.

A lot of us figured that was the end. We had all been in at least one tie game, and a tie was a tie. But, today, it wasn't. A rule written in 1947 was invoked for the first time in NFL history — the sudden-death playoff. The game would continue beyond regulation time until one team scored. Then it would end.

After a three-minute break during which the Giants won the coin toss, the Colts kicked it off. Maynard caught it and ran it back to the twenty. After three plays, we were two feet short of a first down and Chandler punted. This time, Unitas started on his twenty. We held him the first two plays, but, on the third and eight, he connected with Ameche for a first down, barely.

In the next second down, Modzelewski got through and sacked Unitas for an eight-yard loss: third and fifteen. But Unitas connected with Raymond Berry when he saw our covering man, Carl Karilivacz, slip and fall. First down.

The next play involved a trap play to punish Dick Modzelewski for the three sacks he had accomplished that day. Alan Ameche charged through the resultant hole in our line and picked up twenty-three yards to our twenty. Officials unexpectedly called a time-out just then to give time to repair a television cable that had broken. Millions of people were watching.

When play resumed, Katcavage stopped Dupre for no gain. But a second-down slant-in pass to Berry brought the ball to our eight. Ameche took the hand-off next and was nailed by Sam Huff after the gain of a yard. Then, on the second down, Unitas pulled a surprise and lobbed the ball into the air toward Jim Mutscheller and right over Cliff Livingston. Mutscheller kept it and went out of bounds at the one-yard line. Third and one.

We geared up for the run, but not enough. Alan Ameche took the hand-off, but this time he went toward our left-side defenders. Lenny Moore took out Emlen Tunnell while their linemen opened a big hole. Ameche was in and the game was over. The 15,000 Baltimore fans in the Stadium swarmed crazily onto the field — their team had won, 23-17.

Losing the big game was a bitter disappointment — even to someone as philosophical and even-tempered as I was. But, in time we would learn (maybe we even sensed it then) that something more important had happened which made losing that game not so painful. That more important thing was that we had treated our fans to an unforgettable performance. The entire season was one long cliffhanger: we Giants had kept emerging from one impossible situation after another between September and early December to make it to this game. And then we gave them a spectacular finish that was a bigger-than-life replay of the season, but with a surprise ending.

You see, the cardinal sin in professional sports is not losing the game. What is much worse than losing is boring the fans. During the autumn of 1958, our fans were kept in suspense that built each week in intensity which was finally relieved in one furious and noisy crescendo at the last possible moment. Steven Spielberg could not have written a better script.

And the fact that there was no script made it even better. Every Sunday afternoon with the New York Giants was gamblers' heaven. Nothing was predictable.

Putting all this showmanship and horse-racing together in 1958 made the championship game between the Giants and the Colts one of the most important ever played in the NFL. Timing had a lot to do with it. By 1958 the television set had become a fixture in most American homes — so that the entire nation got a taste of what the New Yorkers were so excited about. The result was that professional football was catapulted into the national prominence it still enjoys today. We emerged from the shadow of college football and came into our own, so that the three thousand dollars and change each of us Giants collected for playing in that game in no way reflected the significance of what had happened. Without knowing it, we had made history.

12

BETWEEN
SEASONS ON
THE CIRCUIT

In 1959, I signed a contract with a booking agency and began to travel the rhythm and blues entertainment circuit. I was lonely a lot of times and I felt out of place. Two-facedness and cynicism seemed to be requirements for success in this world, and those were things I refused to buy into.

Happily, I discovered that they were not absolute requirements, either. That first contract, in fact, was to lead to about twenty singles and an album with Bobby Darin. I also had several of my own songs published and performed, such as "Deputy Dog," which Sam the Sham and the Pharoahs made a hit.

That summer, before I had to report to camp, I talked a cousin, Lawrence "Pop" Coleman, into going on the road with me and helping. He laughed at my automobile, a Chevy.

"You're supposed to be a big deal, a professional football player," Pop said, "and you're driving a Chevy?" So I bought a pink Cadillac. If Elvis could have one, so could I!

They called me the "300-pound Perry Como." I went on a rhythm and blues tour with a group led by Jerry Butler and The Coasters. Ernie Cato was with us. He was a big draw because of his hit record, "Mother-in-Law." Also in that tour were Curtis Mayfield, Carl "Tarheel" Slim and Little Ann, Baby Washington, and the Five Keys. Later I got the chance to work with Little Willie John, Gladys Knight and the Pips, and even Chuck Berry.

I was master of ceremonies at many of the concerts. It was an exciting time because black entertainers were just beginning to break out of the ghetto and into the broader entertainment world that had been exclusively white for so long.

It was also a treacherous time. Girls threw themselves at anyone they perceived to be a celebrity. The all-night parties left me feeling uncomfortable. I hadn't seen that kind of stuff in the NFL. Maybe I was just naive, but I don't think so. In the fifties the players in the NFL reflected the mainstream of American society and, by today's standards, that was pretty straight-laced.

I had one particularly unnerving experience. In an arena somewhere in South Carolina one night, a group of young toughs came into a restroom that had been reserved for performers. I explained this to them, politely, and asked them to make use of the other facilities in the building.

Instead of leaving, the leader turned around and called in his buddies.

I said, "Hey, brother, if something is missing here, you'll be blamed. Why don't you go on down to the other men's room?"

He still didn't pay any attention to me, and the guys came on into the room.

"Hey, man, didn't you hear what I said?" I protested.

The guy turned to me finally, "You got your mother-in-law with you?"

"My who?"

"Your mother-in-law."

"What are you talkin' about?"

"I mean, are you heeled?"

"C'mon, brother, speak English," I asked.

He looked disgusted and said, "You carryin' a weapon?"

I didn't have a picture as a young boy. This is my baby brother, Rufus Carl "Baba."

This isn't my baby picture either, even though my tooth is missing.

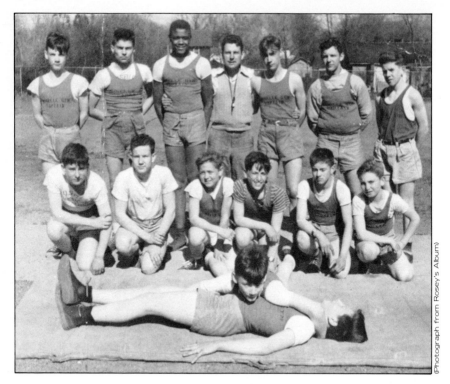

We were just kids, and we all grew up. Coach Ryder,
Robert Hoffman, Dallas Jacobs, Vincent Dienchy,
Robert Squirrel.

Me and the fellas hanging out.
Jerry Barner, Tommy Holmes, Charlie Smith, Isaac
Dwyer, Richard Hunn, Richard Burrell and me.

I know who I am, you know who you are, we know
who we are, thank you very much!

Ruth Gillis, Alvin Bernstein, Robert Bradford, Sylvia Hein, Lolly
Messersmith, Elizabeth Pickett, Bob Shannon, Lucille Wesolowski,
Alfred Siegel, Edward Jakielasjck, Audrey Meitmann, Carol Powell,
Mr. Rice.

Coach Ralph Arminio taught us to be the very best. Top row left to right: C. Therkeldsen, J. Dobson, A. Bienstein, D. Line, R. Clew, R. Mc Millian, R. Hunn, S. Yankeelow, R. Souels, R. Robst, V. Lassiter, Second Row: D. Jacobs, R. Halkovitch, R. Hoffman, J. Dryer, W. McLoed, B. Galish, C. Franklin, First Row: Me, K. Pettigrew, C. Wolf, J. Franklin, T. Holmes, V. Matthews, J. Barner.

I don't always make ugly faces — but when you go for the record it's okay. Where's the crowd?

That sure was a big fellow. He had on the wrong number and I'm tired of playing in the mud. But for the sake of the team we keep on going. Number 50, Bill Galish, is on my side, but will he get there on time to help out? Oh well, one more flop in the mud.

FOOTBALL IN REVIEW

Roselle came into the 1950 county picture as a weak sister, expected to take at the most, three or four games. Here at A. C. H. S. we knew better. Our coaches had watched this group come up for years and said "Fifty is the year" and it was.

GRIER AND GALISH PICKED ON ALL STATE TEAM

Roosevelt Grier, the big gun on our eleven, made the all county eleven first string along with Bill Galish. Johnny Krahnert, Tom Holmes, Jerry Barner, Bill MacMillian and Bob Hoffman were awarded Honorable Mention. Big "Roose" went onto make all State group two tackle, while Bill made second string center.

This year's eleven will go down in the school history as the team that broke the eight year jinx.

I cheered and cheered. I love it when I'm on the winning team.

Grier Sets Record

With the Lion sports teams nearing the half-way mark this spring, the trackmen and golfers are leading the field.

Coach Rutherford regards his team as stronger than the unbeaten unit of last year.

Chick Werner's trackmen have participated in two relays and a dual meet. At Penn Relays, Art Pollard, sophomore sprinter, captured the 100-yard dash, then proceeded to grab the 300-yard honors at the Ohio Relays, Rosey Grier set a Lion record of 52'9½" for the shotput.

It was big Rosey Grier, Lion football tackle, who had the fans on edge. Grier broke the shotput mark five times, each heave setting a new record. His best toss came on his fifth try, a put of 55'8¼".

Penn State Wins Annapolis Meet

ANNAPOLIS, April 16 (A). — Penn State, with Art Pollard and Rosey Grier leading the way, easily defeated Navy and Penn in a triangular track meet today. The scores were Penn State 81 5/6, Navy 55 1/6, Penn 25.

Pollard captured the 100 and 220-yard dash events and Grier took the shot put and discus.

(Photograph from Pennsylvania State College)

Where is everybody? I'm all alone!

He's Weight Man
Rosey Grier, giant tackle of Linden, N.J., will co-captain the 1955 Penn State track and field team.

Trackmen Win in Final Event
Relay Victory Clinches 68-63 Win Over Navy

DICK McDOWELL

Record shattering performances in six events, climaxed by the mile relay's sizzling 3:17 clocking, brought the Penn State track and field team its first dual meet win Saturday — a 68-63 margin over formidable Navy.

Running in the last event of the afternoon, the Lion quartet pulled the Nittanies out of a 63-63 tie, bringing victory with a dramatic touch that had screaming fans on their feet.

But drama played its part throughout the entire meet as records fell with a rapid degree of regularity. In all four Penn State marks and six meet records were smashed.

Grier Betters Shot Mark

Rosey Grier put the shot 55 feet 8¼ inches, bettering both the Penn State and the meet record which he previously had held. His old mark, set just two weeks ago, stood at 52 feet 9½ inches. Charlie Blockson finished second.

Blockson, who has been pushing Grier in the weight events all season, smashed Grier's old mark of 151 feet 4 inches in the discus when he tossed the dish 157 feet 10 inches. This bettered both the Penn State record and the meet record.

Relay Team Sets Record

The other new mark was set by the relay team. The Lion quartet — Pollard, Dave Leathem, Roy Brunjes, and Sax — whipped around the oval in 3:17, good enough for a new meet and Penn State record.

In all the Nittany thinclads gathered in 11 first places in the 15 events run. Brunjes, Doug Moorhead, and captain Dan Lorch all turned in first place performances. Grier also captured one more first place.

Grier's other win came in the javelin where he fired the spear 196 feet 5¼ inches. Navy's Jim Rothrock and Chuck Monson held down the second and third place positions.

The Summary:

POLE VAULT — 1. Lorch (PS) and Pierce (N). 3. Hutchinson (PS) and Howell (N). Height: 13'0"
SHOT PUT — 1. Grier (PS). 2. Blockson (PS).3. May (N). Distance: 55'8¼"
HIGH JUMP — 1. Pierce (N) and Thalman (N). 3. Hutchinson (PS) and Walker (N). Height: 6'1"
BROAD JUMP — 1. Thalman (N). 2. Harrison (N). Johnson (PS). Distance: 22'7½"
DISCUS THROW — 1. Blockson (PS). 2. Grier (PS). 3. Hawkins (N). Distance: 157'10"
MILE RUN — Moorhead (PS). 2. Hurt (N). 3. Chillrud (PS). Time: 4:21.8
440 DASH — 1 Sax (PS).2. Czaja (N). 3. O'Hara (N) Time: 48.9
100 DASH — 1. Pollard (PS).2. Whatley (N). Rittenburg (N). Time: 9.7
JAVELIN THROW — 1. Grier (PS).2. Rothrock (N). 3. Monson (N). Distance: 196'5½"

Grier, Blockson Set for IC4A Title Meet

The explosive power of Rosey Grier and Charlie "Blockbuster" Blockson will be one of the strong points for the Lions when they tangle in next Saturday's IC4A indoor track and field championships at Madison Square Garden.

For the past two seasons these two muscular giants have "pushed" each other after record, leaving numerous revisions of the shot put mark in their wake.

"I don't recall," said Nittany track coach Chick Werner, "of ever having heard of two shotputters placing in the championships before."

Werner was referring to last year's IC4A title meet when Grier placed fourth and Blockson third.

Grier and Blockson have shattered meet and school marks in the weight events with machine gun-like rapidity.

Blockson exploded for a new Penn State indoor shot put critereon last season in the championships with a heave of 51'3½", eclipsing the 51'1½" standard set earlier in the year by Grier. The discus throw is Blockson's specialty, but this event is not included in indoor competition. Blockson erased Grier's Penn State discus record in last season's meet with Navy when he flipped the plate 157'10".

Although both have competed in only one meet so far indoors this season — a quadrangular battle with Michigan State, Missouri, and Ohio State last Saturday at East Lansing, Mich. — another record was sent to oblivion. Grier smashed Blockson's Nittany indoor shot put mark with a toss of 51'10¾". That heave copped first place. Blockson's 50'11"

throw missed second place by one and one-half inches in the quadrangular meet.

It was in last year's meet with Navy that Grier obliterated his own outdoor shot put mark with a sensational heave of 55'8¼" — a new Penn State record that still stands.

Grier, a 6-4, 240-pound senior, uses an unorthodox stance in the shot put. Unlike most shotputters, Grier stands in the shot put circle with his back to the board. When he unleashes from his crouch he counts on a speedy turn to ignite the fuse which will set off his dynamite-like power. Parry O'Brien, Olympic shot put champion and the only 60 foot shot putter in history, uses a similar stance.

Blockson and Grier have been spurred on by competition from other outstanding weightmen. But their finest performances can be attributed to the friendly competition between one another — a competition which has turned them into two of the nation's top ranking weightmen.

Yes, it's me!

Jesse Arnelle, Mickey Bernstein, Rosey

Grier Eyes Record In Meet Tomorrow

by DICK McDOWELL

Breaking the Penn State shot put record is fast becoming a habit with big Rosey Grier, the Lions outstanding weight man. Grier has bettered the record three times in the last two years and may do it again tomorrow when Penn State meets Navy on Beaver Field.

If he does, it will be the third week in succession that the 245-pound muscle man, who doubles as a football tackle in the fall, has topped his original mark. Ironically, Grier's biggest competitor for the honor is his roommate, Charlie Blockson, who held the record briefly this winter.

Penn State's track duel with Navy on Beaver Field tomorrow, will start at 1 p.m. instead of 2 p.m. as is listed on the spring sports schedules. The time has been moved up because of the Blue and White game, scheduled to begin at 3 p.m. Field events will begin at 1 p.m. and running events will get underway at 1:30.

Blockson set the new mark in the 1953-54 Indoor IC4A meet in Madison Square Garden in March when he powered the shot 51'3½", more than two inches better than Grier's best performance to that date.

Grier had erased Chuch Drazanovich's name from the books in 1952 when he tossed the 16-pound ball 51'1/8" against Army in an indoor dual meet. Draz's mark was set in 1950, an even 51 feet.

Then came the 1953 spring season and Grier took over again. In the Ohio Relays he jumped back ahead of roommate Blockson with a 52'9½" performance and a new record stood. A week later in the Penn Relays, he stepped into the circle and topped the old record again, this time with 52'3½" heave.

Tomorrow the pair will be at it again. The experts feel that Grier is hitting his stride and will continue to improve. But they don't strike out the possibility that Blockson who is rumored to be "out to get" Rosey's mark, could shuffle ahead once again. The friendly rivalry, however, has probably helped improve both men's performances.

It might be interesting to see how the two roommates would get along if they should ever happen to tie.

Selections Made All-East

Four Lion Gridders Are Named

Four Penn State gridders, Co-captain Tony Rados, Roosevelt Grier, Jim Garrity, and Lenny Moore, were mentioned on several of the all-East elevens selected by various newspapers and magazines throughout the nation.

Collier's magazine, which conducts one of the most exhaustive polls in the country, picked Rados to fill one of the four backfield positions. Rados, who hit the national spotlight with his sensational passing and quarterbacking of the Nittany Lions this season, holds almost every passing record in the Penn. State record book.

Garrity Picked by INS

Garrity placed on the all-East squad chosen by the International News Service, while Rados and Moore were named to the second team. Grier was given honorable mention on the Newspaper Editors Association team. The American Football Coaches Association picked Rados as all-East quarterback.

New York Giants 1955

This team became a real family to me and I loved all the guys.

1956

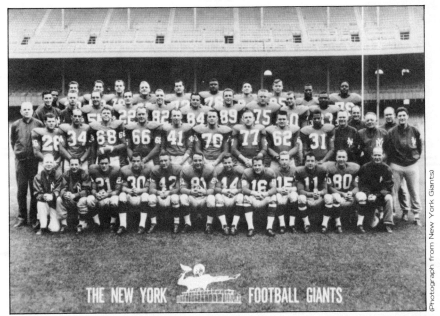

Champions! We won as a team.

In this group is Congressman Jack Kemp. Find him. I want his autograph!

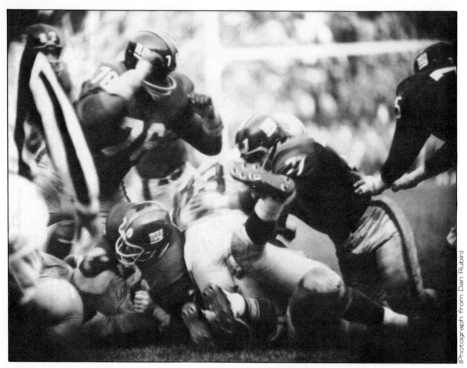

(Photograph from Dan Rubin)

I'm coming in, fellas, and I'm going to hit somebody!

(Photograph from Rosey's Album)

(Photograph from Rosey's Album)

Sometimes when I get tired I kneel down, but before they snap the ball, I get up. But I'm always watching for the action.

When the ball moves, I break through — but sometimes I pose.

'Top Athlete' Award Won By Grier In Area Poll

by MILT FARB

One of the finest defensive players in the National Football League will be the recipient this month of the Chris Zusi Memorial Award, emblematic of Union County's "outstanding athlete — pro or amateur — of 1962."

Roosevelt "Rosey" Grier 290-pound tackle from Linden whose powerful defensive play enabled the New York Giants to win their last nine regular-season games and clinch the Eastern Division title, was named the sixth Zusi Memorial winner in a poll conducted by the Elizabeth Sports-for-Charity Committee.

The silver memorial bowl, donated annually by Benson T. Gold, Elizabeth lumber executive and close friend of the late Zusi, will be presented to Grier at the Hot Stove League dinner a week from tomorrow night at Singer Recreation Hall.

Zusi, former Daily Journal sports editor who was chairman of the Sports-for-Charity Committee lost his life in an auto accident six years ago.

Consistent Performer

Grier, a consistent performer with the Giants for the last seven years and rated one of the most valuable defensive men in the NFL, was a unanimous winner of the Zusi Award, being picked first on all seven ballots.

The second biggest man in the National Football League — Rosey is outweighed only by Detroit tackle Roger Brown, a 300-pounder — Grier also turned in an outstanding performance in the championship playoff against the Green Bay Packers at Yankee Stadium. He yielded little yardage to Jim Taylor and Paul Hornung as the Packers won the game by the margin of three field goals.

Bred in Union County, Grier was an All-Union County and All-State football lineman at Roselle High School under Coach Ralph Arminio. He also starred for three years at Penn State and was an All-East selection in his senior year. Rosey also was a standout weight thrower on the Roselle High and Penn State track teams.

The front four in discussion.

Mo, we are the real workers here!

We want that ball — hand it over!

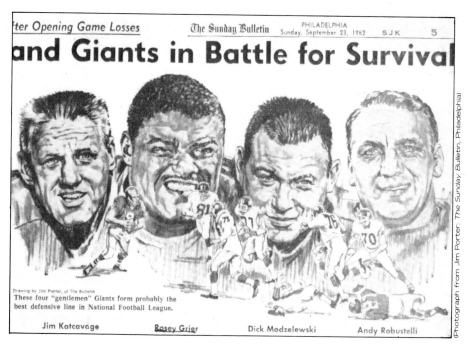

and Giants in Battle for Survival

Drawing by Jim Porter, of The Bulletin

These four "gentlemen" Giants form probably the best defensive line in National Football League.

Jim Katcavage   Rosey Grier   Dick Modzelewski   Andy Robustelli

We don't need favors. We take what we want!

(Photograph from New York Giants)

I told you, Mo, we were the real workers around here.
Where are the other guys?

"No, of course not."

"Well, I am," he said menacingly.

I was due out on the stage in a few minutes and my costume was dazzling white. The only thing I could think of in that moment was how it would look all spattered with blood. So I said, "Hey, man, you can have the whole place."

Up until that incident I had actually believed that being a public figure, especially a popular athlete and entertainer, gave one a measure of universal favor and respect. For the most part, that had been my experience. But that night I learned that there are some people for whom the reverse seems to be true — for whom public figures, benign or not, are targets of hostility and, sometimes, violence.

I found the same patterns of racial discrimination in the world of entertainers that I had found in athletics. We black artists were usually allowed to tour only black communities. And they were expected to produce only certain styles of music — other styles, notably those that had the broadest and most popular appeal, were the domain of white entertainers.

Jerry Butler recorded a magnificent rendition of "Moon River." It was beautiful, but none of the deejays on the "regular" stations would plug it. Instead they plugged Andy Williams' version. Years later, Andy agreed with me that it wasn't fair, but that was the way things were. It was a practice in the trade called "covering." Any time a black artist wrote or recorded a hit song, it was "covered" by a white artist. Pat Boone, a good friend of mine today, covered a number of Little Richard's songs and made hit after hit.

Ed Sullivan did push Little Willie John, and opportunities opened up to a few black artists. Those were the exceptions that proved the rule which established as firm a quota system as any that prevailed in the athletic world.

Black performers were kept in the rhythm and blues field and on "soul" radio stations. Breaks for them were few and far between, considering the huge extent of the market that existed then as now. For me, the financial rewards of working in the entertainment world then were seldom great enough for me to show a profit.

Of course, there were many black entertainers who made a good living at what they did. It took me a long time to understand how things worked. I got one of my first lessons from Curtis Mayfield who was Jerry Butler's guitar player and co-wrote many of his hit songs. Curtis had started out with The Impressions, and he began talking about going back to work with them. That puzzled me. Here was a successful guy enjoying what he was doing, making good money with a measure of security that must have made him the envy of hundreds of less established musicians. But, instead of staying put, he was contemplating a move that might put his whole professional life into jeopardy — going out on his own to be a lead singer. But the very year he made that move, he became one of the biggest black artists in America. Curtis obviously understood things that were not apparent to me.

But I did learn enough to know that every athlete and entertainer — black or white — needs someone with expertise in business affairs who will protect their interests. Without such a person, they will surely get taken, and not just from the private sector, either. The government will wear them out if they don't know what their rights are.

That understanding has grown through years of hard experience. Whenever it came time, back in the fifties, for me to negotiate my contract with the Giants, it went something like this: "I've had a good year this year," I'd say, "what do you want to pay me?" In answer to my question, Wellington Mara would name an amount that must have been well within his budget and to his liking. And I would respond, "Oh, okay. Good."

But, in 1959, I was learning. And there came a day that year when I refused to say, "Oh, okay," and, instead, I and some of my black team-mates on the Giants team took a stand.

13

GROWING
WITH THE NFL

I picked up weight that summer on the entertainment tour. And that posed a problem because Coach Howell had told me I could weigh no more than 280 pounds when I reported to training camp in the late summer. I won't tell you how far above Coach Howell's mark I was, but it was more than a couple of pounds. Finally, as the end of the tour and the day I would have to weigh in at Winooski drew nearer, I knew I had to do something. But what?

It finally occurred to me that I could make use of our travel time between stops on the entertainment tour. We were using a big bus for the troupe, and we often drove slowly on back country roads — slowly enough that I could get out and run alongside from time to time. It was a killer, but I did a lot of running beside that bus — and I endured the jokes and kidding of the stage crew and the others as they cheered me on from inside the bus.

The two big pieces of conversation at the opening of camp that year were that Rosey Grier had made the prescribed weigh-in on the nose, and that Vince Lombardi had accepted the job of head coach for the Green Bay Packers, a down-and-out team in the Western Conference. We wished Vince luck because the Packers had not had a season better than 6-6 throughout the 1950s (but, in 1959, under Lombardi, they went to 7-5). Coach Lombardi was replaced by Allie

Sherman who had been an assistant coach under Steve Owen. Back in 1954, when Jim Lee Howell had gotten the promotion to head coach, Sherman had left to coach the Winnipeg team of the Canadian League, and then had come back, in 1957 (while I was in the army), to work as a scout for the Giants.

Life in camp was not as exciting or exhausting as it had been when we were rookies. To relieve the boredom, a bunch of us conspired to go AWOL one night. It promised to be at least a diversion, if not an adventure. Bed check and lights out were at eleven o'clock each evening. Our plan called for us to meet as soon after that as possible in a field just outside the camp. It took me thirty minutes to sneak out of the building, and the other guys were waiting for me. At last, we were all out and the excitement could begin!

Then it dawned on me. I was in (or on the outskirts of) Winooski, Vermont, not New York City. The others had made friends in town and had somewhere to go. "Why am I sneaking out? I don't have anywhere to go," I thought.

I sat alone out in that field all night because I didn't feel like trying to sneak back into the building. That taught me a lesson: If you are going to break the rules, at least have a plan.

However, even when I had a plan, my midnight escapades had a way of running afoul. On another occasion, in Utah, I decided to go out at night. This time, I made plans the week before. On Saturday night, I would meet a taxi across the field from camp which would take me into town to rendezvous with some friends. The hour arrived, I sneaked out of the building and started walking across the field. About halfway across, I heard something in the underbrush, and I was certain it was a snake. Rattlers are plentiful in Utah. I took off at a dead run in the dark and, suddenly, wham! I fell into a deep hole and sprained my ankle. I limped the rest of the way to the taxi, however, and kept my appointment. But my ankle was no good for several days after that.

I have a recurring dream about snakes. In it I am running, but not fast enough to escape them. Arthur used to torment me when we were boys in Georgia by yelling, "Coachwhip!" when we would be out on a peaceful and uneventful walk. That always sent me running off in terror while Arthur laughed uproariously. Coachwhip snakes are common in the South, and, though harmless, they grow to be four, and sometimes five feet in length. The lore among children was that if one of these enormous coachwhips got you, it would tie itself around you and whip you to death.

My recurring dream comes infrequently now, but, for a long time, I dreamt it nearly every night. During those sieges I learned to awaken myself and stop the dream.

But back to Winooski, Vermont, and 1959. After losing the championship game against the Colts the previous season, Landry began to work us defensemen overtime. "The press is calling you the finest clutch defense in the NFL," Tom said, "but you weren't good enough to stop Unitas and Berry in their overtime scoring drive last December. I know it was the end of a long game, and you were tired. But the Colts were tired, too. This season, we have to be in better shape and we need to get our strategy and tactics perfected."

We all sat and listened — Sam Huff, Harland Svare, Cliff Livingston, Tom Scott, Andy Robustelli, Jim Katcavage, Dick Modzelewski, Dick Lynch, Jimmy Patton, Emlen Tunnell, Dick Nolan, Ed Hughes, Lindon Crow, and the others. Who could argue? He was right. His new-fangled defense had worked time and again. The slipups had come when we had reverted to our old ways.

We played an early exhibition game against the Packers up in Bangor, Maine. It did seem strange to see Vince Lombardi standing on the wrong side of the field. But we showed Tom Landry that we had taken him seriously; the final score was 14-0.

The exhibition season that year took us down to Dallas, Texas. The city did not yet have an NFL team, so we and the Colts — the championship contestants of the previous season — were sent down there to dazzle the local citizenry and generally arouse interest in the game and the league.

We black players knew what going to Dallas meant: the white players would stay in one hotel and we would be housed in another one that was presumably more suited to our race. It was always that way in the South. It was awkward, because we had to take a bus to the hotel where the white coaching staff and players were staying for meetings and the like. But, when it came time to eat, we had to get back in the bus and go someplace where it was okay for blacks to eat.

The annoyance I felt toward this system was reflected when I was fined on one or two occasions for being late to practice or returning to the hotel after curfew. It was tough, if you were black, to get a cab to pick you up in the South, and I refused to get frantic about meeting schedules under those conditions. Otherwise, though, most of us who were black tolerated these momentary encounters with "Jim Crow" pretty readily. We were just glad we didn't have to live in the South any longer.

And we derived what benefits we could from the system as long as we had to be subjected to it. The segregation, for example, gave us a chance to be by ourselves where team officials had less control over our hours and behavior. Also, most owners tended to give black players a little extra money to make us feel better.

But, in 1959 in Dallas, we had a change of heart. It may have been provoked by the promotional nature of the trip that called for all the players to attend a pre-game party downtown where we could be gazed at by local businessmen who might be interested in backing an NFL franchise for Dallas.

Whatever the reason, some of the Colts players who were black — Lenny Moore among them — called us and said they didn't think any of us ought to go to the party. Em Tunnell, Rosey Brown, Mel Triplett and I agreed. The time had come for us to take a stand. We told the black rookies about it and they followed our lead. To state our case, we showed up where the whole team was supposed to board a bus to go to the party. All the white players got on the bus, but most of us blacks stayed down on the sidewalk.

Coach Howell got off the bus and came over to where we were standing, "What's the matter, fellas? Don't you want to go to the party?"

"Coach," I said, "we decided we're not going because we're not allowed to stay in the same hotel with you and the other players."

He looked a little perplexed and then said, "But no one ever mentioned anything about this before."

"We shouldn't have ever had to," I replied.

"I can't argue with that, but we aren't trying to change the world, all we're trying to do is play football."

"I'm sorry, coach, but the time has come for us to take a stand."

Wellington Mara had been listening and that's when he came over. "We didn't know you felt like this," he said, "and, in the future, I promise we won't go anywhere we can't stay together. But if you don't go to this banquet, you don't get paid, and you don't play in this game. That may not bother you, but it may hurt the rookies. For their sake, I ask you to relent this time. I've given you my word about next time."

He was right about the rookies. We discussed it among ourselves and decided to get on the bus. When we got to the banquet, we discovered that none of the black players from Baltimore were there. We wondered if we might have given in too easily. We had to wait until the following year before we had the answer to that question. To our relief, Mara kept his word. That was the last time the team was housed in separate hotels. I understand it was the last occurrence of segregated housing in the entire NFL.

That was the only incident of that sort to occur while I was with the Giants. There was no prejudice among the team members. We all got along great. The quota system was still intact, however. Only six positions were open to blacks on the Giants team in those years.

Most of the NFL teams maintained that quota system, allowing no more than six black players on a squad (some, notably the Redskins, allowed none). And, usually, two of those six players had to play the same position. That arrangement was called "stacking." I knew of no black player in those days who was a center, a quarterback, or a linebacker. I believe the idea was that black ballplayers were not smart enough to play those positions. Most of us held line positions, although Em Tunnell and Mel Triplett did hold down jobs in their respective backfields.

The 1959 regular season opened in Los Angeles with a game against the Rams. We Giants all stayed together in the Disneyland Hotel, by the way. We didn't play the Rams every season because they were a Western Conference team. But on the five previous occasions when we had met them, we had lost to them. This time we won, 23-21. Charlie Conerly had an especially great day, completing 21 of 31 passes for a gain of 321 yards.

The next Sunday we went to Philadelphia where the Eagles handed us our worst drubbing in a long time, 49-21. You can believe that Tom Landry did a little extra coaching of our defensive squad after we had allowed seventy points in only two games. It was some of the worst playing we ever did together.

The next week in Cleveland, however, we got our act together and beat the Browns, 10-6. Jim Brown rushed 22 times but got only 86 yards. Don Chandler did some fine punting in that game, too.

With our early season road games out of the way, we arrived at the Stadium with a 2-1 record that tied us with Philadelphia for first place in the conference. And we were scheduled to meet Philadelphia for a rematch. That brought out the fans, nearly 69,000 of them, who were not disappointed. Harland Svare actually scored a touchdown on a pass interception which he carried seventy yards. The final score was 24-7 which put us at the top of the conference.

After that, we packed our bags again and headed for Pittsburgh. It was an exciting game in which Ed Huff picked up a fumbled ball and carried it five yards into the end zone. The score stood at 21-16 in the final minutes of the last quarter, and the Steelers had pushed us down to the six-yard line where we took a stand to keep that slender five-point lead. Tom Tracy, the second-best runner in the Eastern Conference, tried to pierce the right side of our line on three successive attempts. When the final gun sounded, the score remained 21-16.

Back at the Stadium, 67,837 New Yorkers crowded in to watch us repress Lombardi's Packers. Pat Summerall kicked two field goals from the 49 in that game. The victory brought us to the middle of the season with a 5-1 record, a game ahead of the Browns and the Eagles who had each lost two. We defensemen had special reason to be proud of our stats. No other team in the NFL was yielding as few yards against the run as were we. Our average was 2.7 yards per carry.

But our next game was with the Cardinals who had a rushing average of 5.3 yards per play. And the odds were upped because Charlie Conerly was out with a bad ankle. That, of course, only inspired us to try harder, which we did. There were no touchdowns in that game by either team. The final score was 9-3 on the basis of three field goals by Pat. We held the Cards to 108 yards on the ground and 63 in the air, far below their previous average.

Those games were the beginning of one of the more incredible phenomena in the NFL's history. We were leading the entire league in victories, but, for the equivalent of nearly three games in a row, we did not score a single touchdown. All of our points were scored by Pat Summerall.

The second game of our no-touchdown stretch, in which Charlie Conerly remained sidelined, was against Pittsburgh. They beat us 14-9, which brought our record to 6-2, in a tie for first place with the Browns.

The next week we went out to Bloomington, Minnesota, to play the Cards. The odd location was still another part of the NFL's expansion plans. With the growing interest of the television networks after that 1958 championship game with the Colts, the fever to start new football clubs was spreading across the country (it was at this same time that the fledgling AFL staged its first draft).

Charlie Conerly's ankle was not entirely mended, but he played in spite of that, in the second half. During the first half, Pat Summerall kicked three field goals in the conclusion of his improbable stretch of scoring. During that second half, Charlie tossed a pair of touchdown passes to bring us back into the mainstream of conventional football. The final score was Giants 30, Cards 20. When Pete Rozelle heard the score, he asked if Summerall had kicked ten field goals!

The Washington Redskins came to the Big Apple the next Sunday to help us celebrate Charlie Conerly Day. Nearly 61,000 fans showed up, too, to watch us trump the 'Skins, 45-14. Those were the most points we had scored since the 1956 championship game against the Bears. We were all happy for Charlie who got a lot of nice gifts that day.

Coach Howell was worried that we might grow overconfident and posted a sign in the locker room that week which read:

REMEMBER
PAST PERFORMANCES
MEAN NOTHING.
THE BROWNS ARE COMING
AND THEY WILL BE —
Burning
Revengeful
Obnoxious
Well Fired-Up
Nasty
Seeking Salvation.

Yes, Mr. Howell, we got the message, loud and clear. We steeled ourselves to face off against Jim Brown one more time, and 68,436 fans came to watch. We had the most loyal and enthusiastic fans any club could ever hope for. One of them, Bob Sheppard, our public address announcer, even got lyrical in describing us:

> These are four that carry fear:
> Robustelli, Katcavage, Modzelewski, and Grier!
> These are three that runners find tough:
> Livingston, Svare, and husky Sam Huff!
> And these four make the passers reluctant to throw:
> Nolan and Lynch, Patton and Crow!

That was music to our ears, and the game itself was something else. We held Jim Brown to a measly 50 yards in 15 carries. And we shattered the Browns, 48-7. Then, as the game was in its final minutes, the fans came apart at the seams. At least a thousand of them came pouring onto the field and tore down the goal posts — something unheard of in pro ball. They also encircled the Browns' bench, and Paul Brown shouted to his players to run for the lockers, which they did.

Nobody exactly knew what to do at first, but then Sheppard's voice came over the loudspeakers: "This game will be forfeited unless the fans leave the field," he announced authoritatively. That struck fear in my heart and I did my part to help herd the exuberant (and often drunken) fans back into the stands.

It took twenty minutes to restore order. The game was resumed and the Browns took their loss with dignity and went back to Cleveland. The next week we beat Washington easily and brought our record to 10-2. We were the first team in the Eastern Conference to win ten games in a season since 1953.

That gained us the Eastern Conference title and brought us again to a showdown with the Baltimore Colts for the world championship. This time it would be held in Baltimore where the fans were, if anything, more fanatical than in New York. They roared from the coin toss until the final gun.

As I stood for the national anthem, I thought about the beating we'd taken the year before, and I was ready! Art Spinney and Jim Parker were two of the Colts' best linemen. Mo faced Parker and I was opposite Spinney. Spinney had made negative remarks about my play in an earlier game between our two teams when I was injured and also in the 1958 championship game. I sent word to Spinney by Lenny Moore telling him to be ready.

The game was as brutal and rough as any I had ever played in. We were ferocious and so were they. But my idea of winning was to win by playing fair. To deliberately go out to hurt a player wasn't my idea of fair, and I wasn't going to be a part of it. At one point I caught Johnny Unitas with the ball and drove him over backwards, and his knee was caught under him. I could have hurt him badly without any trouble, and some of my teammates were saying, "Take him down. Take him down!"

But I said, "No, I'm bringing him up."

Dick Yelvington, one of our offensive tackles later made Eugene "Big Daddy" Lipscomb of the Colts mad. So, Dick came over to me on the sideline and said, "Rosey, would you like to play my position?"

He knew he had a patsy because I had been bugging Dick to let me play his position on field goals and extra points. So I moved into the offensive line for the next play. But, when the ball was snapped, Big Daddy almost killed me.

When I picked myself up after the play, I said, "Big Daddy, why did you do that?"

"Rosey! Hey, I didn't know it was you. I thought you were Dick Yelvington. I wanted to smash him. Sorry, man."

Later, I asked Yelvington why he didn't tell me Big Daddy was angry and he just laughed.

Pat Summerall bought us nine points with field goals, and we were leading 9-7 as the second half of the game got underway. In another hard-fought drive, our offensemen made it down to the Colts' 28 where it was fourth down and about a yard to go. I expected to go in with Pat for another field goal attempt, but the coach called a running play for Alex Webster. Sadly, he didn't make it and the Colts took over. After that, it was all downhill. One of the Colts' defensive backs, Johnny Sample, intercepted two of Charlie Conerly's passes and carried one of them forty-one yards for a touchdown. Johnny Unitas threw two touchdown passes and carried the ball himself for a third. In the same time, we managed only one touchdown. The score was 31-16.

Perhaps this is the place to talk a little about the violence of NFL football as I experienced it — both as a dispenser and receiver of it. I loved the roughness of football — you have to if you're going to play the game. But I always believed firmly that there was such a thing as unnecessary roughness. We were playing the Cleveland Browns once, and I saw a Giant spitting on Jim Brown and twisting his legs. I reached down and punched my teammate.

"We don't win games playing like that," I told him.

But we Giants were extremely loyal to one another and we would fight anyone on an opposing team who deliberately hit on one of us. It wasn't just team spirit. It was self-preservation. We understood that anyone who tried to injure a teammate badly enough to put him out of commission, and got away with it, would be likely to do it to another one of us in the next game.

A number of teams had what we called "hatchet men" who seemed to enjoy injuring players on opposing teams. Once or twice over the years, players with that sort of reputation showed up on the Giants' roster. I did my best to restrain them when I could. And our coaches did not condone that sort of thing if they became aware of it. Confrontation seldom did much good, because most hatchet men are convinced they only do it to help their teams win. Most of us regarded such conduct as unsportsmanlike, if not sick behavior.

There was a Pittsburgh Steeler in the late fifties who had a reputation for being a hatchet man. As more and more athletes suffered injuries, some of them serious, at his hands, the question of what to do about him actually came up in a team meeting with Coach Howell.

"I'm not telling you to go after him deliberately," Howell said. "but if you are near him, if he is in your play and you get a chance, put him on the ground. If you don't, I guarantee he will put you on the ground." That is the only time I remember a coach actually giving us permission to get someone.

In the game with the Steelers which followed that talk, I had a personal encounter with the man in question. It happened when Em Tunnell intercepted a pass. I turned and started to run a blocking pattern to help clear the way for Em to run the ball back as far as he could. In the process, I came up against Mr. Hatchet, the one the coach had warned us about. He grabbed me by my helmet and my face mask and almost broke my neck.

After the whistle blew on that play, I went up to him and said, "Everybody's after your tail and I know it. I don't play that way. But if you ever do what you just did to me again, I will put you out."

He never came after me again.

I avoided intentional violence on the field, unless I thought it had to be done for the sake of the team. For example, if someone was trying to injure our quarterback, it didn't matter whether it was Heinrich or Conerly, then we went after theirs. That sent a clear signal to our opponents, "If you take out our man in anything but normal play, we're going to take out yours."

Sometimes, we appealed matters like this to the referee. The NFL refs were and are a hard-working bunch of men who do their best under trying conditions. In many cases, they could threaten a penalty or have a quick discussion with the team captains about losing a game on a silly penalty at a crucial time.

But, if neither our warning play nor the referee had the desired effect, we had one other recourse. In the next huddle, we would call a "bootsie." That meant the player closest to the hatchet man would tackle him to bring him down to earth. Then the rest of us would do what was necessary to put him out of the game. Sometimes that meant a broken arm or leg.

It wasn't nice and I didn't like it, but it was necessary. We felt that such a player wasn't fit to play football because he refused to play according to the rules.

A person reaps what he sows. I was caught in awkward positions many times during play — positions that made me vulnerable to injury. And I watched a lot of my opponents pass up the opportunity to do me harm. I made a point, after the game, to let them know I had noticed their kindness and to thank them for it.

Sometimes they told me they had done it because they had seen me do the same thing when I had had the opportunity to hurt someone. I saved Jim Brown on a number of occasions when he was in danger of having his leg broken by an overzealous member of my team. Jim Brown was a great athlete who played clean and was good for the game.

The NFL was growing in 1959, and, in the early months of 1960, it began to show. The Dallas team was born at the end of the season, and Tom Landry went to be its coach. The Chicago Cardinals moved to St. Louis. And Pete Rozelle was elected the new commissioner of the league, replacing Bert Bell who had headed the league since 1946, and who had died of a heart attack on October 11, 1959, while watching the Eagles play his beloved Steelers at Franklin Field in Philadelphia.

I had been growing, too. And some old things in me were dying and making room for the new. When I had come to the league in 1955, I was a wide-eyed boy who regarded the coaches more as teammates than as bosses. The veterans on the squad were my brothers. But, in the years that had followed, my perspective changed.

I began to see the business side of football as various teammates were traded to other teams. Players were treated like merchandise. Whenever they had outlived their usefulness to the team, they were traded to some other club which needed what they had to offer.

It was even more painful when coaches and managers saw some player on another team whom they adjudged a better player at a given position than whoever was playing that position on our team already. It grieved me to see how readily they tossed a faithful team player on the ash heap in favor of some newcomer. Only a few exceptional or favored people were kept on the payroll once their playing days were over. Those people became coaches, scouts, managers, or administrators in some capacity.

I found such cold-heartedness painful, especially if it affected someone whose companionship I had come to value. At first I reacted to trades with brokenheartedness that made me retreat into myself. It was hard for me to understand the business side of the game.

My pain also grew into a resentment. That resentment was fed when I saw some of the phony stuff that went on. The way that some players were chosen for the Pro Bowl sometimes had little to do with the way they played football. For example, some players, I learned, had participation in the bowl guaranteed to them in their contracts. Now, that's something!

Like a lot of men before me, I was learning my way around in the pros. I loved football, but to me it was just a game, not do or die. I wanted to win, but it didn't kill me if we lost. I had no sights on being the greatest football player to ever live. I just wanted to have fun and grow up to be a man.

I was disappointed at our losses to the Colts in two successive championship games. It was tough to make it that far and then lose. But, if you play your best, that is all that can be expected. Sometimes someone else is better on a given day.

I had a long way to go, but I was learning, one day at a time. Still, I didn't have any inkling of how much it was going to cost me to become the man I dreamed I could be.

14

THE DAWNING OF A NEW DECADE

The tour I went on in 1959 with Jerry Butler, Curtis Mayfield, The Coasters, and Ernie Cato, as I've already shown, started me thinking. To cite a cliché — my consciousness was being heightened. From the man who was too timid to complain about the thoughtlessness of a fellow bus passenger in 1958, I changed in little more than a year so that I was ready to act as spokesman when the coach asked us why we wouldn't get on the bus. I was changing because things were happening around me that emboldened me, things of which I was becoming increasingly aware.

What were those things? They had started, of course, years before. I had been named for the man whose attitudes toward racial discrimination awakened a flicker of hope in the hearts of millions of black people. When Harry Truman inherited the presidency from Franklin Roosevelt, he had carried the torch further by integrating the armed forces. In Korea, black and white Americans fought and bled in the same foxholes for the first time.

But, in those situations, black people were still beholden to the largesse of white people. We needed to stand and speak for ourselves, and the man who came forth to help us do that was a fellow Georgian named Martin Luther King, Jr. King had been born in Atlanta just three and a half years before I was born a little farther south in Cuthbert.

While I was finishing high school in New Jersey, he was setting out on his career as a Baptist preacher. In 1954, when I was still in Penn State, he became pastor of the Dexter Avenue Baptist Church in Montgomery, Alabama.

The next year, Rosa Lee Parks, a black citizen of Montgomery, took a seat near the front of the bus and then disobeyed the driver's order to move when he saw that a white passenger had nowhere to sit but in the back. Mrs. Parks, a seamstress, was arrested for violating the city ordinance that required "colored people" to sit in the rear section of public buses.

News of the incident outraged the black community which responded to a young pastor's call for all blacks in the city to boycott city buses. That young pastor, of course, was Martin Luther King. King had studied the non-violent methods of Ghandhi in the Indian struggle to rid the subcontinent of British domination. Now he was putting those methods to work in order to rid Montgomery of racial discrimination.

The black citizens of Montgomery wore out a lot of shoe leather to accomplish that boycott. But they constituted a significant percentage of the system's clientele. Without their bus tokens, the local transit authority began to feel the pinch. And the entire business community of Montgomery was seriously affected in turn, because black customers no longer rode the buses into the shopping districts.

The white city fathers fought back ferociously. King was jailed and brought to trial for inhibiting trade as the boycott dragged on through the summer of 1956. But, finally, on November 13, when King's trial was winding down and he was almost convinced he had lost the battle, a reporter handed him a note which said the Supreme Court had upheld that day the ruling of a Federal District Court which had held Montgomery's segregation laws unconstitutional. That, at last, broke the back of white resistance, and the law which required Rosa Parks to ride in the back of the bus was abolished. The boycott had lasted an unbelievable 382 days.

It started as an isolated incident, but it grew into a mass movement during 1956, the year the Giants and I were winning the world championship. The next year, while I was in the army, saw the crisis at Central High School in Little Rock, Arkansas. There Governor Orval Faubus ordered out the National Guard to keep the school from being integrated by federal authorities (who were complying with the 1954 Supreme Court decision that had overthrown the old "separate but equal" interpretation from 1896). At that, President Eisenhower took a hand. He federalized the National Guardsmen and dispatched regular troops — units of the 101st Airborne Division — to the scene to escort the handful of black students through the front door of the school. It was a dramatic and powerful event which sent a clear signal to the entire nation that this movement could not be stopped.

But I did not follow these events closely at the time. When I picked up a newspaper, it was to read the sports section. I hardly ever watched Chet Huntley and David Brinkley read the news on NBC. Current events did not interest me. My world revolved around athletics, black entertainment, and my family. I had the dumb idea that as a well-known athlete and entertainer, I ought not to get involved in politics because my voice would influence my listeners disproportionately. It was, of course, an inane rationalization for my self-protective and cowardly instincts.

But I was still a black person who was becoming increasingly aware of the ways racial prejudice was affecting me. The little bits and clips of information that reached me about Rosa Parks, and Martin Luther King, and Orval Faubus touched something in me that had been simmering beneath the surface from those days of my childhood when I had first heard the story of Cy Saul. King was working hard to make us all aware of the problem and the need for change — and he was succeeding with me, slowly, perhaps, but surely.

So, it is not astonishing that, as I and the other Giants dusted ourselves off from the defeat the Colts had handed us in the final days of 1959, I was developing a full-fledged social consciousness. With the dawn of the new decade, I found myself increasingly interested in the news about Martin Luther King. I also took note of a young senator from Massachusetts who was out stumping for the Democratic presidential nomination that year, John Fitzgerald Kennedy.

President Eisenhower was in the last year of his second term. A recent amendment to the Constitution said he was not permitted to run for a third term. So, around the middle of the next football season, we would know who was going to succeed him. Vice-President Nixon might get my vote, if I cast it. He came to watch us play the championship game against the Colts, and I heard he was rooting for New York.

The spring of 1960 was marked for me by the development of a new romance. Back in 1956, I had gone down to Montclair, New Jersey, to try to recruit a promising young high school football player for Penn State. His name was Aubrey Lewis. I failed in my mission (Aubrey went to Notre Dame and then on to the Chicago Bears), but, while I was there, I met his sister, Bernice. Bernice was involved in an unhappy marriage, and she and her daughter were living at home. I liked Bernice, but, at first, I didn't know she was married, and by the time her divorce became final in 1959, we were a serious couple.

It was that year, on May 2, when Francis Gary Powers was shot down over the Soviet Union while flying a secret spy plane called a U-2. I, like many Americans, was pleased to learn that we were keeping track of the Russians in that way.

The Olympics were held that summer in Rome. A young amateur boxer named Cassius Marcellus Clay, a light-heavyweight from Louisville, was part of the American team. He took the gold medal in his division. An American named Nieder put the shot over sixty-four feet and broke Perry O'Brien's 1956 Olympic record. Another American named Oerter hurled the discus 194 feet, 2 inches, to break his own 1956 record.

After the Olympics and the passage of my twenty-eighth birthday, it was time to report to summer camp where no one had been hired to replace Tom Landry as defensive coach. His duties were divided among three player-coaches: Robustelli for the line, Svare for the linebackers, and Patton for the secondary.

The preseason games took us to Toronto, New Jersey, Kentucky, and New Haven for various exhibition games. The game in New Haven was at the Yale Bowl against the Lions. It was the first time that site had been used for pro ball in its long history.

We opened the regular season in San Francisco where Charlie Conerly injured his arm and had to be replaced by a new man, George Shaw. We won the game, 21-19. The next week we went to play the Cardinals for the first time in St. Louis. Injuries deprived us not only of Conerly, but also of Alex Webster and Don Chandler. But, again, we won, 35-14.

That brought us to Pittsburgh where we gave the fans a thriller — though not of the sort they were hoping for. Charlie replaced Shaw at quarterback late in the game, but it looked like it was too late. With only a minute left to play, we were still trailing, 17-12, and we had gotten no further than the Steelers' 42. Only a touchdown would pull this one out of the fire. Charlie put one up high and Gifford ran downfield close to the end zone. There on the six, Frank leaped in the air, but our hearts sank as we watched Steeler Fred "The Hammer" Williamson make a simultaneous leap and grab the ball. It was over. But no! As Williamson came down with the ball, Frank ripped it out of his hands and dashed in for the winning touchdown.

And so we headed home to New York with a 3-0 record that put us in first place in the conference. Mayor Wagner invited us to City Hall that week which he had declared to be New York Football Giants Week. He read a proclamation and shook hands with all of us.

Things political were taking more and more of the spotlight right about then. The contest between Vice-President Nixon and Senator Kennedy was a dead heat. Kennedy even paid us a visit in our locker room and talked like he knew a little something about football, but I was still more inclined to vote for Nixon. Kennedy's Irish Catholicism made him seem remote from my life — even though I liked him a little better in the television debates between him and the Vice-President.

Shortly before the election, however, something happened that changed my mind. Martin Luther King, Jr., was jailed on Wednesday, October 19, for his participation in a lunch counter sit-in at Rich's snack bar in Atlanta; the charge was trespassing.

On Saturday, Atlanta's Mayor Hartsfield announced that, on the personal recommendation of Senator Kennedy, he had reached an agreement with student leaders that called for the release of King and all other incarcerated Negroes.

King, however, remained imprisoned because authorities in adjacent DeKalb County wanted to arraign him for violating probation that had resulted from a traffic violation there the previous spring. On Tuesday morning, October 25, Judge Mitchell of DeKalb County found King guilty of violating probation and sentenced him to four months at hard labor in Reidsville State Penitentiary. DeKalb County was Klan country. Blacks had been imprisoned there and never heard from again.

The night after his trial before Judge Mitchell, King was whisked off to Reidsville Penitentiary where he was outfitted in a prison uniform and placed in a cell block with the prison's most hardened criminals.

News of this reached the world the next day, Wednesday, and created international outrage. Telegrams poured into the White House, but Eisenhower was reluctant to intervene in local affairs. However, Candidate John F. Kennedy decided to call Coretta King.

The long-distance operator announced him and then she heard, "How are you, Mrs. King?"

"I'm doing nicely, thank you, Senator," she replied.

"I was just thinking about you," Kennedy continued. "I understand you are expecting a child. This situation involving your husband must be very difficult for you."

Mrs. King admitted it was.

"Well, I just wanted you to know that I am concerned and we are going to do everything we can to help."

Robert Kennedy phoned the astonished Judge Mitchell to inquire if King's case would allow bail. The next day, October 27, Mitchell granted King's attorney's request for the release of his client which had been filed on the afternoon of October 26. The attorney, Donald Hollowell was his name, flew to Reidsville in a small plane — accompanied by three other small planes with reporters — and secured King's release on Friday.

News of the Kennedy role in King's release spread through the black community with the distribution of two million copies of a small pamphlet entitled, *"No Comment Nixon" versus a Candidate with a Heart, Senator Kennedy: The Case of Martin Luther King,* which recounted the Kennedy phone calls in King's behalf and stressed Nixon's silence.

One of those pamphlets came into my hands just days before the election that would be held on Tuesday, November 8. As I read, my heart was touched and my mind was changed. I was not alone, either. Analysts of that election concluded that news of that episode in the black community was responsible for the last-minute shift of millions of black votes to Senator Kennedy — whose edge in the popular vote in November was a mere 112,881 votes. One of those votes was cast in Linden, New Jersey, by Roosevelt Grier. I was voting in a presidential election for the first time in my life.

In the meantime, the football season had kept moving right along. The fourth game, a 24-all tie with the Redskins, was a letdown after all the hoopla of New York Football Giants Week and the visit to Mayor Wagner's office. And things only got worse when we dropped the next game to the Cards, 20-13.

After those dismal performances in the Stadium, we left for Cleveland where we hoped for better luck. The stands were crammed with 82,872 fans, the largest crowd the Browns had ever drawn in their hometown, who got to watch us maintain our dominance over this powerhouse team. We held Jim Brown to twenty-nine yards on eleven attempts, the worst of his season. And we beat them, 17-13. Katcavage's fumble recoveries had a lot to do with our winning score.

The next week we faced Pittsburgh in a contest that saw Pat Summerall pull it out of the hat with still another last-second game-winning field goal. That brought our record to 5-1-1, a game behind the Eagles with 6-1. And our next two games would be against the Eagles. We would play first in New York and then in Philadelphia.

After the big stampede near the end of our 1959 game with the Browns, when the fans had come running onto the field and nearly caused us to forfeit the game, Wellington Mara had decided to discontinue selling standing-room tickets for the Stadium. That meant that today, when we would fight with the Eagles for first place, 20,000 fans could not get in to see the game. The bleachers were filled, however, with the 63,571 who did get in.

Things went well — except that Jim Katcavage sustained an injury that took him out of the game — and we went to the lockers at halftime leading the Eagles 10-0. In the second half, Norm Van Brocklin, the Eagles' quarterback, threw a touchdown pass that brought the score to 10-7. We dug in harder to hold on to our lead, but, in the last five minutes of the game, they pushed us back inside field goal range where their kicker made it and the game was tied 10-10.

George Shaw was at quarterback to lead the drive to regain our lead. With a third down and inches to go, however, the handoff to Mel Triplett was bungled. Eagles' defender Jimmy Carr picked up the fumbled ball and ran it thirty-eight yards for a touchdown. Now we had to come from behind, 17-10.

Shaw was making good progress. He hit Schnelker with a nice pass. Then, as the clock ticked down, he connected with Frank Gifford. Frank clutched the ball tightly and ran for the sidelines to stop the clock. I watched as Chuck Bednarik, an Eagle linebacker who had been a teammate of mine in the 1957 Pro Bowl, was bearing down on Frank. Only inches from the line, they collided with a sickening whack. Frank crumpled lifelessly to the ground and Bednarik danced for joy. We were incensed by his apparently sadistic joy in bringing down our best scorer, for we could see that Frank had been hurt.

Frank was badly injured, in fact. He had suffered a concussion and was near death for a few minutes. An ambulance was called to take him directly to the hospital. After the game, Bednarik came over to ask about Frank, and we asked him why he'd been leaping for joy when he saw Frank go down like that.

"That wasn't what I was jumping about," he explained. "What I saw was the ball go free and get picked up by one of my teammates. It was only after that when I turned around and saw that Frankie was in trouble. . . ."

At that point, our team physician, Doc Sweeney, interrupted our talk. He had spotted Bednarik just a moment before. Doc was a real partisan when it came to the Giants. He picked up his bag and came charging down at Chuck, yelling, "I'll kill you, I'll kill you!" Chuck took off and we tried to explain to Doc what we had just heard, but it didn't calm him down much. We were all worried about Frank.

That game was a disaster. Frank was out for the rest of the season (to his credit, Chuck Bednarik sent Frank a basket of fruit in the hospital), and so was Jim Katcavage who had suffered a broken shoulder. Those two being out was especially tough and it showed when we blew a lead and dropped the next game to the Eagles down in Franklin Field, 31-23. That was our last shot at the title for the 1960 season.

The next game brought us face to face, for the first time, with the Dallas Cowboys. It was strange, as it had been with Lombardi, to see Coach Landry across the field that day. We played sturdily and ran up a 21-7 lead, but the Cowboys recovered five fumbles and had managed to tie us at 31 points when the game was over.

The next-to-the-last game of the season was played in a snowstorm down in Washington. There must have been six inches' accumulation on that field before the game was over, but we beat them 17-3.

We got the formal announcement after that game from Coach Howell that he was going to retire at the end of the season. I felt especially sad, even though it came as no surprise. Jim Lee Howell had meant a lot to me.

The season finale was held at the Stadium against our traditional rivals, the Cleveland Browns. We had dominated them steadily since 1958 and we continued to do it in this game. Going into the fourth quarter, we had held them to three touchdowns, and it was close. But we fell apart again in that last period and the Browns rolled up 27 points. They beat us, 48-34, and we finished the season in third place in the Conference, behind the Eagles and the Browns.

It was a sad way to end Coach Howell's era with the team. But his record stood for itself. In the seven seasons since 1953, he had led the team to three Conference titles and the decisive league championship of 1956. We had won fifty-three games in those years, lost twenty-seven, and tied four. I was glad to learn that Jim Lee would not disappear entirely. Mara gave him a job in the front office.

On Friday, January 20, 1961, twelve days after the Pro Bowl, John Kennedy was sworn into office by Chief Justice Earl Warren as the thirty-fifth President of the United States. I watched the ceremonies on television and found myself stirred by his challenge to ask myself what I could do for my country. It made me think: I was helping to keep a lot of football fans entertained while I was having fun playing the game. When it was finished, would that be all that could be said for me? I hoped not.

With the coming of 1961, my relationship with Bernice continued to develop. However, my enthusiasm for it was on a steady decline. It was time either to get married or break it off. And, since I didn't have what it took to break it off, I was in the process of talking myself into marriage.

My sister Alice was listening to me do just that one day, and finally she said, "Roosevelt, if you really don't want to get married, you shouldn't do it. Marriage is a serious commitment. Unless you're sure and really in love, you ought to wait."

But I was not one to take advice and, besides, I didn't want to feel guilty for hurting Bernice or embarrassing her. So I decided to go ahead and get married. The day of the wedding came and I had still made no public announcement of my plans to marry. I had to go up to New York City to do some radio interviews that morning. It was only then that I started to let the cat out of the bag to various people in the studio. I said things like, "I'm going to get married, but if it doesn't work out, I'm leaving."

No more reluctant groom ever stood before a preacher to say his *I do's* than I that day. That familiar hatred of being shackled with responsibility put a shroud over what should have been a festive day. I was an odd bird. I longed for the closeness of a family, but I wanted nothing to do with being a husband and father.

Bernice was an attractive and pleasant woman who went out of her way to avoid placing any unusual demands on me. My feelings had almost nothing to do with her personally. She did drink more than I would have liked, but had I been less cold and indifferent toward her, she might have been less inclined to drink. I don't know.

But I do know the real problem was my abhorrence of familial responsibilities. I think now that I never got over feeling robbed of my childhood by the demands of life on the farm. Consequently, I kept looking for a family in which I could be the child. Institutions, like the university and the professional football club, allowed me to indulge this desire more readily than a woman would have. My relationships with institutions were certainly superior to my relationships with women.

In case there was any doubt that I preferred the role of child to that of adult, Bernice and I set up housekeeping in the downstairs of my mom's house in Linden. Except for my first couple of years with the Giants, when I stayed at a room in the Hudson Hotel during the season, this had been my home base, all year long.

Allie Sherman took over as head coach of the Giants after Jim Lee Howell moved out of the office that spring. Mara had tried to convince Lombardi to come back to take the job, but when Lombardi declined, Sherman was the logical choice. It was strange to think about my own response to Allie. I had worried about racial prejudice from the "good ol' boys" who ran the team when I got there in 1955, namely, Jim Lee from Arkansas and others. But, as it turned out, I found my affinity for them as fellow Southerners was almost total. Allie Sherman, on the other hand, was not a Southerner, but a pure-blooded son of Brooklyn. I had almost nothing in common with him — the affinity was not there. But he was a good football coach and I respected him.

This was also the year that the Giants at last found a quarter-back who was good enough to relieve Charlie Conerly, the oldest player in the NFL. His name was Yelberton Abraham "Y.A." Tittle who was thirty-five years old and played for the 49ers. He didn't cost much — he was traded straight across for a young guard named Lou Cordileone. When Lou heard the news, he asked the right question: "Just me?"

The team also picked up a new pass receiver — to fill the spot left empty by Frank Gifford — on a trade from the Rams. His name was Del Shofner. He was tall, skinny, and he had ulcers — but he knew how to catch passes. My good friend, Mel Triplett, was traded to the Minnesota Vikings in 1961 where he played for two seasons. At the end of his career, he had gained 2865 yards and made fourteen touchdowns.

Speaking of the Vikings, they were new that year. Their addition to the league brought the total number of teams in the NFL to fourteen, and the schedule was extended to include fourteen instead of twelve games a season. The Dallas Cowboys were attached to the Eastern Conference as part of the rearranging. There was a time in the 1950s when the terms Eastern and Western had some geographic relevance in the league's denominations, but no longer.

Another big change that came with the fall of 1961 was that we did not open the season on the road. Our first game was at the Stadium against the Cards who defeated us 21-10.

We left town the next week for four games on the road. The first stop was in Pittsburgh where we stopped the Steelers 17-14. One of the most memorable defensive situations I ever found myself faced with in the NFL developed in that game against Pittsburgh. The quarterback came out of the huddle and approached the center. But, before he touched the center, he abruptly stood upright, turned toward his backs and started walking back to them. He gave every appearance of being confused and needing to clarify something in the backfield before he could initiate the play.

We all started to relax on our side of the line, but I noticed that none of the linemen facing me had relaxed even slightly. Following my instincts and training, I tensed and played the ball. And, just as I did, the center snapped it to the back toward whom the quarterback was walking.

They had hoped to sneak that one by us. But I hit that line with all the force I could muster, burst through and brought down the ball carrier before they had a chance to make it work. It still stands in my memory as one of my most satisfying moments while playing in the NFL.

After that, it was on to Washington to help the Redskins inaugurate their new stadium. Interestingly, the Washington team had been compelled to forswear its long-standing policy against hiring any black athletes as part of the deal whereby they got the new digs. I think there were one or two black faces on their bench that day. The Giants took the game, 24-21.

Next stop was Philadelphia. The Eagles had finished first the previous year, and so far in their first three games of this season they had piled up eighty points. So, characteristically, we defenders responded to the challenge by restricting them to five first downs, twenty-eight yards on the ground, and six completions out of twenty-one passing attempts. The final score, 24-9, was in our favor.

Then we went back to Dallas for the first time since the incident in 1959 before the exhibition game with the Colts. So, before we did anything else, we broke the color barrier in the hotel that housed us — all one team. Then we went out to the stadium and finished off the Cowboys, 31-10. We returned to New York with a 4-1 record that gave us a first-place tie in the Conference with the Eagles.

The Rams came to the Stadium that next week for one of our irregular encounters with them. Tittle had been replacing Charlie increasingly as the season progressed, and he started the game this day. But our early 10-0 lead faded to a 14-10 Rams' advantage late in the game. When Sherman sent Conerly onto the field, the stands went crazy. The old war-horse was back, and he came through — we won, 24-14.

We lost the next week in a return match with the Cowboys, this time in New York and on Kyle Rote Day. With that game behind us, the season was half over and we stood 5-2, one place behind the 6-1 Eagles.

Game eight was a cinch. We flooded the Redskins, 53-0, a game in which the defense came up with two safeties. But the Eagles won theirs and we still trailed them by a game. The issue would be decided the next Sunday when we would play the Philadelphians.

Tittle and Shofner were doing wonderful things for our offense, and they came through against the Eagles. It was a 38-21 New York triumph that included three interceptions by our defensive squad. We were tied for first place in the conference with the Eagles; each of us with a 7-2 record.

Our offensive scores demonstrated a fresh potency in our team. We took the Steelers in the next game, 42-21, which brought our point-total for three consecutive games to 133, a record-breaking sum. After that, we brought the record up to 9-2 by humbling the Browns, 37-21.

More and more of our fans were watching us on television. In a growing Sunday tradition, the motels along the parkway leading up to New Haven (from where Giants' home games could be legally broad-cast) were sold out to mobs of Giant fans who came only to use the TVs and the chairs.

The season played out spectacularly. After a loss to Lombardi's Packers, we went on to beat the Eagles and tie the Browns, bringing our record to 10-3-1. That put us just ahead of the Eagles who had

10-4. Once again, the New York Giants were the Eastern Conference champions. This year the world title would be decided in Green Bay where Lombardi's magic was working its wonders.

We played that final game in freezing weather — the thermometer was well below freezing in fact. And — what can I say? — the Packers tore us up. The final score was an embarrassing 37-0.

I went home to Linden to get warm.

15

NEW GLORY
FOR THE
OLD TEAM

It was in February of 1962, while we were still thawing out from our visit to the frozen turf in Green Bay, that Colonel John Glenn got everyone's attention by orbiting the earth, the first American astronaut to do so. That year was also the occasion for Charlie Conerly, Kyle Rote, and Pat Summerall to retire from football. Frank Gifford came back that year, this time as a flanker rather than as a running back — safer for his head.

Harland Svare, a long-time linebacker of the defensive squad, stopped playing in 1961, but had continued on as an assistant coach. In the spring of 1962, he got the call from Los Angeles to join Bob Waterfield's coaching staff. Waterfield would retire after the 1962 season and Harland would succeed to the job of Rams' head coach thereafter. He took Ray Wietecha with him and collected two other former Giants, Don Heinrich and Bob Schnelker, to help fill out the Rams' coaching roster.

In the South, voter registration drives and Freedom Riders were in the news. All sorts of groups had organized by this time to help in the crusade. In addition to the NAACP, we were growing used to hearing about the SCLC (Southern Christian Leadership Council), CORE (Congress of Racial Equality), and SNCC (Student Non-Violent Coordinating Committee). The pressure was building.

The 1962 season would mark my seventh term of service in the NFL with the Giants (it would have been my eighth, except for my tour of duty with the army in 1957). There's something symbolic about seven; anyway, I was a veteran who was turning thirty. I attached no significance to those facts at the time, but it was there, nevertheless.

It was a great satisfaction to me in 1962, to be honored with the Chris Zusi Memorial Award. The award is given each year to the outstanding Union County athlete — pro or amateur. It is always nice to be honored in your hometown.

My marriage was reasonably happy in those days. Bernice did her thing and I did mine. She had little interest in professional football, and, after we got married, she gradually stopped coming to the games.

Allie Sherman led us into another winning season, although we did drop our opener against the Browns, 17-7. But Tittle and Shofner got their act going in the second game, against the Eagles, while we on the defense blocked three field goal attempts and intercepted three passes. We won, 29-13.

A new defensive back who came to us on a trade with the Cowboys, Erich Barnes, helped us beat the Steelers the following week. He intercepted a pass in the end zone in the last two minutes of play, which allowed us to hang on to a four-point lead. The next week we got to watch Y. A. Tittle do some fancy playing while we trounced the Cards, 31-14.

But the next week in our home opener against the Steelers at the Stadium, the tables were turned. "Big Daddy" Lipscomb (traded from Baltimore) and Ernie Stautner sacked Tittle repeatedly, and we lost 20-17. As was our custom, we looked around to see where we were in the conference after the first four or five games. At 3-2, we were one slot behind Washington which was 3-0-2.

Don Chandler took over the field goal kicking responsibilities after Pat Summerall retired. And, in our next game, against the Lions, his three points in the third period made the difference. Of course the defense had something to boast about: Sam Huff blocked a kick, and, in the final twenty seconds of the game, Erich Barnes deflected a pass from quarterback Milt Plum (whom I remembered from Penn State) that was headed straight for a receiver who was standing on the goal

144

line. In that way, we held on and won 17-14. It was an upset according to the oddsmakers.

But our unexpected triumph went largely unnoticed. The whole nation was distracted during the latter part of October by the Cuban Missile Crisis. American spy planes had spotted Soviet missile installations in Cuba, a bold and sinister move that President Kennedy could not let pass unchallenged. It was then that he announced to the nation what was going on and that he was imposing a naval blockade on Cuba.

Everyone tensed. Would the Soviet ships coming with the next shipment of missiles engage our blockading vessels in a fight? Talk of full-scale mobilization was heard everywhere that week. I wondered if I might have to go back into the army. But it turned out well when the Soviet ships turned around and went back where they had come from. With continued pressure from us, they also eventually removed the missiles they had already installed on Castro's island. By the end of that week, however, the crisis was largely resolved and life began to return to normal.

With 4-2 we still trailed Washington with 4-0-2. So, wouldn't you know? — we were scheduled to meet the 'Skins at the Stadium the next Sunday. The game was attended so heavily that a thousand fans parked their cars in the Polo Grounds parking lot and hiked over the 155th Street bridge across the East River to get to the Stadium. One motel along the Connecticut Turnpike with 158 rooms was booked that day with 500 customers. The turnpike and the parkway in Connecticut were both jammed that morning with fans going to rent rooms where they could watch the game on television.

They got a good show. Y. A. Tittle threw seven touchdown passes that day, a feat accomplished by only two other quarterbacks. We urged him to try to break the record and get eight, but he modestly declined — said it would be showing off since we were ahead by so much. The final score was 49-20.

Our first-place standing was confirmed the following week when we beat the Cards, 31-28, at the same time the Redskins lost to Dallas. After that, we met the Cowboys — who had scored 41, 42, 24, and 38 points in their previous four games. We kept them down — Don Meredith and Eddie LeBaron were Landry's shuttle quarterbacks that day — to ten points, while Tittle and his troops piled up forty-one points.

We sewed up the conference title the following week by swamping the Redskins, 42-24. Emlen Tunnell, who had gone to Green Bay in 1959 where he played through the '61 season, was back with the Giants in 1962 as a scout. In the tradition of all our scouts, he warned us not to underestimate our next opponents, the Philadelphia Eagles.

It was a good thing he did, because they gave us a terrific fight on a cold and snowy Sunday afternoon. Chandler got us four field goals and set a Giants record. The defensive line stopped Eagles' rusher Theron Sapp on a fourth-and-two late in the game, and pulled a second save in the game's last minute. The score was Giants, 19, Eagles, 14.

During the remainder of the season, which was marked by a catastrophic newspaper strike in New York, we beat the Bears, the Browns, and the Cowboys — which brought our record to 12-2. Not too shabby.

What followed was the world championship showdown — once again with Green Bay, but this time in New York at the Stadium where the weather was as bad as, if not worse than, it had been in Green Bay the previous year. The greatest number of fans to crowd into the Stadium since Mara had abolished standing room, 64,892 of them, came that day.

The Packers opened the scoring with a twenty-six-yard field goal by Jerry Kramer. Then, in the second period, one of our backs fumbled the ball on our 28 and Green Bay recovered. A pass by Hornung and a run by Taylor pierced our defense for a Packer touchdown after which Kramer kicked the extra point. At halftime the score was 10-0. It was anybody's ball game.

We came back into the game fired up to win — so fired up, in fact, that we forced the Packers to punt from their own fifteen. Erich Barnes blocked the punt and the ball hit the ground. Jim Collier, who was just a rookie, grabbed it and ran in for a touchdown. Chandler's kick for the extra point was good, and the defensive squad felt mighty proud.

Green Bay tried to start another drive, but again we forced them to punt. However, this time our receiver, Sam Horner, fumbled the ball on the return. Green Bay recovered with better field position and again drove to within field goal distance where Kramer scored a second time. The score was 13-7.

Our offensive squad managed to get the ball all the way to the seventeen (thanks to a penalty against Green Bay). But, after that, the penalty flags were all against us. After a while, we were back on our own forty-eight and the drive was dead.

Still fired up as we went back onto the field, the Giants' defense wouldn't let Green Bay go anywhere. We held their powerful offense in check as the game settled into a bone-crushing defensive duel, until, in the final two minutes, Kramer kicked a third field goal from the thirty. When the gun sounded, ending the game, the score was 16-7 in favor of Green Bay. In spite of the loss, it was hard not to feel proud of our work. I had never been in so intense a contest when so much of the outcome of the game had depended on the defense. It made me look ahead eagerly to the coming season and the chance to try our mettle for a third time against the Packers.

Nineteen-sixty-three would be a significant year for the nation and for me personally. It is a year many Americans remember vividly as the one in which John Kennedy was assassinated by Lee Harvey Oswald in Dallas. Football fans may also remember that "Big Daddy" Lipscomb died on May 10, 1963. He had been a formidable opponent and I mourned his passing — all the more because it was allegedly from a drug overdose.

The Civil War centennial was in full swing — although it had to be celebrated circumspectly, since its chief issue was still unresolved. Nineteen-sixty-three marked the hundredth anniversary of the Gettysburg Address, in which we resolved that this nation, conceived in liberty and dedicated to the proposition that all men are created equal, would have a new birth of freedom. And, yet, in 1963, the question of that freedom and equality was still a matter of strenuous debate and bitter violence.

Birmingham, Alabama, where Police Chief "Bull" Connor was achieving national notoriety in his ongoing confrontation with Martin Luther King, Jr., was the location of some particularly troubling incidents. Demonstrators tried repeatedly to march on City Hall and were repelled with increasingly unrestrained violence by Connor's men. The demonstrations only grew larger and the boycott against white businesses kept getting tighter.

On April 10, 1963, city officials in Birmingham secured an injunction barring racial demonstrations. They thought it would stop King's

Southern Christian Leadership Conference campaign in its tracks, robbing King of his desired publicity and dampening the fervor of the black community. But King announced that he saw it as his duty to violate this immoral injunction and that he would do so on Good Friday, April 12. Accompanied by Ralph Abernathy and Al Hibbler, the popular blind blues singer, King led some fifty hymn-singing volunteers on yet another trek toward City Hall. Chanting "Freedom has come to Birmingham!" nearly a thousand blacks lined their route. An infuriated Bull Connor, now assisted by a squad of snarling, snapping police dogs, ordered their arrest.

King composed his "Letter from the Birmingham Jail" — which quieted numerous critics of civil disobedience and won significant new support for "Freedom Now."

Coretta King, having given birth to a baby only two weeks before, grew distressed when her husband did not call her from jail to assure her he was all right. Her distress was not helped by rumors that he had been hanged.

Finally, on the advice and urging of Wyatt T. Walker, King's executive assistant, she tried to reach President Kennedy by phone. She knew he was in Palm Beach, Florida, visiting his ailing father. After an unsuccessful attempt to reach him through the White House, an Atlanta operator helped her get the number of the Kennedy headquarters in Palm Beach. Happily, Pierre Salinger, the president's press secretary, took the call. He listened to Coretta's story and promised to speak to the president promptly so that he could call her back soon.

About forty-five minutes later, Coretta received a call from Attorney General Robert F. Kennedy who explained that his brother was with their father. He said that he would call the Birmingham jail immediately to find out how Coretta's husband was faring. Then, he said, he would call her right back.

The attorney general called Coretta back in a few hours to report that her husband was well, although he had been unable to arrange for him to call his wife.

That call was followed the next evening by another, this time from the president himself. He had, he reported, succeeded in securing permission for King to call his wife from jail. "He should be calling you soon," he said. Furthermore, FBI agents had been in touch with her husband and had ascertained that he was, indeed, in good health and spirits. King was released from jail sometime before the end of April.

In the meantime, on April 21 a white man named William L. Moore who was a member of CORE set out from Chattanooga, Tennessee, on something he called a "freedom walk." He was a Baltimore letter carrier and he planned to walk down through Alabama and into Mississippi to deliver a letter of protest against segregation to Governor Ross Barnett. He wore a sandwich-board emblazoned with the words: "Equal Rights for All — Mississippi or Bust," but his journey ended on April 23 ten miles outside of Gadsden, Alabama, where his body was found with bullet wounds in the neck and head.

Eight black people from Birmingham, led by Diane Nash Bevel, went up to Gadsden to carry on from where Moore had been gunned down. All were jailed. After that, a group of blacks and whites from CORE and SNCC started a second freedom walk from Chattanooga on May 1. They were trailed and tormented by nearly a hundred cars filled with whites who shouted, "Kill them!" and threw bottles and rocks. As the walk continued across the Alabama state line, the marchers were attacked by highway patrolmen with cattle prods and then arrested.

The next day, Thursday, May 2, more than a thousand black children, some as young as six, marched out of the Sixteenth Street Baptist Church in Birmingham to demonstrate for an end to segregation. The cameras rolled as these children sang "We Shall Overcome" and chanted freedom slogans. When Connor's brutal police moved in to arrest the demonstrators, they knelt to pray. And, when they were carted off to the patrol wagons waiting to take them to jail, they skipped and danced about gleefully.

The next day, a thousand more children came to the church to receive their demonstration assignments. Connor ordered his men to block the exits from the church and thus trapped about half the protestors inside. Then he and his men attacked those who had already come outside and gathered in the park in front of the church. They wielded their nightsticks brutally against the youngsters, and their dogs injured several of them nastily. Some of the horrified adult onlookers hurled bricks and bottles at the police, which provoked Connor to new heights of violence. He ordered firemen to turn their high-pressure hoses on the demonstrators. The water ripped bark off trees, clothes off the children, and cut their skin. The nation watched on television that night as the water hoses blasted black men, women, and children against buildings and down slippery streets. By that night, more than 1300 young people were in jail.

The struggle continued for another week, and each night we watched new atrocities committed by Connor's men, using dogs, cattle prods, and hoses. It was sickening and as disturbing as anything I had ever seen. But the conscience of the nation was being awakened and sympathy for the black cause was growing with every blast of the fire hoses. On May 10 a racial accord between the SCLC and a representative committee of white civic leaders was signed that represented a great victory for King's movement and cause.

But the reaction of white supremacists grew more extreme as they felt themselves being driven further back into a corner. They turned increasingly to the instruments of terrorism — bombings and murder. The homes of civil rights leaders were put to the torch; gasoline bombs were hurled into the windows of black businesses; shotguns, machine guns, and pistols were employed to wound and kill. It was in the midst of this mayhem, on June 11, 1963, that Medgar Evers, the NAACP field secretary in Mississippi, was murdered by a sniper lying in wait late at night near his home.

Only hours before Evers' assassination, however, the first black students to register at the University of Alabama did so as a result of a federal court order. Only a year before, we had been treated to the dramatic confrontation that accompanied the entrance of the first black student to Ole Miss — the University of Mississippi. Now, in 1963, President Kennedy took a bold step that headed off a similar confrontation with George Wallace on the Alabama campus. In a televised address to the nation, he said:

> *It ought to be possible for American students of any color to attend any public institution without having to be backed up by troops. It ought to be possible for American consumers of any color to receive equal service in places of public accommodation, such as hotels and restaurants and theaters and retail stores, without being forced to resort to demonstrations in the streets, and it ought to be possible for American citizens of any color to register and to vote in a free election without interference or fear of reprisal. . . .*

In short, every American ought to have the right to be treated as he would wish to be treated, as one would wish his children to be treated. But this is not the case. . . .

If an American, because his skin is black, cannot eat lunch in a restaurant open to the public; if he cannot send his children to the best school available; if he cannot vote for the public officials who represent him; if, in short, he cannot enjoy the full and free life which all of us want, then who among us would be content to have the color of his skin changed and stand in his place?

Who among us would then be content with the counsels of patience and delay? One hundred years of delay have passed since President Lincoln freed the slaves, yet their heirs, their grandsons, are not fully free. They are not yet freed from the bonds of injustice; they are not yet freed from social and economic oppression. And this nation, for all its hopes and all its boasts, will not be fully free until all its citizens are free.

It was a week after that address that Kennedy asked Congress to enact the most comprehensive civil-rights legislation in history. We had come a long way from that first day of December in 1955 when Rosa Parks had said "no" to the bus driver in Montgomery.

But my attention to the momentous events of 1963 was distracted that summer by the approach of football season and a momentous event in my own life.

During Easter weekend in New York, an interviewer had asked me on the air about talk that I was to be traded. "Talk about trades is the favorite gossip of the off-season," I told her. "The coaches have always threatened me about my weight, and I admit I love to eat. But I'm just as fast off the ball as I was in college, and I usually have my weight in line in time for summer training camp."

That Monday, April 15, the Giants' office was flooded with phone calls by fans (who had apparently already finished their income tax returns) concerned that the rumor might be true and wanting reassurance that it was not. I had, after all, become a familiar face and name to them. Wellington Mara himself called me to tell me about these phone calls, and he promised me, "We wouldn't trade you, Rosey."

The word of the team's owner was good enough to me. I rested easy and let myself grow more excited about plans to win the championship in the fall. Then, during the first week of July, I got a call from Allie Sherman. "Rosey," he said, "I thought I should be the first to tell you that you have been traded to the Rams for John LoVotere and a high draft choice."

"You have got to be kidding," I laughed, hoping this was a joke.

"I'm sorry, but I'm not. Let me tell you, though, that the Rams are eager to have you. It was they who started the ball rolling on this deal. Harland Svare and the others want you out there with them very badly."

After he said, "I'm not," the rest of his words were almost inaudible. I was stunned. In a way, this was harder to take than my father's death. At least I had had time to prepare for that — I had seen it coming. But I had ignored whatever hints I might have gotten of this. It hit me hard. The Giants had been more than an employer to me. As I've already described, I related to the team and the organization as if it were my family, and I felt as if I had been handed divorce papers.

The management was aware of the nature of my attachment to the Giants, and they worried enough about how I would take the news that they sent a teammate, Rosey Brown, out to my house, so that he would just "happen" to be there when I got the call from Coach Sherman. At least, I believe that is why he was there that day, although I can't prove it. He tried to say comforting and encouraging things to me after I told him about the call, but, of course, I didn't let him know how I really felt. And, in my pique, I resented the fact that he didn't break the news to me himself, so that I would have been better prepared for the coach's call. But it could be he knew nothing more than I did and that his being there was just a coincidence.

The news hit the streets on July 8. For about four hours that day, I was besieged by phone calls from friends, relatives and fans who told me how sorry they were. They wanted to cheer me up, but, of course, nothing worked. After that, I seemed to hear "Rosey Grier's been traded" everywhere I went.

Grief is a process no one can escape. And so I engaged in a grieving reverie about my years with the Giants. I remembered 1956 fondly, the year of that final make-up semester at Penn State to get my degree.

Then, in the fall, we had taken the world championship by defeating the Chicago Bears so soundly. After that came the Pro Bowl — and then the army, robbing me of my opportunity to capitalize on the successes of the previous season. Now, it was happening again. We were not the world champs, but we had just finished one of our best seasons ever. The Giants were the Eastern Conference champs, but I was going to be playing with the Rams whose record in the Western Conference was not nearly so spectacular. I was being robbed again. It was a first-class pity party.

I went around for days in a deep gloom. I didn't know what to do. My life had been the Giants. The Rams seemed remote and foreign. I took no comfort from Sherman's words about Svare and the others. Instead, I thought about how unfair it was because I had never been particularly assertive during salary negotiations. I regarded myself as the most loyal team member they had. How could they do this thing?

Before July got much older, I said my goodbyes in New York and New Jersey (Bernice was used to me being away at camp, and she was mildly ambivalent about the thought of moving to California). Then, on July 14, I was treated to a birthday party for the first time in my life (no kidding!). It was a surprise affair thrown by some of my friends. I was thirty-one. Shortly after that, I put myself, zombie-like, onto a plane for Los Angeles.

16

TRANSPLANTED
TO RAMS LAND

When I first got to L.A., two of my new teammates picked me up at the airport and took me over to the camp. Needless to say, I was not prepared to feel positive about my new situation. But the fact remained that the Rams had not been in contention for the championship for several years.

The Rams started in Cleveland in 1936 during the second attempt to get an American Football League going. The league collapsed in 1937 and the Rams became an NFL team (the Cleveland Browns were a post-World-War-II phenomenon). As the NFL Cleveland Rams they took the world championship in 1945. In 1946, Los Angeles millionaire Dan Reeves finally managed to get them transported to Los Angeles, after having made an untimely purchase of them in 1941.

What Reeves did was no small accomplishment. It turned the NFL into a truly national organization for the first time. Many of his fellow owners complained bitterly about the trouble of transporting their teams all that distance for games, and Reeves was able to gain league approval only after he guaranteed a bonus — sometimes as high as $5000 — to visiting teams.

Dan Reeves also deserves credit for being the first owner to hire a black player. In 1946, he signed UCLA halfback Kenny Washington to a Ram contract and broke the color line in pro football.

In 1950, Reeves showed his ability to innovate again by experimenting with telecasts of Rams' games. Some people feared this new-fangled idea would diminish attendance at sports events, but, instead, it seemed to bring the fans flocking in ever greater numbers to the home games in the Memorial Coliseum. The Coliseum, built for the 1932 Olympics, is a monster of a place which can seat nearly 100,000 people. The net result was that the Rams started setting NFL attendance records.

In that same year, 1950, the Rams fought their way to the Western Conference championship. That, in turn, brought them nose-to-nose with the Cleveland Browns for the championship. The Rams held the lead through most of that game, but a last-minute field goal by Lou "The Toe" Groza had given it to the Browns.

In 1951, with a team that included Bob Waterfield, Norm Van Brocklin, Elroy "Crazylegs" Hirsch, Tank Younger, and Tom Fears, the Rams took the world championship — Lou Groza and the Browns notwithstanding.

The next year, a young black named Richard Lane walked into the Rams' office — much as Emlen Tunnell had walked into the Giants' office only a few years earlier — and got himself hired as a defensive back. His nickname, "Night Train," derived from the association that grew between Lane and Tom Fears. Lane went regularly to Fears' room in the evenings to get help learning the intricate plays being designed by assistant coach Hamp Pool. It seemed that every time Lane came for help, a popular recording of "Night Train" was playing on Fears' turntable. The two became closely associated in the minds of the rest of the players who started calling Dick by the nickname that made history.

After a slump period, the Rams regained ascendancy under Sid Gillman and took the conference title again in 1955. But in a third showdown with the mighty Browns, they were unable to wrest the big title for themselves again. In 1956, they went to the cellar. After more lacklustre seasons, they plummeted to a 2-10-0 season in 1959, in spite of having Ollie Matson on the team. Gillman resigned and was succeeded by Waterfield for two seasons. During the next two seasons, the Rams were 4-7-1 and 4-10 (the move to the fourteen-game season in 1961 did not help them at all). In 1962, Harland Svare was hired to coach the Rams. Dan Reeves was still the owner, although he shared that status with a handful of other investors.

156

When I arrived in the midsummer of 1963, the Rams had come off still another losing season in 1962. It was little wonder. The first thing I noticed about the two fellows who picked me up at Los Angeles International Airport was the way they were talking individual statistics.

Thoughts of the team were noticeably absent. Perhaps the star-celebrity mentality of Hollywood had affected these two, I thought as we drove to the camp at Chapman College, a small liberal arts school down in Orange County, southeast of Los Angeles. But, when we got to camp, I quickly learned that my two hosts were not exceptions, by any means. Everywhere I turned, I heard "I did this," or "I did that." Each player was only concerned with how many tackles he had made, how many touchdowns, or how many receptions. And, to make matters worse, the black ballplayers were lined up in competition against the white ballplayers and vice versa.

No one was talking about winning. If playing at Penn State and for New York had taught me anything, it was that football is the ultimate team sport. To win a game requires the best efforts of every member of the team — not of a few supposed stars. The championship mentality consists largely of the willingness to lay aside the desire for individual glory and to take up the standard of the team — unswervingly.

It was good to see the old Giants — Harland Svare, Bob Schnelker, Don Heinrich, and Raymond Wietecha — again. They knew what I was talking about, and they knew the Rams needed it. But, being coaches now instead of players (not to mention the fact that they were all white men), they were at a disadvantage when it came to convincing the players. That was where I came in. Right from my first day with the Rams, I refused to join anyone's clique. I announced that I came to Los Angeles to hold the line. And I began to talk about winning through teamwork.

It was an entirely new role for me, being the veteran preaching the principles of team play to the squad. When I played with the Giants, I had, in one sense, always remained a rookie. I was the team jokester and goof-off — always good for a laugh or a wisecrack. For example, once when Jim Lee Howell was trying to get us fired up just before a game with the Eagles, he reported to us that one of our scouts had said that Philadelphia wasn't tough. The story in which this remark was reported had been clipped and tacked on the Eagles' bulletin board.

"The Eagles are mad!" shouted Jim Lee that day. "What are we going to do about it?"

I couldn't resist. "Maybe," I volunteered, "we ought to apologize to them."

That wasn't the answer Jim Lee had been looking for, but it got a laugh — which was all that mattered to me in those days.

Now, in 1963, I could no longer be the court jester. Instead, I found myself called to be a prophet to my teammates.

In those first days, some of the black players told me how prejudiced Red Phillips and Carroll Dale were. I listened, but when they finished talking, I said, "I hear what you're saying, but I'm gonna prove you wrong, brother." And I made friends with Red and Carroll. I hung out with them and shot the breeze until we got to be good friends.

Then, one day during practice and while I was somewhere else, Phillips and one of the black players got into a fight. Phillips called him a "nigger" during the fight which, of course, only made things worse. Word of this had not gotten back to me when I was talking to Red later that day. Red, however, apparently thought I had heard about it.

"Rosey," he said, "I'm really sorry."

"What about?" I asked.

"I called the halfback a 'nigger' today," he said.

"You did?" my voice conveyed my disapproval.

"Yeah," he said, "and I'm really sorry about that."

"What are you telling me for?"

"Well, you're a friend. I just wanted to let you know I was sorry."

I smiled, "You didn't call me a nigger, Red. Don't you think you'd better tell the halfback you're sorry?"

He laughed, "I guess you're right." And he did it.

Incidents like that made the Rams begin saying, "Rosey's brought us the championship attitude." That gave me more to live up to, of course — and the biggest challenge for me was my weight.

I weighed 314 lbs. when I went to the Rams, and that made Harland nervous. That sort of bulk slows a man on his way to greet the quarterback. The team had to weigh in every Thursday. Harland explained the rule he had established for me: "Rosey, I want you to weigh no more that 284 pounds. I'm gonna fine you a hundred dollars for every pound over that figure that registers on this scale at the Thursday weigh-in."

Now that was motivation! I had one week to lose thirty pounds or three thousand dollars. I put on a rubber suit and worked out until I was sweating profusely. Then I worked out longer. Finally, when I was about to drown in my own perspiration, I jumped in a sauna or whirlpool bath. Then came the hard part: eating less!

But, when I showed up at the next weigh-in, there were whistles and catcalls when they saw my girlish figure. The scale registered 283. "Har," I grinned, "how about a little bonus for being under?"

"Nothing doin', Rose," he smiled back. "Keep up the good work."

And I did. It was an ongoing struggle in the years that followed, but never again did I have to lose as much as that first time. And, every Thursday, I made or bettered the mark — well, every Thursday except one. Now it can be told: there was one time I jammed the scales so they would not register over 284, and I got away with it. But I only tried that once — and that was an emergency.

On Wednesday, August 28, came another of those momentous events that made 1963 memorable. Over two hundred thousand people — black and white — converged on Washington, D.C., to express their support for the passage of the civil rights bill President Kennedy had submitted to Congress in the spring. It was the largest crowd of its kind to ever assemble in the city, and the police were nervous — at first. But it also turned out to be one of the most decently behaved groups ever to have gathered near the Capitol.

They congregated between the Washington Monument and the Lincoln Memorial. Odetta, Mahalia Jackson, Joan Baez, Bob Dylan, and Peter, Paul, and Mary all led in song. And the crowd patiently endured the endless introductions and remarks of dignitaries. At the last, however, Martin Luther King, Jr., was introduced by Roy Wilkins who explained that King had been "assigned the rousements." We black people knew what that meant, and he did his job well.

"Five score years ago," King began, "a great American in whose symbolic shadow we stand, signed the Emancipation Declaration. . . ." In surveying the century that followed, he lamented the fact that too little had changed. The Declaration of Independence, he said, had been passed to black people like a bad check — it had come back marked with the words: Insufficient Funds. "But," King shouted, "we refuse to believe that the bank of justice is bankrupt. We refuse to believe that there are insufficient funds in the great vaults of opportunity of this nation."

He praised all those like A. Philip Randolph, the aged founder of the Brotherhood of Sleeping Car Porters and vice-president of the AFL-CIO, who had carried on the struggle through long years of suffering. And he called for a fulfillment of the long-deferred promises now. To make clear to the nation and world what blacks wanted, he said,

> We can never be satisfied as long as our bodies, heavy with the fatigue of travel, cannot gain lodging in the motels of the highways and the hotels of the cities. We cannot be satisfied as long as the Negro's basic mobility is from a smaller ghetto to a larger one. We can never be satisfied as long as our children are stripped of their selfhood and robbed of their dignity by signs stating: "For Whites Only." We cannot be satisfied as long as the Negro in Mississippi cannot vote and the Negro in New York believes he has nothing for which to vote. No, no, we are not satisfied and we will not be satisfied until justice rolls down like the waters and righteousness like a mighty stream.

As he neared the end of his historic oration, he talked of his dream.

> I have a dream that one day on the red hills of Georgia the sons of former slaves and the sons of former slaveowners will be able to sit down together at the table of brotherhood. I have a dream that one day even the State of Mississippi, sweltering with the heat of injustice, sweltering with the heat of oppression, will be transformed into an oasis of freedom and justice. I have a dream that my four little children will one day live in a nation where they will not be judged by the color of their skin but by the content of their character. I have a dream today. . . .

160

He ended with words which few of us who heard them will ever forget:

When we let freedom ring, when we let it ring from every village and every hamlet, from every state and every city, we will be able to speed up that day when all God's children, black men and white men, Jews and Gentiles, Protestants and Catholics, will be able to join hands and sing in the words of that old Negro spiritual, "Free at last! Free at last! Thank God Almighty, we are free at last!"

The struggle in Birmingham continued and grew more grim, however. In September, two dozen black youths defied the orders of Governor George Wallace by desegregating several previously all-white Birmingham public schools. Shortly after that, a bomb, made of fifteen sticks of dynamite, exploded in the Sixteenth Street Baptist Church which had been used as a staging area for the demonstrations in the spring. The explosion occurred on a Sunday morning, so that dozens of Sunday School children were injured. Four black girls — two were fourteen, one was eleven, and the other, ten years old — were found dead in the debris. They had been changing into choir robes in the basement. Later that same day, one of Bull Connor's policemen shot a black youngster in the back with a shotgun, and killed him. A black thirteen-year-old boy was also shot to death by some white boys while riding his bicycle that day.

Those horrifying events moved me even more deeply than had Martin Luther King's words. When I saw the pictures of those girls' broken bodies, something broke inside me. Whatever fear or selfishness had kept me aloof from the struggle for black equality was shattered that day. I was broken. But it was like the breaking of a shell that allowed someone new to emerge — someone more whole and real. I began to see that I was a selfish person who cared too much about myself and not enough about other people.

After that day I found that I cared about every child I came across as never before. I wanted to do whatever I could to help them grow and be happy. And I recommitted myself to the principle with which my high school principal had challenged me years before: athletes need to stand as examples of all that is good and wholesome.

For example, I started speaking up if I found myself with a group of men who found it necessary to use foul language, especially if there were youngsters within hearing. I would say, "Hey, fellas, there are some young kids watching us over there. We shouldn't be talking like this."

I dropped the notion that people in my position shouldn't try to use their influence, and, instead, I began to feel that I was in a unique position to help my country and my people. But I didn't know what I could do about people not caring about one another.

Of course, I was not alone in being affected by the incredible and bloody violence that was being rained down on Alabama's blacks — mainly by Klansmen and members of the White Citizens' Council in and around Birmingham. Those events, more than any others, won great sympathy for the black civil rights movement within the main line of the American population.

That same month, in the brief space of time between the close of training camp and the opening of the regular season, I sent back to New Jersey for Bernice and Denise. When they arrived in Los Angeles, we rented an apartment on Longwood Avenue. Our reunion was neither sweet nor sour; I got them moved in and then rejoined the team. I still hadn't broken out of the shell that made it impossible for me to enjoy being a husband and father.

What I came back to with the Rams was my first experience with a losing team since I had started playing football. The season began on September 14 when we played and lost to the Detroit Lions, 23-2. When we finished playing our regulation fourteen football games — the last was a loss in Baltimore to the Colts, 19-16, on December 15 — we had won only five of them and lost nine, putting us in sixth place among the seven teams of the Western Conference. I watched from afar as the New York Giants topped the Eastern Conference with eleven wins and only three losses (they met Chicago for the championship, but, again, missed it).

The third game of that season took us to Cleveland for the weekend of September 28-29. That was the occasion of my most successful curfew-breaking episode. This time, I was ready. I had a list of things to do and places to see which I followed dutifully. I didn't know much about Cleveland and it wasn't as much fun as I had hoped it would be. But, at least it broke the routine and monotony. We lost to the Browns on Sunday, 20-6.

At the end of the fifth game of the season, we had lost to the Chicago Bears, 52 to 14. Now, at that time, nobody should have lost to the Chicago Bears, 52 to 14. And, worse, it marked our fifth straight loss of the season. We had played more than a third of our ball games without winning a single one. After that, Svare called practice the next day.

"But Coach," one guy complained, "when we play on Sunday, we don't practice on Monday."

Svare said, "That's right. When you *play* on Sunday, you don't practice on Monday."

When we went out for practice that Monday, we thought he was going to kill us. But his method worked. The next Sunday, October 20, we eked out a narrow win against the Vikings, 27-24, in the Coliseum. But a win is a win, and we got Monday the 21st off. And never again while Harland was coach did we permit any team to score so many points against us. Pain is a wonderful teacher.

On Friday, November 22, we were out on the practice field, and, a little after ten-thirty in the morning, Harland Svare came walking out. I don't know what it was, just something about the way he looked and walked. . . anyway, I kept watching him.

"Okay, men, gather round," he called out solemnly.

We bunched around him in the usual fashion, curious to hear the reason for his tone and somber expression.

"President Kennedy," he began, "was shot just a while ago in Dallas. The announcer on the radio says they're getting conflicting reports about his condition, but at least one says he's been killed."

All of us milled around after that, not knowing how to handle our feelings or what to do.

One of the black players on the team whispered to me, "That's another honky we won't have to worry about."

I couldn't be angry. I just looked at him and walked down to the other end of the field by myself. My heart just sank — someone had actually shot the President of the United States! I began to weep.

We couldn't keep our minds on practice, and what practice we accomplished was half-hearted. By early afternoon, the president's death was confirmed beyond all doubt.

I, like everyone, was stunned beyond belief. I could recall how sad my folks were in 1945 when the death of President Roosevelt was announced, but this — the violence and bloodshed cutting a man off in his prime — everything had to stop for a while. I sat at home with Bernice and Denise and watched the whole tragic scene unfold on a black-and-white television set.

Somehow, we managed to play a football game that Sunday. It was the eleventh game of the season, and we defeated the Colts at the Coliseum, 17-16. I would have preferred not to have played that game.

The radio, newspapers, and television were full of background on the Kennedys — the family, the parents, Jackie, Caroline, and John. On the day of the funeral, Monday, I saw little John's salute to his dad. Man, that really broke me up.

I felt compassion for the family and for the country. I saw photographs of the new President, Lyndon B. Johnson, as he was sworn in, and I watched Jackie during all of the things that happened. I was sad for a long time after that.

Nineteen-sixty-three was a hard year. Almost no one was sad to see it pass and to leave its ugly and troublesome incidents behind. For me, the historic events of that year only thickened the cloud of gloom created by my own personal crisis.

And yet, as I look back now, those events — personal and national — were changing me and forging me in a way I desperately needed. In the old adage of athletes, "no pain, no gain." The pain of my separation from the Giants was helping me to make gains I would need in order to be ready for the next chapter in my life.

17

TAKING ROOT
IN THE WEST

In spite of the Rams' poor showing in the league in 1963, something memorable and important for the team did happen that season. It was during the 1963 season that the now-famous "Fearsome Foursome" first played together.

Harland Svare learned a lot of what he knew about coaching from Tom Landry. That, together with his own experience as a defensive linebacker with the Giants, made him especially good in developing a strong defense. "The heart of Harland's defensive system," he explained, "is the four-man front line. And that's why I wanted you, Rosey. To start with, I had my two ends, Deacon and Lamar, but the tackles were still missing. Last year Merlin showed up from Utah and, right away, I knew I had one tackle. Now you're here, a veteran, and we can get to work."

It was strange to be the oldest man on the front line and to have credentials that made me the leader of the pack. It was also strange to share the line with someone who was taller than I. Lamar stood six-foot-seven!

So, who were these other hulks Harland was introducing me to? Lamar Lundy was next to me in age, having been born, in Richmond, Indiana, in 1935. At Purdue he turned in performances as an honor student, a football player, and a basketball player. In those respects, he reminded me of Jesse Arnelle, my teammate from Penn State days. He was light, only around 260 pounds. He started out of college with the Rams as a tight end in 1957, but became a defensive end in 1960. Early in our acquaintance, I began to recognize Lamar as an extraordinarily consistent player — more so than any other lineman with whom I had played, and that included me. A good strong intellectual man, he was a great ballplayer.

Next was Deacon Jones at six-foot-five and 275 pounds. He was born in Eatonville, Florida, in 1938, and had proven a notable all-round athlete at Hungerwood High School in his home town. His real name was David, but he earned the nickname by leading his squad in prayer. He attended South Carolina State after high school and there got involved in the civil rights movement by participating in some lunch-counter demonstrations. That had gotten him on the receiving end of fire hoses and dogs' fangs, and he'd even been thrown in jail.

In 1961, the Rams drafted him as an obscure fourteenth-round pick. But he was to become, in his prime, the game's most feared pass rusher. He was called the "Secretary of Defense" and was tremendously fast, running the 100-yard dash in 9.8 seconds. He played left defensive position.

I mentioned earlier how I developed the head slap that helped me get by offensive linemen and at the quarterback. Deacon Jones copied the technique and then developed it to such perfection that it was outlawed. Today, as Norm Schachter, the well-known NFL referee (now retired), explains, "All players are prohibited from striking, swinging at or clubbing another player on the head, neck or face with the heel, back side of the hand, wrist, forearm, elbow or clasped hands. It is a 15-yard penalty and automatic first down" (*Close Calls*, Morrow, 1981, p. 139). Oh well, it was fun while it lasted.

Last, but — need I say it? — not least, was Merlin Olsen, born in Logan, Utah, in 1940. Merlin is also six-foot-five and weighed 280 pounds — and he wears size 15 shoes, one on each foot. He was an All-American at Utah State where he finished in 1961, at which time the Rams quickly snapped him up. Now, as was said above, he was just coming off his rookie year. Had we known it then, he still had fourteen more seasons to go with the Rams before retirement. Some people snicker today because Merlin sells flowers on television, but not me — my name's Rosey, after all.

The four of us became good friends quickly, and, as we played football shoulder-to-shoulder, we proved to be so good at what we did that we eventually formed the core of the team's leadership. Before long, some sportswriter came up with the nickname, "Fearsome Foursome," and it stuck. Having been on a winning team whose biggest asset was its defense, I knew the importance of a defensive line and of leadership. The Rams' defense later became the greatest line ever assembled on a national football field. The media developed the publicity for the Fearsome Foursome without us doing anything to promote ourselves except playing football every Sunday.

Merlin did a good job of explaining why that happened in an interview he gave a *Los Angeles Times* staff writer, Mal Florence, in 1985. "We helped people appreciate. . .the team effort that a defensive line initiates. . . We were one of the first teams to incorporate stunts into blitzes and dogs as a regular part of defensive patterns."

[Before I go on with Merlin's remarks, some definition of the term "dogs" is in order. This one will enlighten the uninitiated and warm the hearts of trivia buffs everywhere. *Red dog* was a term made popular during the 1960s to describe the headlong charge across the line of one or more linebackers in an effort to sack the quarterback; that is, a blitz.

[In 1949, in a game between the Chicago Bears and the Chicago Cardinals, the Bears' Ed "Catfish" Cody, a fullback playing linebacker for the first time, charged into the offensive backfield and spilled the quarterback thirteen times. "He looked like a 'mad dog' coming through there," said one of the Bear coaches, a little proudly.

[In time, every team began using linebackers in this way. The term "dog" remained as a code word. With some teams, "white dog" meant one linebacker charged; "blue dog," two linebackers charged, and "red dog" meant all three crashing through. — adapted from *Pro Football, A to Z*, p. 238].

Now, to continue with Merlin's remarks about why the four of us became so fearsome. "We decided our opponents couldn't double team [English: gang up on] all four of us. Somebody will be one-on-one, and he'll get the quarterback. There were times when teams would double team all four of us, or change their blocking patterns just to hold us down — which was a nice compliment.

"It got so bad in Detroit one year that they ran one-man patterns against us, using all of their other people to keep out the defensive line. So it was everyone they had except the quarterback and one receiver to keep the four of us off the quarterback."

The question was, if we were so good, why did we have losing seasons in 1963, 1964, and 1965? We led the entire league or were near the top in rushing defense and sacks during those years. Why didn't the team win games? Mal Florence asked Merlin.

"If you analyze the defensive stats, it's hard to see how it could have happened," Merlin replied. "But it did. I think part of the reason is that we had too many rookies behind the front line who were not good football players. Had we been blessed with a complete defensive team, as we were later on, we could have dominated other teams unmercifully. The number of sacks we got came in spite of the fact that there were always receivers open."

Merlin spent a lot of time thinking up drills. In the interview above, he mentioned the stunts we pulled in our dogs. His drills were the way we perfected the stunts. He and Deacon were unusually intense — dying to get in there, to get the ball, to tackle. I respected them immensely, but I didn't like all those drills.

Lamar was probably the most underrated of all of us. Every season, we had to nurse him to get him ready. Later, we found out that he had allergies, diabetes, arthritis, and a rare muscle disease, myasthenia gravis. Apparently, he played for years on sheer willpower.

Harland Svare was always thinking about how to use us Fearsome Foursome to better advantage. One day, he had a particularly good idea. "Fellas," he said, "from now on, when you're waiting for the next play to begin, I want you to stand tall on the line."

"How come?" we, who were used to kneeling as the appropriate between-plays posture for a defenseman, asked.

" 'Cause you all are tall, and when that offensive squad comes out of its huddle and up to the line of play, I want them to have to see just how towering you are. I want them to feel intimidated by your size and reminded of your reputation."

That got us to thinking about other things we could do which might help to unnerve our opponents. One thing was to talk to them.

We'd harass them verbally when they came up to the line — say things like, "You aren't coming this way, are you, man? What are you thinking about? Are you crazy? The only way you're goin' is back. You can't come this way. This belongs to us, Jack."

The Fearsome Foursome took the defensive system that Tom Landry had conceived and made it sparkle. And, in a series of seasons when our offensive team gave the Los Angeles press corps little to brag about, we provided the copy that helped sell their papers. Those two factors worked together to create a new image for the defensive line. After us came the Doomsday Five, the Purple People Eaters, the Orange Crush, the Steel Curtain, and the other names that sprang up throughout the league. Defensive linemen began to get the credit they deserved — before it was all over, Deacon and Merlin were even inducted into the Hall of Fame. No other defensive line in the history of the NFL has had more than one inductee.

After my first season with these three fine men, I was feeling cheerier. The arrival of 1964 brought new hope. One sign of that new hope was the ratification, on January 23, of a brief and simple amendment to the Constitution of the United States which said, "The right of citizens of the United States to vote in any primary or other election for President or Vice-President, or for senators or representatives in Congress, shall not be denied or abridged by the United States or any state by reason of failure to pay any poll tax or other tax."

Congress later passed the Voting Rights Act which gave the government power to force local communities to register blacks and allow them to vote. The Twenty-fourth Amendment and the Voting Rights Act began to change the political complexion of the nation. Slowly, but surely, the walls erected by the old Jim Crow laws were being torn down.

In the wake of the stormy events of 1963 — notably in Birmingham and Dallas — sympathy for the civil rights legislation that President Kennedy had proposed in 1963 grew rapidly in Congress. The bill was signed into law by President Johnson on July 2, forbidding racial discrimination in hotels, motels, restaurants, and by labor unions and businesses engaged in interstate commerce. At the same time, the new President urged Congress to move forward on a program of legislation he called a "War on Poverty."

But war of another sort loomed on the horizon. On July 30, 1964, South Vietnamese naval vessels raided islands in the Gulf of Tonkin, north of the border that separated North and South Vietnam. Two U.S. destroyers were patrolling not far away. When North Vietnamese patrol boats came out to drive off the South Vietnamese attackers, they also attacked the American ships. The destroyers responded to the attack and sank two of the North Vietnamese boats. Shortly afterwards, an air raid was launched from a carrier against the North Vietnamese base from which the patrol boats had come.

On the basis of this incident, President Johnson asked Congress to give him the power "to take all necessary measures to repel any armed attack against the forces of the United States and to prevent further aggression." Congress passed the Gulf of Tonkin resolution, which gave the President these powers, by an overwhelming majority. We were to spend more than 57,000 lives and the next eleven years trying to prevent further aggression.

At the time, however, the Tonkin incident received only a modicum of attention. None of us had any idea what the nation was in for and we continued on about our lives as usual. And the usual thing for me at midsummer was to report to camp to get ready for the fall season.

Camp went uneventfully and the season began on September 13 in Pittsburgh in a game which we won, 26-14. The following Sunday we tied Detroit in the Coliseum, 17-17, and then beat the Vikings there, 22-13, on September 27. After dropping the fourth game to the Colts, 35-20, the Rams' season stood 2-1-1.

On October 11, we lost to the Bears, 38-17, at Soldiers Field. Back in the Coliseum the next week, we defeated the 49ers, 42-14. That brought us to Green Bay the next week for a game we won, 27-17.

Of five games in November, we emerged victorious from only one when we beat the Eagles, 20-10, in the Coliseum on the 8th. After that, the season held no more wins for us, only a tie with Green Bay in the last game of the year on December 13. The final tally placed us fifth in the conference with a 5-7-2 record — not good, but an improvement over the previous season.

But our nation ended the year on an upbeat note when the Nobel Prize for Peace was awarded to Martin Luther King, Jr. for his work to secure the civil rights of American blacks by non-violent means. The prize was awarded on December 10, the anniversary of Nobel's death.

After the 1964 season, my transition from the Giants to the Rams was complete. It was still hard to be part of a losing team after all those championship years, but the fun of being in the Fearsome Four-some compensated for that. It also helped that I was making better money in Los Angeles than I had in New York.

My marriage to Bernice continued on its desultory course. It survived, in part, because I spent so little time at home. I kept busy with my life, and she with hers. Whenever our lives converged at any length, we were reminded of too many things about which we disagreed. And the bottom line was still the fact that I was not ready to be a family man. Other than that, I was not abusive and I paid the bills dutifully.

Progress toward racial equality seemed steady and real. More and more, blacks were receiving public recognition in other than athletic and entertainment roles. Ralph Bunche was an undersecretary of the United Nations. In 1965, Thurgood Marshall was appointed Solicitor General of the United States; and my old friend, Jesse Arnell, was prac-ticing law in San Francisco. However, most black people in Los Angeles lived in deprived circumstances in a swath of land stretching south from the civic center and that centered in a district known as Watts.

During the spring of that year, on a flight back to L.A. from New York, I was sitting in the coach section. I noticed that another black man was on the plane — sitting up in the first-class section. When he happened to turn around and look in my direction, I saw that it was Martin Luther King, Jr., himself — a man whom I had come to admire and respect as I did no other.

I finally summoned the courage to walk forward and introduce myself. When I arrived by his seat, he looked up and smiled, "Aren't you Roosevelt Grier of the Los Angeles Rams?"

"Yes, sir."

"I thought I recognized you when I saw you in back a little while ago, but I wasn't sure."

"Well," I replied, "I was sure who you were when I saw you, and I wanted to tell you how much I admire you and what you're doing."

"Thank you, that's kind of you to tell me."

"Dr. King, I don't know if I have the courage to march with you, but I sure would like to help the cause."

"Thank you," he paused a moment. "Do you live in Los Angeles?"

"Yes, sir, I do."

"I'll be coming to Los Angeles later this year. Perhaps you could bring along some other athletes who are interested in getting involved in the movement when I'm there."

"I'll try to do that. Thanks for the idea. I guess I better get back to my seat. And thanks again for the work you're doing."

"God bless you," he replied.

I never saw Martin Luther King again. When he came to Los Angeles that summer, I was away at training camp, which makes me glad that I took advantage of that opportunity to meet a truly great American. Seeing and talking to him in person made me feel a surge of hope that things could be better for all Americans if we would do our part.

But I had little idea as to how I might help Martin Luther King or "join the movement" — except that I could send him a donation. And I could try to stand for the principles of love and brotherhood among the people with whom I worked — football players.

And so it was that football began to give me opportunities to speak out and to lead. Every time I got a chance, I talked about love.

"We love one another on this team," I would say.

"What are you telling people we love one another for?" the guys would ask me indignantly. They thought love was a sissy thing.

"Don't go around telling people we love one another. We're men," they would say.

During the taping of a Super Comedy Bowl television special (a few years after my conversation with Dr. King), I told Joe Namath that the Rams came together as a team because we loved one another.

Joe looked at me oddly and then said, "I like guys, but I don't love them. Love is for chicks, man."

The other Rams would tell me to say that we liked one another.

"No, man, we love one another," I told them. "We win because we care about each other. That's how we can all work together for the good of the team." In time, the guys began to let their guards down, and we began to see the team molded into a unit. And those who refused to give up their old ways gradually weeded themselves out. They were replaced by men who could envision the team concept.

I kept saying it, and now you hear guys from all the teams saying they love one another. It is not considered a sissy thing anymore. But, in 1965, in Los Angeles and thoughout the United States, we suffered a serious shortage of love.

18

RAMS,
RIOTS, AND
RENAISSANCE

At seven o'clock in the evening of Wednesday, August 11, 1965, a California highway patrolman pulled over Marquette Frye, age twenty-one, at the corner of Avalon Boulevard and 116th Street in South Los Angeles near Watts. Frye failed a sobriety test and was placed under arrest by the white officer, whose name was Lee Minikus.

The heat had been oppressive for several days prior to this incident — temperatures in the high nineties with high humidity, something Southern Californians are unused to. Because of the weather, a large number of people were out on their porches trying to cool off. A drunk-driving arrest — with the summoning of a patrol car to take away the suspect and a tow truck to impound the car — readily drew a crowd.

Frye's brother, Ronald, 22, was riding with him that day and they were only two blocks from their mother's home when they were pulled over. When Minikus told Ronald Frye that he would not be permitted to drive the car away from the scene, Ronald walked quickly to get his mother, Mrs. Rena Frye, and bring her to the scene so she could retrieve the car, which belonged to her.

Frye and his mother arrived at the scene just as the tow truck, the patrol car, and Minikus' motorcycle partner also arrived. The crowd of onlookers numbered roughly 300. Rena Frye, who was forty-nine, went directly to her son Marquette and began to scold him for drinking. At that, Marquette grew unruly and started to struggle with the patrolman. By the time three more patrolmen arrived, Mrs. Frye had become so upset that she attacked one of the officers. Ronald Frye came to her aid, and, in the melee that ensued, all three Fryes were arrested and taken from the scene. It was then 7:25 P.M.

By that time, the crowd on the sidewalk numbered nearly a thousand people who were becoming increasingly hostile toward the police officers, all of whom were white. Those officers — Los Angeles policemen as well as highway patrolmen — started to withdraw from the scene when someone in the crowd spat on one of them. A man and a woman were arrested in connection with the spitting, and then all the officers departed from the scene. As they drove away, at 7:40, members of the crowd threw rocks at their vehicles, but the officers did not return to make any further arrests.

That crowd of people turned into a mob that began roaming the streets. By 8:15 the first white motorists in the area were stopped and beaten. Soon any car occupied by whites was either stopped or barraged with whatever missiles were near at hand. In several cases, these people's lives were in serious danger, but they were rescued, in each instance, by mercy-loving black people who gave them sanctuary in their homes and transported them, when necessary, to hospitals.

The violence continued through the night, but there was a pause of calm on Thursday — until the evening. Then the mobs reassembled to loot, trash, and set fires. Many of them strode through the streets crying, "Long live Malcolm X," and, "Burn, baby, burn!" On Friday morning, fires were burning over a wide area and the rioters stayed in the streets.

Several hundred National Guardsmen arrived at five o'clock on Friday afternoon to reinforce the 1600 policemen, highway patrolmen, and sheriff's deputies who were trying in vain to subdue the erupting rage of more than five thousand rioters. By midnight on Friday a thousand guardsmen were marching shoulder-to-shoulder through the streets, but at no time was the rioting brought under control. Major calls of looting, burning, and shooting were reported every two or three minutes throughout the night. Snipers fired at and killed two law officers and a fireman.

On Saturday a curfew was imposed on the forty-seven square miles of area engulfed by the riot. So many fires burned in the area that it looked as though it had been subjected to an air raid. Firemen trying to fight the fires were continually harassed by rock-throwers and snipers. By Saturday night the National Guard contingent had grown to 13,900 fully-armed troops who patrolled on foot and in jeeps equipped with light machine guns.

I was out of town at training camp when the riot broke. We were scheduled to play a charity exhibition game with the Cowboys on Sunday in the Coliseum. However, the Coliseum was inside the riot area, at its northwest corner, and the game was postponed. Our apartment on Longwood Avenue was not in the riot area, but I kept in telephone contact with Bernice to make sure she and Denise were safe. On Sunday, a young Oriental man — caught in the act of fleeing from a looted liquor store — was shot and killed by police on Washington Boulevard, less than a mile from our home.

The tremendous show of force on Saturday night slowed the rioting on Sunday. By Tuesday, Mayor Sam Yorty lifted the curfew. That evening we played the postponed exhibition game with the Cowboys at the Coliseum. Smoke was still rising from smoldering buildings to the south, north, and east, and armed guards were everywhere. Only 20,000 fans felt enough courage to show up, and their enthusiasm for the game was modest at best.

Thirty-four people died of gunshot wounds or other injuries in the riots. More than a thousand suffered injuries, including ninety Los Angeles policemen, 136 fire fighters, ten National Guardsmen, twenty-three employees of other government agencies, 773 civilians, most of whom were black. Of the dead, twenty-nine were black people. Besides the officers, fireman, and Oriental man, the other dead man was an Hispanic person.

Coroner's juries inquired into thirty-two of the deaths and found that twenty-six were justifiable homocides, five were felony homocides, and one was accidental. Of the justifiable homocides, sixteen were inflicted by Los Angeles policemen and seven by National Guardsmen.

The estimated loss in property was listed at $40 million. More than 600 buildings were damaged by fire and looting. Of that number, 200 were entirely destroyed by fire (close to 3000 fire alarms sounded during the riot, 1000 of them during Friday and Friday night).

But, as terrible as all these things were, there was yet a more grievous aspect to the riots — which erupted also within the same five-day period in Chicago and Boston. That more grievous aspect was the sense in which they represented a repudiation of Martin Luther King's pacifistic leadership. In 1966 and 1967 even worse riots than the one in Watts broke out in Newark and Detroit, and violence convulsed Boston, Buffalo, Chicago, Dayton, Cleveland, Milwaukee, San Francisco, Cincinnati, New Haven, Providence, Wilmington, Cambridge, and a hundred other cities.

The ghetto holocausts worked together with the war in Asia to dismember the civil-rights alliance and to destroy the consensus for racial reform. The dream of which King spoke on the steps of the Lincoln Memorial in 1963 was deferred.

But, in the fall of 1965, I didn't see all that. The riots passed. On August 24 the governor appointed a commission, headed by John A. McCone, to investigate the riots and to "develop recommendations for action designed to prevent a recurrence of these tragic disorders." Most of us who had not been directly affected by the riots turned our attention back to the daily affairs of our lives.

For me, that meant playing football with the Los Angeles Rams. The thing that had the team buzzing that year was the salary that a rookie quarterback from Alabama named Joe Namath was getting — $400,000 per year. He was signing with one of those obscure AFL teams, the New York Jets. We figured the AFL teams were willing to put out big bucks to get the top players, but, even at that, $400,000 seemed like an unimaginable amount of money for one man to make in a year. We hardly knew what to make of it.

Our regular season of fourteen games opened in Detroit on September 19. The Lions blanked us, 20-0, and we went home to beat Chicago in a close one, 30-28, the next Sunday. After that, sad to report, we lost eight games in a row. Finally, on November 28, we snapped out of it and beat Green Bay in the Coliseum, 21-10 — a feat that helped our morale immensely since the Packers were leading the league and would beat Cleveland at the end of the season for the title (in what was the last world championship contest before the birth of the Super Bowl). My old Giants' teammate, Don Chandler, was now with the Packers. It was good to see him again, even if I did have to work hard to keep from giving him chances to kick field goals against us.

But that game stands out in my memory for a much more important reason — to me, at least — than those I have just mentioned.

Some of these guys can be real pests. Hey, Mo,
where are you?

(Photograph from Bob Olen)

Hey, you guys, he's about to get away. Hurry, hurry, hurry!

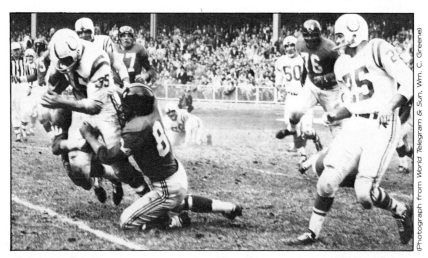

(Photograph from World Telegram & Sun, Wm. C. Greene)

I've got the left leg, you've got the right — let's make a wish!

(Photograph from World Telegram & Sun, Wm. C. Greene)

When I started the game, I knew I had all of it.

If I can get that ball, I'm going to fly.

Somebody's been stealing old number 76.

I sure wish I had learned how to spell "Rosey."

Merlin Olsen, 74; Deacon Jones, 75;
Lamar Lundy, 85; and Me, 76.

Me.

Sometimes we serenaded the quarterbacks
before we broke them up.

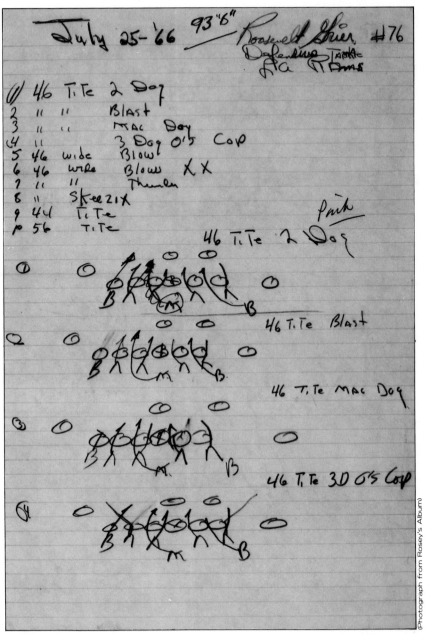

Sometimes they told us how to do it. And if you remembered all those funny looking things, you did it ok — if you remembered.

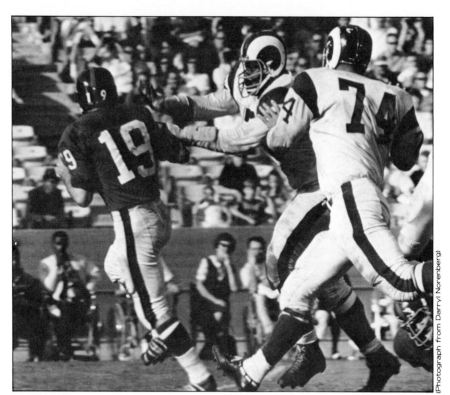

(Photograph from Darryl Norenberg)

One more inch, and I would have had him. Merlin likes quarterbacks too.

I'm ready, coach.

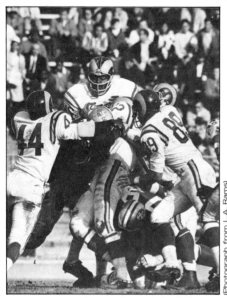

(Photograph from L.A. Rams)

I think I just pulled his head off.

(Photograph from L.A. Rams)

Old soldiers never quit. They just are carried out.

Jimmy Dean, Fess Parker and Me. I'm the black guy.

George Allen doesn't know how to spell "Rosey" either.

You see, it can happen to anyone. I love that little kid.

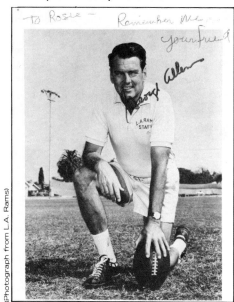

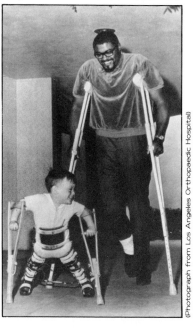

(Photograph from Rosey's Album)

Me and Elvis. "I taught him how to move." Wonder who said that?

My ship came in!

Me and Bob Hope. Can you believe he said Viet Nam was only a few hours by plane?

I want to thank the NAACP for this wonderful trophy.

(Photograph from Rosey's Album)

Me and Tom Jones.
"I taught him all he knows."
Wonder who said that?

(Photograph from L.A. Rams)

The L. A. Coliseum.
Boy, was I nervous.
I wonder if they knew?

(Photograph from Rosey's Album)

Me and Bobby Darin. He
believed enough in me to
produce a record album.

(Photograph from Rosey's Album)

This is it. Bobby Darin was right — you
have to have a cover.

I thank God that I got to know Bobby Kennedy. He taught me how to dream.

For Rosey. From Your Baby Sister
With love always, Marlo

We are free to enjoy.

Captain Kangaroo, can I have your autograph?

No better way to relax than among friends.

I'm not odd because some-times I needlepoint. I know who I am. Do you?

These are the precious few.

To my great friend, Rosey Grier — Jimmy Carter 12-79

Can you believe it? The President spelled "Rosey" right!

They told me I would love the kids in Africa. And I do.

I want you to meet my mom, Ruth Grier. Margie and Little Rosey (on my knee) and our nieces, nephews and friends.

My wife. Such a wonderful lady I married her twice.

I'm going to get this kid a horse.

Hey, Little Rosey. Would you like to trade?

My mom and brother Arthur (behind me).
My cousin Joe Newkirk and my brother
Robert. The other guy was supposed to
be taking the picture. How did he do that?

Margie and two actors.

She started my life — my
mom, Ruthiabelle Grier.

We are a team.

A very precious lady —
my daughter Sheryl.

Margie and an actor.

I really mean
this. You are
called.

Big Rosey and Little
Rosey. We are a team.

He spelled my name right also. Democrat or Republican — they spell right.

*To Rosey Grier
With best wishes,* Ronald Reagan

You should see him now, signed, "A proud father."

Boy, why do I have to wear this suit?

Brother Oral Roberts and me. "You mean I'm a real doctor?" "What do you mean 'honorary'?"

Mrs. Reagan, you and I worked harder to get here.

I'm impressed with these two ladies.

It was a game in which my dream and the dream of every defensive football player came true.

Near the end of the game, the Packers pushed us down to our five-yard line. Bart Starr was at quarterback, and, since Bart had a way of throwing touchdown passes, we figured it was time for a blitz, a play where everybody rushes into the backfield and jumps on the quarterback. So Bart came out of the huddle and yelled, "Hut! 2-8-4, 2-8-4. Everybody go down." And his offensive line got down into position for the play they had just plotted in the huddle.

He took the ball and yelled, "Hut two, hut two!"

Then he backed up with the ball and closed his eyes. While he had his eyes closed, probably thinking, "I'm going to throw a touchdown over the Fearsome Foursome," he heard a voice speak to him.

The voice said, "You'd better open your eyes."

He opened his eyes and staring in his face was Deacon Jones. Now Deacon Jones didn't have anything against Bart personally, but he was generally furious with all quarterbacks. So he leapt on Bart. Then Merlin Olsen leapt on him. And finally, for good measure, Lamar Lundy leapt on him. That left nowhere for me to leap on him. And, just as I was about to feel sorry for myself (almost as sorry as I imagine Bart was feeling for himself at that moment), the ball popped up in the air.

I thought, "Wow, there's the ball and all my life I've been wanting to carry the ball. I'm going to get that ball and go down that sideline, and I'm going to say, 'Hey, Mama, what's happening?' "

Before I finish this story, a confession is in order. I had been waiting, nearly all my life, to get a good chance to carry the ball. Granted, I was part of a generation of defensemen who brought the drama and importance of strong defensive play squarely before the public's eyes. And, back in New York when the crowd would start shouting "DEE-fense!" — it felt great. We were heroes. But, truth be told, we still envied the offensive players who got to handle that funny oval-shaped ball with pointy ends — the Jim Browns, Lenny Moores, Ray Berrys, Frank Giffords, Ollie Matsons — not to mention the flashy quarterbacks who were always throwing or handing off the ball to one of these lucky people.

There is no shout louder, no cheer more joyous, no applause more glorious than for the man who carries the ball for a touchdown or a significant gain. And so, we whose specialty it was to ruin the best efforts of these gallant and fleet-footed men always hungered and thirsted for the rare opportunity to grab that ball and do with it what they did!

My own history as a ball carrier had been either dismal or frustrating. When I was in high school, I went over to the Polo Grounds one Sunday to watch the Giants play football. The Cleveland Browns were in town. They had a rusher named Marion Motley. He took the ball from the quarterback and started to the left, but he could see the Giants were ready for him on the left. There was nowhere to go. In a flash of brilliance, he turned back, reversed his field, and ran all the way back the other way for a touchdown. Even though I was cheering for the Giants, that run of Motley's was still one of the most wonderful things I had ever seen done on a football field. If only, I dreamed, I might be able to do something as dramatic and noteworthy.

Well, in high school football, anything is possible. And it was during those years that I had the most opportunities I was ever given to do some offensive ball carrying — one. It wasn't long after watching Marion Motley's splendid performance that Abraham Clark High School's football team found itself with a fourth down and not far to go to the goal line. Would we kick the field goal or try for six points?

With a giant like me on the team, who was also fast, the choice seemed easy. They put me in at fullback and handed me the ball. Oh, but it felt good as I snuggled it in my arms. I started to run the planned play — to the right. But, like Marion Motley, I could see nowhere to run. Of course, I knew what to do: I wheeled about and ran in the other direction. Somehow, though, it didn't quite work the way it did for Motley. Those defenders were after me in a flash. My ploy had not fooled them even for a moment, and, instead of heading for the goal line, I was running back from the line of scrimmage in an effort to elude my pursuers. They tackled me an humiliating twenty yards back from where the play had started.

My next opportunity to carry the ball came when I was playing for the Giants. I recovered a fumble and started to go for it, but I had only gone two steps when I got tackled.

Then, with the Rams, in a game in Candlestick Park against the 49ers, I had just missed snagging a fumble that popped up into the air. Merlin had grabbed it instead and had a good shot at a long run down the sideline. So keenly did I feel that he had robbed me of an opportunity that I ran up alongside him and asked him to let me carry the ball part of the way. Strangely, he wasn't warm to the idea and rebuffed my suggestion. His attitude was so ungracious that I refused to block for him. That would show him!

Now, with that confession and history in place, we can continue where we left off a few paragraphs back. In case you've forgotten: the ball had just mysteriously popped out of a pile of people consisting of Bart Starr (at the bottom), Deacon Jones, Merlin Olsen, and Lamar Lundy.

The ball struck my hand and fell to the ground. The referee's whistle was still silent — it was a live ball. I jumped on it and covered it up. There it was again, in my arms!

Then I heard a voice, "You can still make it."

I jumped to my feet and started to make my getaway!

A second voice spoke, "Better see who's coming after you."

I looked around, and got my answer. All eleven of the Green Bay Packers were coming straight for me. I was in imminent danger of getting a taste of my own medicine!

Suddenly I wanted nothing better than to be rid of that accursed ball. Seeing no one to whom to toss it, however, and being too proud to fall on it a second time or to throw it out of bounds, I ran for my life. Then, THUD! The first Packer to reach me hit me with a force I'd never felt before. In the pit, where I was used to playing, things got rough, but we seldom got up much speed before we ran into each other — the play was in close and tight. But now I was being hit by big men running at full throttle in high gear!

In a moment, they were all on me with merciless ferocity — seeking to avenge the loss of the ball before they had to leave the field and give place to their own defensive squad. Their vengeance must have been sweet because, when they finally pulled everybody off of me, blood was pouring from my mouth. I had bitten clean through my own tongue!

It was a nasty injury that took me out of the game because it required immediate medical attention. Alas, it was not one of those heroic injuries that gains everyone's sympathy. Instead it was more the embarrassing sort. It damaged the nerves in my tongue and it took me awhile to learn to speak clearly again. To this day, there is some numbness in it. In addition, my head took such a jarring on that play that swelling affected my nasal and auditory passages for several days as well.

But something good came of that incident — besides the fact that the Rams recovered and regained the offensive. The good I have in mind was more personal and internal. It consisted in my being entirely set free from coveting the work of the ball carrier. I was, at last, content to be a defensive tackle.

After beating Green Bay we enjoyed our only win on the road that season, in St. Louis on December 5, 27-3. The next week we humiliated the Eastern Conference champs, the Cleveland Browns, 42-7. Jim Brown led the league in rushing, as usual, that season, but not because of that game.

We finished the season the next weekend at the Coliseum where we lost to the Colts, 20-17. That brought our record to 4-10-0, the most dismal season since I had started playing football (only one team in the entire league, Pittsburgh, performed more poorly). It was also Harland Svare's worst — and last — season with the team. Dan Reeves fired him even before the final tally was in (after that, Harland finished his career as head coach for the Chargers between 1971 and 1973). I was sad to see him go. He was an old friend, and he deserves a lot of credit for having first assembled the Fearsome Foursome.

The man Dan Reeves had in mind to replace Harland was named George Allen. Allen was a coach with unusual talents, and he got his first chance to exercise those talents as a head coach with us. As a measure of how good he was, George Halas and the Bears lodged a lawsuit against him in 1965 when he first accepted Dan Reeves' invitation to come and take over the Rams. He had been an assistant coach (defense) for the Bears since 1958. They knew his merit and didn't want to let him go.

George was a brainy sort of man. After taking a regular degree from Michigan, he went on to earn a Master's degree from Stanford in 1948. He coached two small college teams after that until he got the job with the Bears.

The lawsuit dragged on into 1966, but George finally won it (he had a way of winning) and got on the plane for Los Angeles. Soon after he arrived, he drove out to take a look at our regular practice site, the San Fernando Recreation Center out in the north end of the San Fernando Valley, and to Chapman College, in Orange, California, our summer training camp. "Those places," he announced when he got back, "are the worst I've seen, and the locker rooms are a disgrace. How could any team develop a winning attitude in such surroundings?"

We didn't know. All that was certain was that we had not succeeded in doing it.

"I'll tell you men something," he continued. "Football games are not necessarily won by the best players. They are won by the team with the best attitude."

He moved our regular practice site to Long Beach and he picked Cal State-Fullerton for our summer training camp. They were a lot nicer.

George Allen talked, slept, and breathed football. No other subject interested him — not movies, or women, or money, or baseball, or any other thing. If you talked to George, you talked football.

One of the most unusual things about George was that he didn't care much about rookies. Most coaches had a common strategy for building a championship team. It involved the slow methodical process of making careful draft choices and then building them into a winning team over a period of years. But not George. He looked for immediate results. "The future is now!" was his slogan. Consequently, he placed a premium, not on hot-shot draft choices, but the older, more experienced players.

So, it was difficult to make his team as a rookie. But it was hard to stay on his team, no matter what. When he got done trading and reorganizing the team, only twenty-nine of us who had played in 1965 survived to play in 1966 when seventeen new names appeared on the roster. The Fearsome Foursome all survived, but of the seven linebackers, only two, Dan Currie and Doug Woodlief, survived. I could not remember having seen so many trades in one season.

He also made players take more responsibility by appointing field "generals" and "captains." He introduced specialized practice sessions in which each segment of the team started drilling — learning patterns of play for specific situations and conditions. Those sessions had a lot in common with Merlin Olsen's drills about which I complained earlier.

To us defensemen he preached the "take-away" concept. "If you can take away yardage, points, or momentum from the opposition, you will win," he told us. But he didn't just preach. He gave us specific and definite techniques — like fake signals designed to throw off the opposition. He showed us things we could do to disrupt our opponents' quick-count signals. From the minute he arrived in Los Angeles, George Allen had only one goal: to build the Los Angeles Rams into a winning team.

Nineteen-sixty-six was a significant year for professional football. Since 1959 the American Football League (the fourth and most successful attempt to form a league under that name) had been working hard to compete with the well-established NFL. It got its start when Lamar Hunt, son of Texas millionaire H.L. Hunt, tried and failed to lure an NFL team to Dallas. Not one to give up, he started his own league.

When the AFL first played in 1960, it consisted of the Dallas Texans, the Los Angeles Chargers, the Oakland Raiders, the Denver Broncos, the Houston Oilers, the New York Titans, the Buffalo Bills, and the Boston Patriots. The early years were rough. These teams did not try to scoop up the NFL players and mostly contented themselves with rookies and castoffs. As a result, the crowds at games were often small. Before long, the Los Angeles team moved to San Diego, the Texans went to Kansas City and became the Chiefs, and the Titans went into bankruptcy court, only to emerge, Phoenix-like, as the Jets.

But, even with the readjustments and slowly growing crowds, it was nip and tuck until 1964, when the league got a contract from NBC which agreed to pay $36 million for the exclusive right to televise AFL games. After that, the AFL began to compete formidably with the NFL. In 1966, Oakland announced that it had Roman Gabriel, our leading quarterback on the Rams, under contract (in the end, Dan Reeves and George Sherman convinced Roman to stay with us). After that, word spread that John Brodie of the 49ers was going to the Oilers.

Pete Rozelle and the NFL owners saw the handwriting on the wall: it was time for a merger. Not ones to let grass grow under their feet, the two commissioners, Pete Rozelle and Al Davis, signed an agreement on June 8, 1966. The new league would be comprised of twenty-four teams and would expand to twenty-six by 1968. The constituents of the old leagues, however, would continue to play separate schedules until 1970, at which time the merger would be complete. Beginning at the end of the 1966 season, early in 1967, the winners of the NFL championship would meet the winners of the AFL in the Super Bowl.

The 1966 season got underway in Atlanta, Georgia, on September 11. The Falcons got their start when the NFL awarded a franchise to Rankin M. Smith on June 30, 1965, so they hadn't been around long. Nevertheless, they fought hard and gave us a good game which we won, 19-14. For me, it was special to play professional football for the first time in the state of my birth.

The Chicago Bears met us the next Sunday in the Coliseum and we beat them handily, 31-17. Winning the first two games of our season was something that had not happened since I had come with the Rams. Coach Allen was already making a difference.

After that we lost to Green Bay on their turf and then beat San Francisco and Detroit. Five games into the season we were 4-1. That felt good. It exceeded by a country mile the record for the first five games since I had come in 1963.

But that was on October 9. We did not win another game until November 13, dropping four in a row to Minnesota, Chicago, Baltimore, and San Francisco. And whom were we due to meet on November 13? None other than the New York Giants in the first and only regular season game in which I would oppose them. It was strange, though, most of the faces sitting across the field that day on the Giants' bench were unfamiliar to me. Of my old teammates, I saw only Jim Katcavage, Del Shofner, Joe Morrison, and Jim Patton. Allie Sherman was still the coach.

If it had been any comfort to me, the Giants had had only one winning season, 1963, since I had left. In 1965 they went 7-7-0, and now they came to Los Angeles to grapple with us. The outcome was lopsided, the biggest win the Rams rolled up that season, 55-14. That brought us to a 5-5-0 record for the season with four games yet to be played.

On November 20 and 27 we beat Minnesota and Baltimore, avenging the losses they had dealt us earlier in the season. Then, on December 4, we dispensed with Detroit for the second time that season,

23-3. Now the Rams' record was a respectable 8-5. No matter what happened, we would end up with a winning season for the first time since 1958.

The last game of the season promised to be a thriller. The Green Bay Packers were coming to Los Angeles on December 18 — after a bye weekend for us, which came as a result of having started our season a week earlier than usual. The Packers were at the height of their power and they arrived at the Coliseum with an 11-2-0 record, the best among all the twenty-four teams of the newly-merging NFL-AFL.

With our 8-5 record, you would have thought that we were the underdogs, but not so. The oddsmakers gave us an edge of three and a half points, mostly because Bart Starr, the Packers' star quarterback, would be out with injuries. There were other considerations, too. The Packers already had the Western Conference title sewed up, so there was nothing at stake for them in this game. We, on the other hand, did have something at stake. Winning this game would give us second place in the Western Conference which would put us in the Playoff Bowl against the Eastern Conference runners-up in Miami on January 8. And, finally, we had lost to Green Bay (24-13) in Wisconsin on September 25, after which Coach Allen had vowed, "We'll beat 'em in L.A."

It so happened that Deacon, Lamar, Merlin and I had started singing together, and earlier this same year we had gotten booked for some appearances on shows like "Hollywood Palace." Our reputation as the Fearsome Foursome made us a ready hit with the fans who loved the novelty of four big linemen trying to make a little harmony. And we didn't sound too bad. Someone wrote new words to fit the tune of a popular Calypso song, "Day-O." It was always a big hit with our audiences. One verse went like this:

Day-o, Day-o,
Green Bay come, and I wanta go home.
Oh, please, Mr. Coach, won't you be a good fella?
Green Bay come, and I wanta go home.
It's starting to rain, and I need an umbrella.
Green Bay come, and I wanta go home.
Those six-foot, seven-foot, eight-foot guys!
Green Bay come, and I wanta go home.
I think Bart Starr is getting wise.
Green Bay come, and I wanta go home.
Day-o, Day-o.

Not surprisingly, the game drew the largest Coliseum crowd of our season, 72,416. Green Bay took the lead early in the game with a seventy-six-yard pass interception that led to a touchdown for them. Zeke Bratkowski handled the quarterbacking opposite our Roman Gabriel. Zeke's passing got them a second touchdown, but Gabe's good throw to McKeever got fumbled on the Packers' five where they recovered. A field goal by Don Chandler brought their first half total to 17. In the meantime, our kicker Bruce Gossett made first-half field goals that spanned 36, 30, and 17 yards to net us nine points.

By the time we went to the lockers at halftime, we had suffered a number of injuries. Several of the fellows had concussions, and Merlin got a sprained knee.

During the third period we held each other scoreless as the two teams' tough defensive units showed their stuff. But in the fourth quarter they drove us sixty-two yards down field and took another score. It was 24-9, and, suddenly, the battle was on. We dug in afresh on defense and the offense got fancy. In a fourth-and-nine situation, they sent in our punter, Jon Kilgore, who took the ball and passed it to Claude Crabb for a 47-yard pick up. That lined a final eleven-yard run by Gabe into the end zone (24-16).

The Packers came back and our resistance faltered enough to let Don Chandler get another field goal — this one traveled forty-seven yards and brought the score to 27-16. Our offense came back strong. Gabe hurled a high one to Steve Heckard that bought us fifty yards. A little later, Marlin McKeever took a short toss from Gabe and made the touchdown (27-23). Only thirty-four seconds were left on the clock, so we tried for the onside kick (the short kick — it has to travel at least ten yards, after which it may be recovered by the kicking team if no member of the opposing team is able to touch it first). Sadly, one of the Packers got to it first. They ran out the clock and our season came to an abrupt end.

We finished third in the Western Conference of seven teams — a game behind the Colts and four behind the Packers. It felt good, in spite of the loss at the end of the season, to be breathing the higher-altitude air after having ended the 1965 season in the basement. George Allen had turned us into a winning team in one short season, an amazing accomplishment. Our eagerness to start the 1967 season was only tempered by our need to get our injured men back in shape. After that, there would be no stopping us. But how was I to know? . . .

19

THE BIG AND
THE BIGGER
SURPRISES

After the end of the 1966 season and a little time to recuperate, the Fearsome Foursome hit the entertainment circuit — with ever more reason to sing "Green Bay Come and I Wanta Go Home!" Our itinerary eventually brought us to San Diego where we appeared on a network TV variety show with Kay Stevens and others.

After a rehearsal, we were standing around talking, and Kay said, "You four make quite a team. They had to pay a handsome penny to get you on this show." She was smiling broadly.

Deacon said, "Hey, Momma, when you're as good as we are, you gotta pay to get us!"

Everybody laughed at his joke, and then Kay continued in a slightly less lighthearted vein, "But I'll bet you still make your real livings off football, right?"

"Yeah, just barely," Deacon answered with another laugh.

"Hey, if you don't like what they're paying you, why don't you organize?"

"You mean like the Players' Association?" Merlin asked.

"No, actually, I was just thinking of the four of you. I'll bet you might get old Dan Reeves to cough up a million dollars if you negotiated your contract as a unit."

That got a big laugh from us, and then the subject changed. But later, as we talked about it among ourselves, we realized we might be able to do better as a group than as separate individuals. We didn't want to hold up anybody, but, after we started talking about it among ourselves, we discovered that none of us believed we were getting a fair shake. Kay Stevens got us thinking.

I felt reluctant because I was almost thirty-five and might not be playing much longer. Yet it was an intriguing idea. The longer I played football, the more I came to believe that I and my fellow players had been taken advantage of in our contracts.

That was the result of athletes negotiating directly with owners. There is no way a rookie just out of college can negotiate a contract in his own best interest. He cannot understand how much athletics is going to take out of him over a period of years.

When I signed my first contract with the Giants in 1955, it never occurred to me to ask for more than they were offering me. Most of us back then were still a little astounded that anyone would pay us to play a game at which we had so much fun. People got paid to do things they didn't particularly enjoy. And even when an occasional player came along with a little more savvy, the owners of the teams refused to talk to any agent or lawyer. Furthermore, when we signed our contracts, they told us not to let each other know what we were making.

As a result of those attitudes and circumstances, few of us were paid enough to make a good living. Instead of money, our reward, according to management, was in playing the game we loved and hearing the cheers of the fans.

And, it has to be recognized that in those days there was not as much money in football as there is today. Television made a dramatic change in the economics of football which has led to the astronomical contract negotiations about which we read and hear today.

When all that money is being tossed about, does anyone stop to think about the fans who pay to watch the games? How many Americans are struggling to earn enough to keep their families housed and clothed?

The owners have to make a fair profit, and the players have to make a living, but things today have gotten out of proportion, and the little guy, the customer, is getting hurt. If we are not careful, this attitude could kill the game.

Excuse me, I seem to have mounted my soap box. Anyone who knows me will not be surprised. But I'll get off it and back to my story now.

The summer of 1967, as I mentioned when I talked about the Watts' riots in 1965, brought ever more gruesome and heartbreaking disorders — particularly to Detroit and Newark. The ones in Newark were the bloodiest. I had spent the second half of my growing up years in the shadow of Newark, and I had seen the life there close-up in those days when I went to visit my older brother James.

As the fifties gave way to the sixties, whatever glory Newark had once possessed was gone. The black unemployment rate there was the highest in the nation, together with the rate of condemned housing units, crime, new cases of tuberculosis, and mortality among women giving birth. The majority of Newark's population was black, but the city's administration was almost entirely white and notorious for its callousness and corruption. The city had long been on the verge of a race war.

And so, on Wednesday, July 12, the violence erupted in response to a rumor that a black taxi driver had been arrested and beaten to death by police. Looting began immediately (it had taken over twenty-four hours for it to begin in Los Angeles), and was quickly followed by arson. On the second night, the police began using live ammunition and killed five blacks. Then, as the riot began to abate, the state's governor sent in the National Guard. Over the weekend guardsmen fired thirteen thousand rounds of ammunition in the city killing twenty more blacks and wounding some 1200. Thirteen hundred blacks were arrested and property damage was fixed at $10 million.

What happened to the rioting blacks of Newark in terms of the sternly militaristic response of the white administration of the city and the state was white backlash. And against what or whom were whites lashing back? To understand the answer to that question, we need to look back to an incident in Mississippi in 1966.

In 1966, Stokely Carmichael of SNCC (most people called it "snick") was grabbing the limelight from Martin Luther King who was struggling in vain to keep the unity of the civil-rights movement intact.

King preached non-violence, but not Stokely. Few white people failed to note his threatening invocation of a new spirit in Greenwood, Mississippi, in 1966 during a march organized in response to the shooting of James Meredith.

Emerging from a brief jailing in Greenwood, Carmichael found a large crowd waiting to welcome him. The crowd was already in a hostile mood when Carmichael jumped to the back of a flatbed truck and gave the raised-arm, clenched-fist salute. "This is the twenty-seventh time I have been arrested," he announced, "and I ain't going to jail no more! The way we gonna stop them white men from whippin' us is to take over. We been saying freedom for six years and we ain't got nothin'. What we gonna start saying now is Black Power!" And then, in good preacher-style, he started to repeat in a rhythmic, chant-like manner, "We. . . want. . .Black. . .Power!"

Some in the crowd began to join him. And, as Carmichael continued his chant, the response of the crowd grew into a loud and angry litany. Then Carmichael yelled, "That's right! That's what we want. Now, from now on, when they ask you what you want, you know what to tell them. What do you want?"

"Black Power!" the crowd roared.

"What do you want?"

"BLACK POWER!"

"What do you want? Say it again!"

"BLACK POWER! BLACK POWER! BLACK POWER!"

Martin Luther King was there, but Carmichael had captured the moment. King's protest that "We must never seek power exclusively for the Negro, but the sharing of power with white people" went largely unnoticed and unheeded. He got his answer a few days later, on June 26, when the march reached Jackson. Most of the marchers were shouting "Black Power!" — without coaxing or coaching. Then Floyd McKissick, the newly-elected leader of CORE, speaking at the final rally announced, "Nineteen-sixty-six shall be remembered as the year we left our imposed status as Negroes and became Black Men. . .1966 is the year of the concept of Black Power."

Few of King's white supporters who had marched with him for so long stood beside him that day. And what I saw on television a year later in 1967 while Newark burned was only a further demonstration that white sympathy for the plight of poor black people was draining away quickly.

While most of us former-Negroes-now-turned-black-people recognized that Stokely Carmichael and Floyd McKissick had struck a chord, we were unwilling to follow them on the course that eventually led Carmichael into the Black Panthers and thence on to full-fledged insurgency and anarchism with trips to Cuba and North Vietnam.

Instead, we employed their slogan usually in more domesticated ways. Black Power was a fine slogan, particularly because it never gained any single clear definition. Soon everyone was using it to mean whatever they wanted it to mean. For the revolutionaries it meant guerilla warfare, for liberals it was a call to reform, and for conservatives it spoke of self-help. But, in spite of the confusion, it helped to call attention, as the civil rights movement had failed to do, to the needs of poor people and to the root of their plight: powerlessness. In this way it pointed to the need to restructure our nation's economic and political institutions on the basis of a transformed value structure.

Furthermore, Black Power made us proud to be black, and that was something we needed in order to achieve true equality. Black became beautiful. We started throwing away hair straighteners and skin bleaches, and began instead to affirm our own culture with joy. I, for example, became unashamed to own up to the fact that I'd eaten 'possum. Instead, as you've already noticed, I'll heartily recommend it as a taste sensation and give a recipe for it to anyone who will listen. My colleague James Brown sang it like it was: "Say it loud — I'm black and I'm proud." Many of us searched out our African heritages. Cassius Clay and Lew Alcindor were among the thousands who took Arabic names, and some of the black athletes who took medals at the XIX Olympiad in Mexico City gave the clenched-fist salute. It all struck white people, at first, as ominous and foreboding. But it was a necessary, if painful, step of growing up for black Americans.

In the meantime, my own personal growing up continued without let up. As usual, I didn't feel ready for the next stage when it came — unannounced.

I reported to Chapman College down in Orange for summer training camp on schedule (and hopeful that I would be more assertive when I negotiated my next contract with the Rams). It was good to be getting back into condition. At thirty-five, it was taking a little longer than it had when I was twenty-five, but not much. The camp proceeded vigorously and I could tell that the team was getting ready to have a bigger winning season than it had in 1966 — although it didn't seem that way the night we were playing an exhibition game with the Kansas City Chiefs.

The Chiefs were, after all, mere upstarts from the American Football League. The merger between the NFL and the AFL was moving forward, but it was difficult for us to take the AFL teams seriously yet. Perhaps because of that, the Chiefs were slaughtering us. They got us down 24 to 3 in the first half!

Then, just as the half was about to end, they called a dinky screen play. In a screen play, the offensive linemen drop back as though to form a cup, but they just "brush block" the charging defensive linemen, like me. Then, instead of forming a cup, they re-form near the sideline in front of a pass receiver. The receiver takes a short toss from the quarterback and then moves upfield behind the screen of blockers. They weren't very subtle about getting set up to make this sort of play and I quickly saw what they had in mind.

As soon as the ball was snapped, I pushed through the line and put myself squarely between the quarterback and his intended receiver, the Chiefs' Mike Garrett. Poor Mike, I was all over him. Then, just as the ref blew the whistle, I felt a nasty pain on the backside of my right leg near the ankle. I thought somebody had clipped me. I looked around to get the number of whoever had done it so that I could return the favor later in the game. But no one was there — all the other players were at least seven yards from me.

Suddenly, that leg gave out and I was sitting on the ground looking at my feet. I tried to move my right toe and my ankle, but nothing happened. While I was sitting there, Garrett came over and reached down to pull me up.

Proudly, I refused his offer. He, after all, was on the other team.

So I sat there looking at my right foot and trying to make it work. Helplessly, I looked over at the Rams' sidelines. Every one of them, it seemed, was looking at me. I looked back at my foot. No injury had ever stopped me before, except that time in 1958 in the championship game against the Colts. Usually I kept on playing, knowing that the pain would come later. But this time was different. That darned leg just would not work!

George Menefee, the trainer, knew when I got hurt not to bother coming after me, because I invariably refused his help, went back into the game and performed better than ever. But now I found myself looking pathetically in George's direction and waving to him. I realized I was not going to play anymore that day even if they wrapped my foot.

Not only George, but also John Perry, the team's physician, and Dr. Danny Leaventhal, the team's orthopedic specialist, came running out on the field. I told them the problem and Leaventhal felt around on the back of my ankle. The doc didn't say a word to me, but he stood up and announced to the others standing about, "Well, his Achilles tendon has been snapped."

George Menefee and a couple of the players helped me off the field. I was holding my right leg up so my dragging foot wouldn't touch the ground. I was upset that I was hurt, but mostly I worried about how we were going to beat the Chiefs. During halftime, some of the guys — Lamar, Deacon, and Merlin among them — came to see me while I was lying on a table in the locker room.

"Rosey," they said, "we're going to give you the game ball."

I laughed to myself. It was a nice thought, but how were we going to get the game ball if we didn't win? We were down 24 to 3. If we hadn't been able to stop the Chiefs in the first half, how did they expect to do it in the second half — especially without me to help them!?

Then the doctor must have given me something for pain because I don't remember the guys leaving to resume the game. But I will never forget when they came back and brought me that ball. My injury had evidently galvanized them into action. Those Rams had gone back out there and beaten the Chiefs 44 to 24!

"Here's the game ball, Rosey," they proudly announced as they came stomping back into the locker room.

I cannot express what I felt like at that moment. Winning and then giving me that ball said they cared about me, a lot. Few things in my life have ever felt as good as that did. They loved me and they wanted to show it.

After getting the game ball, I was taken to St. John's Hospital. The Achilles tendon attaches the calf muscle to the heel bone. Some excellent doctors on the St. John's staff operated to re-attach mine from where it had snapped loose. Then I went home to convalesce.

The injury put me out of the game for the 1967 season. I traveled to some of the later games and spoke to the players. It was good to see them and to see how well they were doing — although it was sad not to be playing with them. They finished the season 11-1-2, tied with Baltimore and Green Bay for first place in the Western Conference. In the playoffs they beat the Colts, but not the Packers. The Rams would have to wait a bit longer to make it to the Super Bowl. But George Allen was voted Coach of the Year for the amazing turnaround he had accomplished. George Allen was very good at motivating. He used everything he could to motivate his players to go out and play super-natural football.

Being stuck at home except when I went down to the hospital to do my rehabilitation therapy was hard on my marriage. As I said earlier, Bernice and I lasted as long as we did because I wasn't home much. So what happened next helped put off the inevitable divorce just a while longer.

Later that fall, after I had recuperated enough to be pretty steady on my feet, my theatrical agent (I never did have an agent for my football career) gave me a call and asked me to come over to his office. His name was Cal Mason.

"What's up, Cal?" I asked.

"I got a very important call that we need to talk about face-to-face. Just come on over, okay?"

"Okay, I'll be there in an hour."

Once I arrived at his office, he announced. "I got a call this morning from Ethel Kennedy."

"Who?"

"Ethel Kennedy is Robert Kennedy's wife," he replied.

"Yeah, I know about her. I just couldn't believe that's who you really meant."

"She called me in person — it wasn't even her secretary."

"What did she want?"

"She wants you to come to a fund-raising event in Washington. They're raising money to send kids from the ghettos to summer camps. And they like to get the celebrity jocks and other notables out for these events."

"No way, man," I told him. "You know how I feel about plane rides." I believed the correct way to travel was by car, subway, or train. Only out of necessity would I fly.

"Rose, you need to think about this. The Kennedys are important people, not just your average slobs."

"Yeah, but. . . ."

"Look, you've been working at this career of yours part time for more than seven years. With that tendon damaged like it was, the money from football isn't going to last much longer. You need to take this invitation seriously. A lot of people you should meet are going to be there."

"Cal, I'd go if I didn't hate to fly like I do. You know how I get when I'm up in a plane."

"Will you do it if I agree to go with you?"

I looked at him and realized he was serious. I sat silently for several moments, weighing my dread of flying against the shame I would feel if I turned him down. "Okay, Cal," I sighed at last, "you shamed me into it."

Ethel didn't send tickets for us to fly commercially. Instead, a private airplane was chartered to take us. As soon as we got to the airport, I found myself in impressive company. No less than Eddie Fisher, Connie Stevens, and a rock group were on that plane with Cal and me.

After landing in D.C., we were taken to the hotel where the Kennedys were putting us up for the weekend. Two girls were assigned to drive Cal and me around as needed. As soon as we'd freshened up from the flight, they drove us out of town and across the Potomac to the Kennedy residence, Hickory Hill, an ante-bellum mansion in McLean, Virginia.

Ethel Kennedy met us at the door. She greeted each of us warmly and gave me a big hug. I liked her right away. We weren't in the house long before Bobby arrived to greet us. He treated me like an old friend, even punched me fondly in the stomach. I had never been treated so warmly by someone who was a stranger. Bobby Kennedy refused to allow us to remain strangers for even a minute. It was wonderful!

That evening, a number of their friends and supporters came to the house. Bobby said, "Stay with me, Rosey. I want to introduce you to my friends." And everywhere he went, I followed.

He introduced me to people like Lauren Bacall as "my friend, Rosey." I met Byron "Whizzer" White, the supreme court justice who had been appointed by President Kennedy in 1962. Justice White, I found out, had been an All-American halfback at Colorado back in the thirties, and he had played a little pro ball to help finance his law studies. I also met a lot of the stars I admired: Shirley MacLaine, Andy Williams and his wife, Claudine Longet, all the Kennedys, and some well-known newscasters.

I kept saying to myself, "I don't believe this! What am I doing here with all these high-class celebrities?"

Saturday morning, those two girls drove us back out to Hickory Hill again where things were busy as a beehive. All day long, people were at the Kennedy home, but Ethel and Bobby were steadily congenial and pleasant to everybody.

After getting ready on Saturday, the television program in which we were all appearing was taped on Sunday.

That night, after the taping, we went to Averell Harriman's home and partied all night. Harriman was near the end of a long and distinguished career in the service of his country. Heir of the Union Pacific railroad fortune, he had been involved in politics with Franklin D. Roosevelt and the New Deal. Later he had been ambassador to Britain and, later, to the Soviet Union. He was governor of New York during some of the years I played for the Giants. President Kennedy had brought him back into the State Department and, on the night of the party, this seventy-six-year-old man was an ambassador at large and would soon be called upon to serve as chief U.S. negotiator at the Paris peace talks on the war in Vietnam.

However, I didn't "hang out" with the ambassador that night. Instead, I met Peaches and Herb, a terrific singing duet. We hit it off together right away and made a lot of noise singing together. Finally, about five o'clock in the morning, Harriman, who had gone to bed earlier, banged on the floor for us to keep quiet. One has to wonder at his patience in waiting so long to make his wishes known!

The next day, there was an affair at Teddy Kennedy's house. I was so tired from lack of sleep that I faded out. But I was tremendously impressed with the way those people responded to one another, the love and concern they showed.

In the Kennedys, I saw the big-family ideal that I had yearned for all my life. They were a unit, a team, yet the individual wasn't lost in the crowd. Each of them seemed real to the others — was treated with respect and affection. And they were amazingly honest — they "let it all hang out," their feelings, aspirations, and ambitions.

When I got back to California, I sent flowers to Ethel and to Teddy's wife, Joan, thanking them for the great time they had shown me. Also, I sent flowers to the Harrimans. It was a point in my life I can never forget, the bigger surprise that overshadowed the big surprise of my ruptured tendon. Looking back, I have to admit that, if I had been playing football that season, I would have been unable to accept that invitation. At the time, it seemed much as it had in my younger days, that my life kept unfolding and doors kept opening which led me into places and circumstances I could never have anticipated. Perhaps, however, there was a plan.

One day in January, 1968, I was out for a walk with Dog, my beautiful brown boxer, and Little Bit, the toy poodle I had raised from a two-month-old puppy. They made an unusual pair, walking side by side. And Little Bit was very protective of Dog.

As we walked along, I broke into a trot. I had forgotten all about my Achilles tendon, and I continued to forget as we jogged along. Then I stopped and thought, "Wow, my ankle feels fine! I could go back if I wanted to." Funny thing, though, the idea didn't appeal to me that much. I was going to have to think about it a while longer.

Then, a month or two later, I met a man in Hollywood named Bill McFee who asked, "Rosey, what are you going to do if you quit playing football?"

"I don't know," I replied. "I've never planned my life yet. I didn't plan to finish high school or attend college. My life has been one long happening."

McFee smiled. "How would you like to do your own television show?"

"I think I'd like it fine," I answered before I gave myself a chance to think about it. I thought he was "jivin' me." There's a lot more talk than action in Hollywood.

But Bill took me to meet his brother Jerry, a producer for ABC. Before I knew it, I'd signed a contract to do something I'd never thought about before. In the aftermath of the Watts riots, Los Angeles television stations were responding to the recommendations of the McCone commission by running more black programming. It was a matter of being in the right place at the right time.

I became the host of "The Rosey Grier Show" which aired every Saturday afternoon. A half-hour talk and variety show with its own band, it featured a guest each week who was doing something in the community to help people, together with celebrity guest stars. Producer Jim Baker created the format.

We tried to demonstrate that the team concept works. The band members represented several ethnic groups. Band leader, Frankie Ortega, was Spanish. We had a black, an Hawaiian, an Indian, and others — a magnificent mix of people working harmoniously to make a terrific show that ran for three or four years. It even received an Emmy nomination.

Shortly after we began production on the show, I saw a news item that provoked me to call Bobby Kennedy.

20

A PIECE OF
ME BEGINS
TO RUN FREE

It was in March, 1968, that I read reports that Bobby Kennedy was going to run for the presidency and that a lot of people were upset because he was entering the campaign late. I had first met him, of course, during the weekend of the television special, and we had kept in contact since then through letters and mutual friends. That had been enough to establish an unusual bond of friendship between us which I sensed was genuinely mutual. I called him up at Hickory Hill that evening, and he was at home.

"Rosey, good to hear from you," he said when he came to the phone.

"Hi, Bobby. What's this I hear about you running for the nomination? Is it true?"

"Yes, it is. I made the decision less than a week ago."

"I'm going to help you," I announced without further ado.

"That's wonderful, Rosey! I can use all the help I can get. Campaigning is hard work. Is your leg up to it?"

"I'll be fine. You just let me know what you want done."

I had never done anything like this before and I had no idea what to expect. But, very shortly, Bobby began to call for me to go places to speak for him.

"What can somebody like me add to anything you might have to say?" I protested.

"Rosey, I can't be in more than one place at a time. You're a man with a big heart who understands people's problems. Just speak from your heart. When they hear your heart, they'll listen.

"Now," he continued, "the Indiana primary will be on May 7. I want you to meet me there in Indianapolis on April 4. Can you do that?"

"Yes, sir. I'll be there, and anywhere else you want me."

However, neither of us could foresee what would prevent that meeting. On Thursday, April 4, about five o'clock in the afternoon, I was at Los Angeles International Airport preparing to board the flight to Chicago from where I would catch a connecting flight to Indianapolis. I was reading the sports page of the newspaper when I heard my name on the paging system. Bewildered as to who it might be, I got up and went to the phone.

"Mr. Grier?" a stranger's voice inquired.

"Yeah?" I grunted curiously.

"My name is Joan Breden. I'm calling from Bobby Kennedy's campaign headquarters to ask you to stay in California."

"But? . . ."

"Martin Luther King was shot to death in Memphis just about an hour ago. Needless to say, Mr. Kennedy will not be able to continue his Indiana campaign as anticipated. We will be in touch with you as soon as the rally in which you were going to participate is rescheduled."

"I see," I murmured.

After that, I walked around the airport in a daze, lost in thought and grief. Eventually I found a quiet corner in which to sit and weep for a man I loved.

Later I found myself back at my apartment watching the news on television. I was saddened by footage of some people who were rejoicing because King had been killed. Again I wasn't angry, just hurt. A black man had made a tasteless and hateful remark to me when John F. Kennedy was assassinated. Now I saw white people capable of the same sort of behavior. There wasn't a choice between them.

Anyone who challenged our society at such a deep level as did Martin Luther King was liable to assassination. People don't like change, but I didn't understand that then. All I felt or thought about was my pain.

I cried again during the television programs about Dr. King's parents, his wife, and his children. The man who had awakened the conscience of America and done more than any other to unite black people throughout the nation in the common cause was gone.

Black people — like Cy Saul's son — had asked repeatedly, "When is the time? Is now the time to stand up and be a man?"

Martin Luther King had given us the ringing answer to that nagging question. "Freedom now!" had been his cry. In him, our day had come.

King called for racial equality, not merely for the sake of black people, but for the sake of all Americans — because the Constitution must work for everyone or it doesn't work for anyone.

That night, in the deepest ghetto of Indianapolis, Bobby Kennedy announced the horrible news of Dr. King's murder to his listeners who had not yet heard it through the media. They gasped audibly and then listened in stunned silence as he spoke:

> *Martin Luther King dedicated his life to love and to justice for his fellow human beings and he died because of that effort.*
>
> *In this difficult day — in this difficult time for the United States — it is perhaps well to ask what kind of a nation we are and what direction we want to move in. For those of you who are black — considering the evidence there is that white people were responsible — you can be filled with bitterness, with hatred, and a desire for revenge. We can move in that direction as a country, in great polarization — black people amongst black people, white people amongst white, filled with hatred toward one another.*
>
> *Or we can make an effort, as Martin Luther King did, to understand and to comprehend, and to replace that violence, that stain of bloodshed that has spread across our land, with an effort to understand with compassion and love.*

For those of you who are black and are tempted to be filled with hatred and distrust at the injustice of such an act, against all white people, I can only say that I feel in my own heart the same kind of feeling. I had a member of my family killed, but he was killed by a white man. But we have to make an effort in the United States, we have to make an effort to understand, to go beyond these rather difficult times.

My favorite poet was Aeschylus. He wrote: "In our sleep pain which cannot forget falls drop by drop upon the heart until, in our own despair, against our will, comes wisdom through the awful grace of God."

What we need in the United States is not division; what we need in the United States is not hatred; what we need in the United States is not violence or lawlessness, but love and wisdom, and compassion toward one another, and a feeling of justice towards those who still suffer within our country, whether they be white or they be black. . . .

We've had difficult times in the past. We will have difficult times in the future. It is not the end of violence; it is not the end of lawlessness; it is not the end of disorder.

But the vast majority of white people and the vast majority of black people in this country want to live together, want to improve the quality of our life, and want justice for all human beings who abide in our land.

Let us dedicate ourselves to what the Greeks wrote so many years ago: to tame the savageness of man and to make gentle the life of this world. Let us dedicate ourselves to that, and say a prayer for our country and for our people. (From *Robert Kennedy and His Times* by Arthur M. Schlesinger, Ballantine ed., 1978, pp. 939-940.)

I read those words soon after Bobby spoke them, but I saw fires break out around the country and protests against King's murder in city after city. I watched the fires burning, and there was nothing I could do. There was nothing anyone could do but hold on and wait. Somehow we got through it all, and Bobby's campaign started to move again. I got on the plane and flew to Indianapolis.

Many athletes, black and white, were there with Bobby — Oscar Robinson, Lamar Lundy, Wayne Embry, Rafer Johnson, me, and many others. When we finished campaigning that day, Bobby was chatting with us.

After a few minutes, he said to me, "Why don't you bring some of your friends and come on down to the airplane with me. We'll go and visit Ethel."

I thought he meant that Ethel was on the plane, but she was nowhere in sight when we went aboard. The next thing we knew, the pilot's voice came over the intercom telling us to sit down and fasten our safety belts.

I didn't want to appear stupid, so I didn't ask where Ethel was or where we were going. As it turned out, she was at Hickory Hill and the plane was flying to Washington. I couldn't believe we were doing this, getting on a plane without even a shaving kit and flying five hundred miles at a moment's notice. At Hickory Hill, Ethel gave us all hugs. Then we had lunch and played touch football. That evening, we checked into a hotel and got ready for a campaign appearance in Washington the next day (the D.C. primary election was scheduled for the same day as Indiana's). Bobby's lifestyle was not something I was accustomed to, but it was exciting. I was having the adventure of my life.

Wherever I went with him, thousands of people turned out to hear Bobby speak. At some of the places, he asked me to sing "Spanish Harlem." I was amazed when people swooned! Things like that emboldened me to think that I could make a difference. I was timid — shrinking back when I had opportunities to tell people what I thought or felt. I used to feel like a turtle.

My timidity stemmed from my deep distaste for conflict. I felt as if I were always walking on eggs —- fearful that hostility might break out if I weren't careful. I worried lest a black person offend a white person, or a white person hurt a black person's feelings. I was on a perpetual quest for that magic kingdom where everyone would live together in peace and harmony.

But another side of me wanted to get up and say unafraid all the things I felt in my heart. I wanted to be more like Bobby Kennedy who was not afraid to speak his mind, even if people didn't like what he said. Like the time in Indiana when he addressed medical students and faculty at Indiana University. He told them what they didn't like to hear — that our nation's system of health care had failed to meet the urgent medical needs of millions of Americans — the rural and urban poor, blacks and Indians. A black janitor in the balcony shouted, "We want Kennedy!" But a group of students shouted back, "No, we don't!"

The medical students asked where the money would come from to pay for the kind of system of national health care that Kennedy envisioned. Bobby replied, "From you." These men and women who were about to enter upon their lucrative careers knew what he meant and they didn't like it. But Bobby went on:

> Let me say something about the tone of these questions. I look around the room and I don't see many black faces who will become doctors. You can talk about where the money will come from. . . Part of civilized society is to let people go to medical school. You are the privileged ones. . . It's our society, not just our government, that spends twice as much on pets as on the poverty program. It's the poor who carry the major burden of Vietnam. You sit here as white medical students, while black people carry the burden of the fighting in Vietnam. (Schlesinger, p. 948.)

I was thankful for Bobby's courage in calling America — black and white, rich and poor — to come together and stand for what was good and decent. Listening to him gave me fresh courage to speak out and let myself be heard — for good or ill.

It was great fun to campaign with him. But still, every time he called on me to speak, I would shiver because I wanted so much to say what was in my heart — a whole mass of love, a whole mass of desires to see changes, to see the whole world in love and caring about one another, to see everyone pulling together to make the world a better place to live.

On one of the campaign trips, I was walking through the airplane, and Bobby was sitting with a group of men I didn't recognize.

"Rosey," he said, "come on up here and talk to me."

The guys with him began to ask questions about why I thought Bobby should be president and about why I thought black people should support him. I opened my heart and told them I thought he had a feeling for blacks, that he was sensitive to the needs of poor people and sensitive to the yearnings of blacks to contribute to the growth and destiny of the country.

The next day, I picked up a newspaper and could have passed out. The headline read: "Rosey Grier Pinpoints the Why of Kennedy." I thought to myself, some sneaky reporter was lurking around when

I was talking with those men and Bobby yesterday. We'd learned about guys like that in football locker rooms. The team would be talking, and the next day, our conversation would be in the paper. Then we would remember seeing a man standing nearby smiling and realize that he had been a reporter. But who among those men with Bobby the day before on the plane had been a reporter?

I showed the article to Bobby. "Can you imagine a newspaper reporter writing all that down? I didn't know any reporters were on board. Did you?"

Bobby smiled, "All those guys you were talking to?"

I said, "Yeah?"

He grinned, and said, "They were all reporters."

"Man, you didn't tell me I was going to be doing all that stuff!" I was upset.

He just laughed. And, somehow, I couldn't stay angry at him for having tricked me.

Bobby didn't want a lot of policemen around, so it fell to us big sturdy athletes who were with him on the trail to escort him through crowds. Many times I found I had to wrap my arms around his waist and carry him through a crowd while he shook hands and asked for votes.

In San Diego once, he got up on the back of the car. I was holding him tight and the crowd was pulling at his hand.

He said, "Rosey, you're holding me too tight."

"If I don't, you're going to fall down," I told him.

But he said, "Don't hold me so tight."

So I didn't hold him so tightly — and down he went. He and I and Ethel all went down. I was trying to get her out of the way. Finally, we managed to get hold of the seat belt and pulled Bobby back up. I never heard any more about me holding him too tight.

Campaigning with him was fun. Bobby Kennedy attracted people and won their trust because they could feel he liked them and honestly wanted to know what they thought. He took an interest in the people he was with and sought to understand their interests and concerns.

That kind of thing can't be faked. He asked us about football, and he listened carefully while we spoke at length. We told him about the game's problems and what we thought were their solutions.

Whenever Bobby asked me a question, I felt like opening up and telling him everything. He asked about my family, and, again, I spoke a long time — and I never sensed that he was bored or didn't care. He was the first man about whom I had ever felt that way, and I admired him unabashedly. With him I was safe from ridicule, no matter what I said.

He was my friend, and the thing I cherish most from my friendship with Bobby Kennedy was what it taught me about fear. He used to tell me, "You can never fail, if you never quit." By watching and listening to Bobby, I saw that my fear was getting in the way of my life — and it had been for a long time. How I learned that most valuable lesson is bound up in the story of my participation in the primaries, especially in the California primary.

During May, Bobby started dividing his time among Oregon, South Dakota and California. Oregon's primary was set for May 28, South Dakota's and California's for June 4. Lyndon Johnson had decided not to run for another term. His most visible opponent in those spring primaries was Eugene McCarthy, the popular liberal senator from Minnesota. Standing in the wings was the old Democratic campaigner, Hubert Humphrey. When Humphrey entered the race with his "politics of joy" shortly after the assassination of Martin Luther King, it struck me as an inappropriate slogan for such grim times. Even if Dr. King had not been killed, the Tet offensive in Vietnam was chewing up our troops in the bloodiest fighting of the war. It was not a time for joy.

On May 7, Bobby took forty-two percent of the vote in the Indiana primary, after him came Governor Roger Branigan (standing in for Hubert Humphrey) with thirty-one percent and Eugene McCarthy with twenty-seven percent. On the same day in the District of Columbia, where the electorate is heavily black, Kennedy took 62.5 percent against Humphrey's 37.5 percent.

On May 14, Bobby took a decisive 51.5 percent of the vote in the Nebraska primary. McCarthy trailed with 31 percent. Because McCarthy and Bobby were so close in many of their positions, the Nebraska vote was seen as a resounding disavowal of the administration's domestic and foreign (Vietnam) policies.

In any event, as the California primary campaign warmed up, more and more of my time was given over to it. That suited me fine. Nothing in my life had vitalized me like working for this man.

One night Bobby was supposed to come to Venice, a beachside town adjacent to Los Angeles and facing onto Santa Monica Bay. But his plane was delayed, and I had to travel the route that had been announced in the papers and tell people lining the streets that he wasn't coming. I felt terrible because I knew they would be disappointed.

They would see me coming down the street in an open car and, thinking whoever it was must be Bobby, they'd start to yell, "Bobby's coming. Bobby's coming."

When I came by each group, I told them, "He'll come. He won't be here today, but he will come through here."

Sometimes when he was driving through the streets, Bobby would jump out of the car and go over and touch someone's hand, and they would cry. He would say, "Vote for me." Later, when I was campaigning in New York for Paul Dwyer in his race for Bobby's senate seat, a lot of people showed me autographed pictures of Bobby. In some little hole-in-the-wall places that nobody would ever go, people would show me those pictures. "Bobby promised to send me this, and he did," they would say. Bobby loved the poor and insignificant people who are so easily overlooked.

I was learning more, faster than ever before in my life. I enjoyed sitting in the background and listening to conversations about the campaign, seeing how things really worked.

When I think of those months, it seems that I was laughing all the time. "When I'm president, I'm going to make you head of the CIA," Bobby used to tell me. And, of course, there were his endless jokes about his dog Freckles.

Not everyone in the campaign was as congenial as Bobby, however. A big rally was scheduled at the Ambassador Hotel in Los Angeles. The crowds had assembled, both inside the building and out in the parking lot where Bobby was scheduled to speak briefly before going inside. But Bobby, as usual, was behind schedule and had not arrived.

Someone said the people in the parking lot were going to leave, so I went out, got the microphone and began to tell stories about my little dog, Little Bit. Then I began to do routines from my entertainment act (I was working, in those days, at a night club in West Los Angeles — so the song and comedy routines were fresh in my mind). The audience started warming up and, pretty soon, some of the people in the ballroom started wandering out into the lot to join in the fun. Still Bobby hadn't shown.

Finally, enough people had deserted the ballroom to make the staff in charge nervous. That was when one of them came out and slipped me the message to cool it and come inside where they would give me some time with the crowd in there. I cooled my heels in the wings for two hours after that, and still Bobby had failed to appear. But, during that time, I was never invited to speak to the people inside.

Finally, I left for the nightclub where I was working. Ethel heard how I had been treated and called to soothe my feelings. "Let's just forget it," I said. "The important thing is for Bobby to become President."

The next day I was campaigning with a group of other athletes down at the corner of 80th Street and Western Avenue, not far from Watts. Charles Evers, the brother of slain civil rights leader Medgar Evers, was in the middle of the street handing out literature. He himself was entered in the Mississippi Democratic primary for a seat in the House of Representatives. And now he was here in Los Angeles to help Bobby. I considered it a great honor to meet him.

When Bobby finally arrived, we were sitting in a long line on the curb waiting for him. In spite of all that was on his mind and the day's schedule ahead, the first thing he did when he got there was call me over to his car. "Rosey," he said, "I hear they treated you shabbily at the Ambassador last night."

"Hey, it was nothing. Let's get to work," I replied.

"No, this is important. I don't like that sort of thing happening in my campaign. It was an act of petty arrogance and I won't tolerate it. I want you to give me the name of the person who did it."

"Bobby, I appreciate how much you care about me. That's all that counts. Let's get to work."

"I know the pain you felt because I felt it, too, when Ethel told me about it. I want his name, Rosey."

"No, sir," I said, "and that's final."

He said, "Get in the car with me."

"I brought some of my friends along with me — six of 'em," I said. "What about them?"

"Call them over. There'll be room enough for us all."

The car was jammed once the seven of us had crowded in there with Bobby, Ethel and his driver. His car was at the head of a motorcade filled with other members of his party and reporters. We wound our way through those neighborhoods, and everywhere people came out to cheer Bobby on. Finally we came down through Watts where I got out of the car and began circulating in the crowd. Suddenly I realized the whole caravan had stopped. I heard people up front calling me.

"Where's Rosey? Where's Rosey?"

Several of them were yelling for me. They really didn't sound alarmed, more exasperated, but still urgent. I immediately began to make my way through the crowd and found that a young man had jumped up onto the hood of Bobby's car — straddled it like he was riding a horse — and wouldn't get off. Every time anyone came near him, he would cuss them out. No one had been able to get him off the car.

"Hey, man," I asked him, "what're you doing on top of this car? Get offa there, man."

He turned around and recognized me, and here he came. He jumped at me, threw his arms around me and his legs around my waist, and began hugging me. The driver of the car started to drive off, but Bobby wouldn't leave.

"Go ahead," I urged. "Go ahead."

But Bobby wouldn't let them drive on. It took a little while for me to calm the kid down and get him to unwrap himself from me and to depart in peace. But Bobby and his motorcade stayed put until I did. Then I finally got back into the car. It made me feel good to see Bobby refuse to drive off and leave me there. He knew how to count others more important than himself.

Somewhere along the route that day, we picked up a baby. Both Bobby and Ethel loved kids and were always picking them up. So, before we left the vicinity, we had to take this child back to his parents. It was a duty to which the others and I were growing accustomed. Ethel was holding the baby and we needed to get out of the car and take it up to its home. By that time it was early evening. The sun was going down and there was a cool breeze. So, I told Ethel to put on her coat. I was particularly concerned about her because she was pregnant with their eleventh child (she and my mother had that much in common).

"I'm not cold," she protested.

But I was not deterred, and I reached over and put it around her. She looked as if she didn't like it, but that didn't bother me. I was taking good care of her — whether she liked it or not.

Another time, when we were in San Bernardino, Bobby got up on stage and was trembling. The next thing I knew, we were taking him into the men's room. Bobby said, "I feel awful," and threw his coat on the floor and lay down on it.

No candidate can afford to be sick on the campaign trail. . . and here was Bobby lying on the bathroom floor. I got a wet towel and put it on his head, then I picked him up by the waist and had him take a deep breath. Pretty soon, he began to feel better. Then he and one of his associates, Bill Barry, began to discuss what they should give as the reason he left the stage.

Bobby turned to me, "Rosey, what do you think we should tell them?"

"I think you ought to tell them the truth," I answered.

"You're right," he smiled.

Shortly, he walked back out to the podium where he apologized for the delay and explained that he was worn out and had had a little spell, but that he was feeling fine now. Again, I found myself admiring this unusual man.

Truth, to me, is the most important aspect of a person's character. The more truth we have, the more strength we have to love one another.

One night, I was at home in my apartment in Los Angeles, and Bobby's brother-in-law, Stephen Smith, called. He wanted me to speak at the Brentwood Country Club where various celebrities were going to speak on behalf of various candidates. "Bobby wants you to speak on his behalf, Rosey."

"Man, I can't do it," I said. "Bobby is running for the presidency of the United States. He ain't running for just any old job, you know. The Brentwood Country Club is a very exclusive place. Exclusively white. They don't want to hear what I've got to say over there."

"Rosey, you told Bobby you were going to help him. Besides, think about it: Bobby could have asked any one of scores of people who would have jumped at the chance to do this, but Bobby told me he wants you."

"Stephen," I asked, "are you sure about that?"

"Yes, Rosey. This is not a joke. This is something you should do for Bobby."

"Okay, but I think you're making a mistake."

When I got to the club, I knew they'd made a mistake. The lot was full of unbelievable automobiles — Excalibers, "Huntleys and Brinkleys," long Cadillacs, Bentleys, Rolls Royces. My heart sank, but I went on inside where I found a room full of stars and other well-known people were there, eating and drinking. You name them, and they were there, all for their own candidates. Lorne Green had a hit show, "Bonanza," at the time, and he spoke for a long time. Gene Barry and Shelley Winters made speeches, and I tried to hear what they were saying — although it was hard because people were clinking glasses and talking.

Finally, my turn came. "I realize," I said, "I'm not one of you. I'm a football player and the Brentwood Country Club is not exactly my turf.

"If I had you out on a football field, I could drive you all into the dirt," I said, "but I'm not here for me or to show my abilities. I'm not here for my own benefit. I'm here because I met a man named Bobby Kennedy.

"I've traveled all over the country in the past ten weeks, and I've watched people come out and vote for him — in Indiana, and D.C., and in Nebraska. I've been with him and seen the reaction of people, young and old, black and white, yellow and red. They cry just to touch this man. There is something very special about him that makes people want to touch him.

"This nation needs to be brought together, and he is the man who can do it. He has the heart and the compassion to pull us together.

Somewhere in the Bible it says that a house divided against itself cannot stand. I've never read that, but I have heard it's in the Bible. And I know that it's true.

"I've been on the fence about politics all my life. I've never gotten involved. This is my first time to do this. But I know that it is time for every one of us to get involved, because if we're not involved, no one is involved. This campaign is about all of us — you and me — standing together in this house called America.

"All of the states are rooms of this house that is us. It's our nation. It's our world. We need to find a man — maybe Bobby is not your man, but that's not really important. The important thing is that all of us get involved in the processes that were set up for the people to participate in the running of the country."

Suddenly, as I was speaking, I got the uneasy feeling that the people at the tables were listening to me. The glasses had stopped clinking, the murmur of conversation had ceased, and they were looking in my direction.

I glanced behind me, but no one was doing anything back there. The people sitting in back were looking at me, too. So I looked down to see if my zipper was unzipped.

Then it dawned on me that, for the first time in my life, I'd said what I really wanted to say, and it had made sense.

I stood there, a kid from Georgia who had started out in the fields shucking peanuts, and I thought, "What would my papa think if he could see me now?"

When I finished, the audience applauded with warm appreciation. That felt wonderful, but not because of the personal praise. I'd had that applause in football and as an entertainer. It was the joy of seeing that for the first time in my life, after all those years of struggle, my mouth was saying what my heart was feeling.

Several people came up to me afterwards saying things like, "I know what you were saying. I feel the same way you do. Thanks for speaking out."

I finally got over my fear of public speaking that night. How long had I hungered to say exactly what was in my heart? But I had been afraid, unsure of my ability to speak. I had believed that because I was from the South and black, I had no proper background and was unable to express myself. In the movies or on television I had never seen a Southerner — black or white — portrayed in any way but as a villain or as the comic relief.

Before that evening I had thought many times, "What does Bobby Kennedy see in me?" But, after that night, I began to see that I had valuable qualities — particularly honesty and sincerity.

I also saw it is not as important to be grammatically correct as it is to mean what you say.

Many times the best in us fails to surface because we allow ourselves to be beaten down by our own fears and by the negative thinking of other people. But we need only to say what is in our hearts, and to stick to it. We don't have to be great orators or inspiring leaders.

A piece of me began to run free that night. After that, they asked me to make more speeches, and it was an exciting time — not because I was winning converts for Bobby Kennedy, but because I was convincing people to become involved, to believe in the American dream, to love one another.

21

TRIUMPH
BEFORE
TRAGEDY

Things were looking good for our man. The polls and the newspapers and television commentators were all in full swing our way. We had every right to be excited, because we were growing up together. We were learning to pull together — black and white, rich and poor.

None of us was taking victory for granted, however. The night before the California primary, I was too keyed up to sleep. I went out early the next morning, June 4, 1968, and voted.

I had a big discussion with Bernice that day. I'd been away from home a lot, and she felt the Kennedy people were just using me. She didn't understand how I felt about Bobby and that the question of using didn't mean much to me.

Yes, I was "being used" — if that is the right term — to help Bobby establish his credibility with the black community. But that is exactly what I wanted to do, because I was convinced then — and I remain convinced to this day — that Robert F. Kennedy was genuinely seeking to promote the interests of poor and underprivileged people, not only in the United States, but everywhere. He used me because I allowed him to and because the rewards I derived from our relationship more than compensated for what I was able to contribute. And those rewards were personal and emotional, never financial — which is why I valued them so highly. My needs — some of my deepest needs that money could not meet — were being met by my volunteer participation in the campaign to elect Bobby Kennedy president.

People feel "used" when they do not receive adequate compensation for whatever it is they do for others — be those others employers, friends, or relatives. Bernice was not getting adequate compensation from me for being my wife. She felt used in our relationship, and she had a right to feel that way. However, it was easier to exhibit her resentment about that toward the absent "Kennedy machine" than it was to exhibit it toward me face to face. That's the way it is with all of us. I don't blame her.

It was my life, and I shared very little of it with Bernice. I didn't know how to share the important things then. I was not mature enough to understand an adult man-woman relationship — the commitments, the sharing, and the oneness. I tried to love her and Denise by providing material things for them. They needed more than that from me, but I failed to supply it. Only a part of me was learning to run free, and it was not the part they needed.

That evening, I went down to the Ambassador Hotel and watched all the people coming in and all the excitement. In the early part of the evening, I went up to Bobby's suite, and we sat around and talked and laughed and waited for the election returns to come in. A lot of people wandered in and out — among them labor leader Cesar Chavez, newspapermen Jimmy Breslin and Pete Hamill, civil-rights leaders Charles Evers and John Lewis. Ethel was there with some of the children — David, Michael, Courtney, and Kerry. Freckles, their springer spaniel, was also on hand.

I answered the phone once, and it was Pierre Salinger, calling from inside the hotel to say that we were projected to win in South Dakota where the polls had just closed.

Bobby said, "Does he want to talk to me?"

And I said, "No, man, I got it." It felt good to be a part of the team.

As I listened to Bobby and Steve Smith talking, I heard them mention the vote in Oregon that had favored Eugene McCarthy, and I thought, "What does Oregon know, anyhow?"

I started out the door and Bobby told me, "Don't be gone long, Rosey. We'll be going downstairs pretty soon."

"Okay," I replied. Then I went down to the lower floors and roamed around. I had never seen so many cameras in my life. News teams from all over the world were there, because Bobby was of great interest to foreign audiences. He was the brother of the martyred President who had captured the attention and hearts of people outside the United States perhaps more than any other American chief executive. And, now, Bobby was showing himself to be the right man to pick up the fallen torch.

Since that day on the plane when I had spoken unawares to a group of newsmen, I had begun to feel more at home with members of the media. So, by now, I was friendly with a number of them. They were exciting to be around.

I watched them doing their thing, and I felt a sense of belonging. It seemed we were all parts of a puzzle that was coming together — in many ways it was my own personal puzzle — so that I felt I was coming together as a whole person. I was leaving behind those days when there had been at least two Roseys — one on the outside watching and commenting about the one on the inside. It felt good!

In another room, campaign workers were laughing and dancing and hugging one another. That small, ragtag bunch of people was the essence of American society, from top to bottom. We all had a stake in this race. We all had hopes and dreams, and believed we were on the way to bringing our country — splintered by race riots, white backlash, and the Vietnam War — back into unity and harmony.

I went back upstairs and said, "Hey, Bobby. Man, I hope you have something to say tonight because people are going to hear you all over the world."

"I do," he grinned.

Shortly after that, Bobby was called out to another room for an interview. I saw no one from his staff get up to go with him. Apparently, they thought he'd be safe, but I went along with him. I hit the hallway and walked on one side of the hall with him on the other side. He looked over at me — with an expression of appreciation — over the tops of the heads of the people between us.

Then I stood outside the door — in his line of sight — and waited while he did the interview. Whenever he moved, I moved. When he came back out, I was standing there, and we went back to his room.

I tried never to get in his way, but just be where he could see me. I wanted to do the right thing and not be intimidated by his position so much that I wouldn't do what was right for him or the family. Bobby never scolded me for my protectiveness toward him or Ethel or the kids. When he finished, we returned to his suite.

Once in Washington, everyone was talking about Bobby looking tired and saying he should rest, but most of them were afraid to say what they thought. So I said, "Bobby, you'd better go to bed."

They told me I shouldn't say things like that to him, but Bobby never acted like he minded. That day, however, he tried to ignore me. So, in a little while, I said again, "Man, you'd better go to bed. You need to rest." And he went, in a little bit.

"He's going to get mad at you," somebody warned me.

"I don't care if he gets mad," I replied. "He's not big enough to whip me, and, besides, it's for his own good."

I was not in awe of Bobby, but I knew it would be inconsiderate of me to waste his time. He never acted as if he wanted any special consideration, however. He acted as if he wanted friends around him, people that he cared about. It was a pleasure to have a few minutes to spend with him, knowing it was because he liked me and not because I was an important person.

George McGovern, the well-known senator from South Dakota, called to tell Bobby about the primary results in that state. He said Bobby's votes were more than the combined tallies of Humphrey and McCarthy. The farmers and the Indians had almost universally voted for Kennedy.

When it was about time to go downstairs, more people began arriving in the suite. Pierre Salinger, Ted Sorenson, and Larry O'Brien — the old JFK troopers — were there. Rafer Johnson, decathlon champion of the 1964 Olympics, and John Glenn came in. And there was George Plimpton and his wife, and a lot of people I didn't know at all.

Decisions were being made about who was to be with Bobby, who was to do this, and who was to do that. I was told to stick with Ethel, who was six-months pregnant. I loved Ethel, and I understood that she needed me, but I also felt responsible for Bobby.

After Bobby had made his appearance, the plan called for us all to go to The Factory, a well-known nightspot in the area, to wind down.

I was having a problem with the way some of the people were giving orders that night. I have never been receptive to orders from someone who addressed me as an inferior. On the other hand, I will do anything for a person who asks nicely. That night, however, I resisted the temptation to tell my "order-givers" where to get off. Most of them were not members of the regular entourage. They were from regional headquarters and hadn't been around that much. I excused them on those grounds.

As we went down in the elevator, I leaned over and punched Bobby in the stomach and laughed, "You got it, Bobby."

"Yeah," he replied without a smile, "but we've got a lot more work to do."

We walked out of the elevator and into the kitchen where Bobby stopped to shake hands with some of the workers. Everyone was happy and excited. Then we got him up the steps and on stage in the Embassy Room.

People were screaming and yelling. Cameras were flashing, and newsmen were trying to get up close. The podium was filled with microphones. It was chaotic and yet beautiful. They were there to applaud the man I loved because they loved him, too.

Bobby began his remarks by joking with the crowd and thanking those of us who had helped him win the campaign. He mentioned Jesse Unruh and Tom Rees, California politicians. When he expressed his gratitude to the students who had helped, the crowd, which was well populated with young faces, roared and wouldn't let him continue for a few moments. He thanked Steve Smith and his sisters, Pat Lawford and Jean Smith, and all the other (and innumerable) Kennedys. Then he got to Rafer and me. He said, "Rosey Grier said he would take care of anybody who didn't vote for me."

I got a kick out of that, and so did the audience.

Then Bobby went on to congratulate Eugene McCarthy on his good showing and for the courage he had shown by entering the race. And he urged those who supported McCarthy to join in supporting him because both men stood together in the things that mattered.

221

He said we could work together so that what had been going on within the United States over the previous three years — the division, the violence, the disenchantment with our society; the divisions, whether between blacks and whites, between the poor and the affluent, between age groups, or on the war in Vietnam — could be healed. "We can start to work together," he said. "We are a great country, an unselfish country, and a compassionate country. I intend to make that my basis for running."

While Bobby was speaking, a man came up to me and said, "We have arranged for them to come off the right side of the stage." I looked and saw that the area he had indicated was all laid out with a walkway cleared through the crowd.

When Bobby finished speaking, he moved to the back of the platform where we were standing. Then Bobby and Ethel started to move back up front because the crowd kept applauding and didn't want to let them leave. "Bobby, when you get through, come back here to me," I said, because he could always see me over the crowd, like a landmark. "Okay, Rosey," he replied.

He and Ethel waved to the crowd, and took the applause for a few minutes. As they were coming back toward me, Bill Barry said we were to go to the left. Bill had been a special agent with the FBI when Bobby was Attorney General. At that time he was a friend of the family who was in charge of Bobby's security.

"The right is all blocked off for us," I objected.

"No," Bill replied. "We're changing it. It'll be shorter to go left to the freight elevator off the kitchen."

Bobby jumped off the back of the platform with Paul Schrade, a United Auto Workers' official. When they started moving, everyone had to scramble. Rafer Johnson was trapped on the left side of the stage, and the other people who would have been with Bobby were trapped on the right. I jumped off to run after him, but then I remembered my responsibility to take care of Ethel, so I turned back.

Bill Barry helped me get Ethel down off the stage, then we all ran to catch up with Bobby. But all these people were jammed in between, pushing and shoving. One cameraman almost hit Ethel trying to catch up.

22

THE
SHATTERED
DREAM

With Ethel beside me, I could see over the crowd that Bobby was not far ahead of us. I was trying to catch up. Then he turned a corner. That's when the shots rang out. They didn't sound very loud, but they were such sad sounds.

Either I pushed Ethel down or she dropped. I have never been able to reconstruct in my mind exactly what happened. She had a habit of crumpling up whenever she heard the sound of anything like gunfire. However she got to the floor, I fell over her and covered her with my body.

The next thing I remember was taking off and running. I hit the corner opposite the curve in the hall, then I went around the curve and saw a little man with a gun. Bill Barry was struggling with him and shouted, "Take him, Rosey, take him!"

People were grabbing at him, and I flew forward. As I reached to grab hold of the man, someone knocked the gun out of his hand. For a second, it was laying on the table. Then it was back in his hand. I grabbed his leg and pulled him back up onto a big serving table. Some of the newspaper reports said I "threw him up" onto the steel table.

He was trying frantically to get loose. I don't know what he was saying, but he seemed to have superhuman strength. I gave up any thought of being gentle and locked his legs. Jesse Unruh, the powerful California Democratic politician, was grasping at the man also. George Plimpton got hold of his gun hand, but the gun was pointing right into George's face. That gun pointing at my sister's face years before this in New Jersey came vividly to mind at that moment. That flash of memory made this scene in California in 1968 seem even more nightmarish and unreal. I reached up and covered the young man's gun hand, and locked my thumb behind the trigger so it couldn't fire anymore — just as I had with my sister that time in New Jersey. Then I held on and looked around.

I wanted to see who had been shot. I still didn't realize for sure that Bobby had been hit. I could see Paul Schrade lying on the floor, down with a head wound. But I saw none of the five other people who were also wounded that night. I know I saw Bobby lying there, but my mind refused to accept it.

I finally wrenched the gun from the young man's hand. It took all my strength, as big as I was, to pull the gun away from him. People started coming at him and trying to hurt him. They were furious, nearly out of their minds with rage. One man tried to break his leg. I kicked that guy, and Rafer Johnson got up on the table trying to question the suspect. Other people were still trying to hit him from my side, and I had to fight them off. I put the gun in my pocket and began to weep.

Someone said to me that Bobby had only been shot in the side and that he was going to be all right. But I looked at him and saw his right leg up like the man who died next to me when I was a child in Georgia. The similarity between those two scenes haunted me. And I knew something awful had happened, something unthinkable that didn't seem real. One of the young kitchen workers had a rosary and someone had handed it to Bobby. Ethel was putting ice in a towel on his head.

Someone else shouted, "Pray!" That stood out clearly in the middle of all the cursing and screaming. I saw Bobby close his hand over the rosary. He was lying on the concrete floor in the middle of kitchen litter, cigarette butts, and trash — with Ethel beside him. After a while, the police came and took away the man I had been holding, and an ambulance took Bobby to Central Receiving and later to Good Samaritan Hospital for surgery. I sat down on the floor — I didn't know what else to do — and cried.

Rafer came back a little later and asked about the pistol. When I told him it was in my pocket, he asked me to give it to him. I reached in, took it out, and placed it in his hand. George and Freddy Plimpton knew how much I cared personally about Bobby. They were concerned for me and walked with me to a little room where I could be alone for a bit.

Later, I went down to police headquarters and made a statement about what I recalled. But I couldn't stop crying. The shooting happened shortly after midnight on June 5. I went home for a while, then Wednesday morning I got a call from the hospital. So I went down there and found a lot of people sitting around outside who had been there since Bobby was admitted. Some were crying, and some were praying. I went inside and stood around. No one seemed to know what was happening.

I stood in the hallway and hurt when people said they didn't think Bobby was going to make it. Ethel and Jackie — Jackie had just flown in from New York — came through, and Ethel came over and hugged me. She murmured sadly, "My hero."

It amazed me to see her strength and hope. Later that day, when they let me go up to Bobby's room, Ethel was lying on the bed beside him. She looked up, "Hello, Rosey, thank you for coming."

I nodded silently. Bobby lay very still, although he was breathing. Teddy was there, too, along with Jackie, Stephen and Jean Smith, and Pat Lawford. I shook their hands and left very shortly.

A few minutes before two o'clock in the morning on Thursday, just about twenty-six hours after the shooting, Frank Mankiewicz, Bobby's press secretary, came to the room where his friends were and told us that Bobby's heart had just stopped beating — he was gone. Then he went to the press room across the street from the hospital where he reported, with faltering voice, "I have a short announcement to read which I will read at this time. Senator Robert Francis Kennedy died at 1:44 A.M. today, June 6, 1968. With Senator Kennedy at the time of his death were his wife, Ethel; his sisters, Mrs. Stephen Smith and Patricia Lawford; his brother-in-law, Stephen Smith; and Mrs. John F. Kennedy. He was forty-two years old." Frank omitted to mention that Senator Edward Moore Kennedy was there only because he forgot and was himself so upset (Robert Blair Kaiser, *"R.F.K. Must Die!,"* New York: Dutton, 1970, p. 106).

I went back home with an empty, dark, hopeless hole in me. So much enthusiasm, so much hope and so much drive, all gone for nothing. Just like that, like snapping your fingers, everything I'd ever hoped to see in our nation was changed. It seemed as if it all died with Bobby.

Thursday morning, I watched on television as Ethel, the family, and some of Bobby's friends got on a plane to take the body home to New York. I couldn't stop crying when I saw that plane take off. Somewhere in that same time frame I first heard the name of the alleged assassin: Sirhan Sirhan.

I went to the studio that afternoon to do my television show, and couldn't do it. I walked off the set crying again. Later that afternoon, I got a call that Ethel wanted me to join the family at their New York apartment. There was a ticket at the airport for me, and someone would meet me in New York with a limousine to take me to Ethel's. All I had to do was come. I went. At the apartment, there were people everywhere, but I let Ethel know I was there, and she thanked me for coming!

Friday night, we sat up and watched over the body at St. Patrick's Cathedral. People came, and they came, and they came. And they cried. On Saturday morning, the mass was said. Teddy Kennedy spoke movingly and we sang "The Battle Hymn of the Republic." It was hard for me to sing, though.

Then the casket was placed aboard a special funeral train that would travel slowly to Washington for Bobby's burial. At Grand Central Station the line seemed to last forever, all of those people getting on the train. I was told not to stray too far away in case Ethel needed me for anything, so I stayed close by. As the train moved slowly along, people stood along the tracks on either side — up on the banks. Some wept and waved, some stood silently, others stood to attention and saluted.

Near Philadelphia, a train approaching us plowed through some people standing on the track watching for us. Some of them were killed. It was horrible beyond words — grief was added to grief. How much could we take?

As the train neared Washington, Ethel announced, "I want to go through the train and thank everyone." A lot of the people with her thought it would be too much for her, but she really wanted to do it.

So I said, "Let's do it."

I went ahead into each of the cars to tell them she was coming. "Mrs. Kennedy will be arriving here in a few minutes," I would say. "I want all of you to stand up, and I want you to put any beer or anything else like that out of sight. She wants to thank you."

So we went throughout the train, and it was a long one. I don't know how many cars there were, but she went through all of them, thanking each person, one at a time. It was touching to watch.

When we arrived in Washington, I began to help with the logistics, making sure everyone was in the right car and things like that. I was glad to have something to do. At last, all the people were in the cars on the way to the cemetery. Everybody but me. Then someone stopped to pick me up. Once there, we had to make a long trek up to the grave site. I walked with Frank Gifford part of the way. It was something to see all the people I knew and all those I had read about. President Johnson and Lady Bird were there, and Averell Harriman, cabinet officers and justices of the Supreme Court, and more senators and congressmen than I could count.

After the burial, many of Bobby's friends went back to Hickory Hill. I hadn't known him as long as some of the others, but I loved him as much. I slept that night with Bobby, Jr., in his room. Bobby's dog shared the bed with us.

I'm not one for sharing my bed with a dog, and then it got cold (the Kennedys are fresh-air fiends). Consequently, I rose early and went downstairs. I was standing outside and one of the eleven kids, four-year-old Max, was already out there.

"Hi, Rosey," he greeted me.

"Morning, Max," I returned, astonished that he knew my name.

"Rosey, you were there, weren't you?"

"Yes, I was."

"Why did that man kill my dad?"

"Maxwell," I said (his full name was Matthew Maxwell Taylor Kennedy), "some people are full of hate. The man who killed your daddy was one of them. We don't know why he was full of hate, though." I picked him up, put him on my shoulder and started walking. "I don't think we'll ever understand," I continued, "why he did what he did."

Maxwell showed me all the animals on the place, and there were quite a few. Hickory Hill was noted for its "menagerie." He and I became good friends that day. During the rest of my stay at Hickory Hill, he stayed near me. As the day went on, we were able to laugh.

It seemed to me all of us were trying to break through our grief by laughing, all these loving people who cared about Ethel and the family. We stood around and sat around and talked. I tried to get off in a room somewhere by myself where I could give way to sadness, but Ethel wouldn't let me.

She came in and sat down beside me and said, "You can't sit here like this. We've got to go outside and do something. Come on out of here."

I obeyed and, after a while I joined in a game of touch football. It was a hot day, and, after the game, we jumped in the pool to cool off. I don't swim, but I delighted everyone with a bigger-than-usual splash when I cannon-balled into the pool.

Ethel didn't let anyone get downhearted or depressed or sit around and mope. She kept some kind of activity going on all the time to keep our spirits up. The whole time I was with Ethel or any of the family that week, I never remember any of them giving way to grief. The only time I thought Ethel came close to weeping was much later. I called her, and she told me someone's comments about the upcoming trial of Bobby's assassin. The person she named had said a lot of nasty things about Sirhan, displaying a great deal of hostility and anger.

I said, "I don't know why he had to call you up and tell you all of that. Why rake all that up in your memory? We've all got to appear at the trial, and that's time enough to think about what happened."

It seemed as if she broke down for a few minutes and couldn't say anything. I waited and didn't say anything either. In a few minutes, she was composed and back on the phone, and we talked a little longer, then said goodbye.

Bobby Kennedy's abrupt death wrenched me more deeply and catastrophically than I can express. I grieved for him a long time. For years, I agonized about what I could have done differently. "What," I asked myself, "can anyone do to prevent an act of violence against a human being?"

Bobby, quoting Aeschylus, had called us to dedicate ourselves to the task of taming the savageness of man and to make gentle the life of the world. I had to answer that call. I resolved that the rest of my life would be given to that goal as never before. The Rams might have heard me talk about love and comradeship before, but they hadn't heard anything yet.

I had sat too long on the sidelines of life, refusing to do more than be grieved by the suffering that came to my attention. "Someone ought to do something about that," I would say.

"Someone?" Who is that? Usually no one.

Martin Luther King, Jr. showed me that change by non-violent means was possible. Bobby Kennedy had invited me to pay the price of becoming personally involved in that process of change.

"People Make the World What It Is," a song written by a friend of mine, Bobby Womack, says it best.

Before I met Bobby Kennedy, I only knew how to play football and to sing. Granted, the seeds of gentleness were planted mysteriously in my heart during my childhood — perhaps even before my birth. And I had moved as a man with a gentle heart in the violent world of the NFL. It was a contradiction for which I had no resolution. But football had given me a life I would never have enjoyed otherwise. I owed a lot to football, and, yet, I needed more because it had given me little opportunity to express my heart. After I met Bobby, I found all the opportunity I needed.

I loved all Americans — black, white, and otherwise — and I wanted us all to live in freedom, equality and harmony. But I was learning this wasn't possible unless I was willing to make myself part of the struggle.

When I returned to California after the funeral, it was the middle of June. I had to make a decision about my football career. I hated making decisions. I liked it better when they were made for me. That way I didn't have to take the blame for them if they turned out badly. (I know this was immature, but, for what it's worth, a study has shown that people who refuse to take responsibility in this way live longer and healthier lives.)

My habit at this time each year was to work out in preparation for training camp. So, in the name of habit and not making a decision,

I was working out in Pasadena with Deacon Jones, Merlin Olsen, and Merlin's little girl, Kelly, who was about six years old. As we ran around the track, Merlin and Deacon steadily pulled out in front. But, then, a little later, I found that Kelly was setting a pace with which I also could not keep up.

Pretty soon I was trailing well behind them all. So I started to walk — and think. My career as an entertainer had developed slowly and unspectacularly, but steadily, since I had come back from the army with that guitar in 1958. Now, ten years hence, it could probably sustain me if I gave it my full-time attention. And it would allow me even greater freedom to pursue the vision that my friendship with Bobby Kennedy had given me.

Training camp was scheduled to begin, as usual, on July 14. Putting off the final decision as long as possible, I waited until the 14th to call George Allen. "Coach," I said, "this is Rosey Grier. I've made up my mind to retire."

"But, Rose, your tendon's okay, right?"

"Yeah."

"Why don't you come on down here to camp and at least give it a try? What could it hurt?"

"No," I replied after a moment's hesitation. "I don't understand it all, but I know the time has come for me to hang up my cleats once and for all."

23

REMEMBERING
NOT TO FORGET

When I didn't go off to summer training camp, that meant more time to argue with Bernice. Our marriage was deteriorating fast and I found myself looking down the barrel of divorce for the first time. Happily, in terms of reducing the level of conflict between Bernice and me, I still had obligations which got me out of the house.

At the end of August, 1968, came the Democratic National Convention in Chicago. The campaigns that Bobby had waged in Indiana, the District of Columbia, Nebraska, Oregon, South Dakota, and California had won him delegates at this convention, and I was one of those delegates. With Bobby gone, one might have expected that our votes would have shifted to the candidate most similar to Bobby — Eugene McCarthy — and there would be the end of it.

But neither I nor many of the other Kennedy delegates were willing for anything so perfunctory to happen. The issues that had brought on Bobby's candidacy — the war in Vietnam and the need for further racial reform — were still burning hotly. And what burned even more hotly in my heart (and I was not alone in this either) was a love for the man, Robert F. Kennedy, and a reverence for his memory.

We went to Chicago to demand a better America, one sensitive to the needs of the people, not business as usual. The Kennedy delegates called for an end to the fighting in Vietnam so that our troops could return home and so that the funds being spent there could be redirected into the flagging war on poverty.

One day at the convention, Bobby's name was mentioned and the place erupted. The applause and singing went on and on and on. Shirley MacLaine was a member of the California delegation also, and she and I were standing side by side during that demonstration. We kept singing, "His truth is marching on." Bobby's truth — the things he had stood for in this critical era of American history — was marching on and could not be stopped.

Again I found myself in a mystifying new world. Political conventions had never interested me before. I had little idea how they worked. So, to be introduced to the process at the 1968 Democratic Convention was a baptism of fire. That was the convention during which Chicago police clashed bloodily (but not fatally) with rioting students in downtown Chicago a great distance from the convention hall.

The priority of those students, many of whom were in support of McCarthy's candidacy, was to protest the war. As a Kennedy delegate, my priority and that of many of my fellow Kennedy delegates was to see America fulfill its dreams of a democratic society. Most of us who were members of the California delegation did not join the students in the streets.

After years of having my travel and lodging paid for by football teams and the like, I was taken by surprise when I learned delegates have to pay their own way. But I was glad to do it because it represented growth in my commitment to the ideals I wanted to espouse.

A lot of us urged Teddy Kennedy to throw his hat into the ring, but he was reluctant to do it unless he was assured of winning the nomination. And Chicago mayor, Richard Daley, was not going to release his delegates unless Teddy would throw his hat into the ring along with everyone else. Later, Teddy told us he felt that coming into the ring as an open candidate seemed to him like running on the graves of his brothers. The only way he would run was to be brought in by a majority of the convention because they needed him. It was a momentous decision — one only he could make. And I understood it better when I saw the sort of man Richard Daley was. If I were Teddy, I would not have wanted to be at Daley's mercy.

During all this, a black caucus was set up to make sure the politicians dealt with the issues black people were most interested in: unemployment, high interest rates, high insurance rates in the inner cities and other predominantly black communities, and affirmative action programs. We enjoyed some success.

On the whole, however, the convention's outcome was disappointing to us Kennedy delegates. Hubert Humphrey won the nomination, but the party was badly split. In the November election, Humphrey and Muskie ran against Nixon and Agnew. George Wallace of Alabama and General Curtis LeMay ran on the American Independent ticket. The popular election was close. Nixon polled a mere 812,000 votes more than Humphrey in an election in which more than 72 million Americans voted. In the electoral college the vote was more decisive: Nixon, 301, Humphrey, 191, and Wallace, 46.

I got to know Shirley MacLaine fairly well there in Chicago. She had been on the train that took Bobby's body from New York to Washington in June and I was sitting, part of the time, where I happened to hear her talking. She had excellent opinions about a wide variety of subjects. She was outspoken about them all and she laughed hard. I was impressed. But I didn't get to talk with her on the train. I called her secretary and left messages, and her secretary called me back with answers, but we didn't get a chance to connect.

So, we finally met in Chicago, and we latched onto one another. We formed a little group with Rafer Johnson, Warren Beatty and, later on, newsman Sander Vanocur. After that, when I went to New York, I called Shirley and went out with her and Sandy Vanocur.

After the convention, Rafer Johnson and I went on to Hyannis Port, on Cape Cod in Massachusetts. We and a lot of other folks who had helped Bobby were the guests of the Kennedy family for the Labor Day weekend. We were playing touch football, and a little kid kept running in and out between my legs. I couldn't figure out who he was.

Finally I asked Rafer, "Who is this kid?"

He laughed, "That's little John F. Kennedy, Jr., the same one we all watched give the salute at his daddy's funeral in 1963."

"Oh," I said, "that means his mother is here, too?"

"Yeah, would you like to meet her?"

"Sure."

After the game, Rafer introduced us. We had a nodding acquaintance, but that was the first time I really got to meet and talk with Jackie Kennedy. I put my arms around her and said, "You know, I'm going to be here for a little while, and I don't have anyone to be with. How about if you and I hang out together?"

"How do you mean, 'hang out'?" she asked.

"I'd like to get to know you and be friends."

"That sounds all right," she smiled.

So we went in the house and sat down and got acquainted. Both of us were enjoying ourselves and each other, and, after a while, Jackie said, "I have an idea. Let's you and I challenge everyone else on the compound here to a game of touch football!"

"Go for it," I said.

So we wrote invitations to everyone there, including the Secret Service agents who were on duty. No one accepted our invitation, however, which was the cause of a lot of good humor. That was the beginning of a good friendship, of getting to know her and the children.

In the years following that Labor Day in Hyannis Port, I often met Jackie in New York. On one of those occasions I told her, "Jackie, you're really a nice lady. The only problem is, you can never know who likes you for yourself. I'll bet most people do whatever you want them to do. No one will say what they really feel or think, because they are always trying to please you. To me, you're just another lady."

She laughed and said, "I think you're crazy."

But I wanted her to have that experience of being cared about as a person, not because of her family or the family she had married into. Of course, she would always be a former First Lady and a famous person who was followed around by reporters. I wanted her to be able to relax and be herself. I wanted her to be able to laugh.

I would call her and say, "Look, I'm standing down here by the railroad track, and I've got a dime on the track. I'm waiting for a train to come along and flatten it out. Do you want to come down and join me?"

And she would laugh. Or I would say, "I'll meet you on the corner of Fifth Avenue and 74th Street, and I want you to be there at 4:15 P.M., not before and not after."

Again, she would laugh, but she would get there right on time. Once I met her like that and kept looking for the limousine that I figured she would have following her.

She said, "Well, where are we going?"

I kept looking around for the car, but I said, "Where do you want to go?"

She said, "To a movie," and we kept walking. Finally, she said, "Well, are we going to a movie or not?"

I said, "Yeah," and we ran to catch a cab.

Wherever we went in New York, the cab drivers or other people would see me first and say, "Hi, Rosey." While they were talking to me, they would zero in on the lady with me and realize who it was. It was always fun to watch their surprised reactions.

Most people we met on our adventures into "ordinary" life were pleasant, but not all. We picked Caroline up from the home of one of her friends once and stopped to get some ice cream. While we were in the store, this lady walked up to Jackie and started talking. "You and I have something in common," she announced without so much as introducing herself.

Jackie politely replied, "Oh, yes?"

"Yes, my daughter died the same day your husband was killed."

I could have gone right through the floor. I stepped in quickly to change the subject.

Jackie didn't like all the Secret Service protection, the feeling of someone following her around all the time. Once I took her from Hyannis Port to the airport to go christen a ship. As I watched her plane take off, I saw a guy in a car talking on a radio.

I went over and said, "What are you doing?"

He was from the Secret Service and asked me not to tell her because she didn't want them to follow her everywhere she went. But they did anyway. They had to follow orders or lose their jobs.

Jackie is a wise and sensitive person. I think running around with me from time to time gave her a break from her normal routines. One time, in her apartment in New York, I was telling her about "water bombs." "When I was a kid," I explained, "we would take cups of water and pour them out the window on people. Then we ran and hid." She thought that was a funny idea. We were drinking coffee, so we put it into paper cups, went over to the window, and poured it on people walking up Fifth Avenue. Of course, we were on the 15th floor so not enough would reach street level to get anyone wet. It was harmless, but we got a kick out of imagining the headlines if someone called the police.

She suggested, "Jackie Kennedy and Rosey Grier Arrested."

I said, "What makes you think your name should be first? It would be 'Rosey Grier and Jackie Kennedy Arrested.'" And we laughed like a couple of kids.

Back in California after the Labor Day holiday, my relationship with Bernice kept on eroding until one night things came to a head, and I walked out. I called a friend to come and get me. Our relationship had gotten to be all hurt, and I caused much of that hurt. The breakup was precipitated by a lot of things — the trauma of Bobby's death, of leaving football, and of my own immaturity in terms of how one should take care of a marriage. I wasn't living the life of a married man. I lived as if I didn't have a wife.

So I went into the divorce courts and gave up everything except an automobile and the clothes on my back. I stayed with a friend for a couple of nights after I first moved out and then found a room in a hotel.

During that time, an agent mentioned to me one day that singer-actor Ed Ames was leaving the Daniel Boone television series. He said the producers of the show wanted me to try out for the part. So, at the appointed time, I went down to the studio for a screen test.

"You got the part of Gabe Cooper, an Indian chief who was a black man who had been captured as a child and raised by the Indians," the casting director told me after the screen test.

"That's good," I said.

"Aren't you happy?" he asked.

"Yeah, I'm happy," I said unconvincingly.

"You could have fooled me," he replied.

I didn't tell him, but I was worried. "Now, how am I going to do this?" I asked myself. I suppose, too, that my ability to express excitement was more diminished than ever after what I had gone through with Bobby Kennedy, not to mention the other changes that were happening.

"Daniel Boone" — in which the title role was capably handled by veteran actor Fess Parker — had first aired on September 24, 1964, and was enjoying unusual success. It was an honor to be invited to audition for it and an even greater one to get a part. I did not get the part Ed Ames had played — Mingo. The part of Gabe Cooper had been employed on a semi-regular basis prior to my taking it. But, after my first episode as Gabe, he became a regular.

I was on the show over a year before it was canceled in 1970. I especially enjoyed the interaction with country singer and actor Jimmy Dean. We had so much fun with jokes and ad libs that sometimes the cameras would have to be stopped because we kept breaking each other up.

An episode that demanded more acting ability than I knew I had was the one in which Ethel Waters played my elderly mother who was a slave. In this episode, Daniel Boone helped me to find her. We put her on a wagon and were taking her to where she could end her days as a free woman, but she was ill and it was questionable whether she would survive the trip.

Finally, it was clear she was dying — the woman who had given me birth but whom I had never known. The script called for some poignant scenes at her bedside in which I would have to give a convincing performance.

To make matters tougher, Ethel was nearly seventy by then and not hearty enough to be on hand for whatever shooting that did not involve her face. Consequently, I said my heartfelt and grieving lines to a reclining stagehand who lay in Ethel's place before me! Sometimes it was hard to maintain the required solemnity.

My decision to retire from football was turning out not to have been a mistake. Work in the entertainment business was keeping the rent paid and groceries on the table. Beginning in 1967, I was hired from time to time to do parts in movies. The first one, *In Cold Blood*, was the film version of Truman Capote's chilling account of the apparently motiveless and gruesome murder of a farm family in Kansas by two young men who were apprehended and executed for the crime. I also had parts in *Skyjacked, To Kill a Cop, The Glove, Timber Tramp*, and *Mr. Carter's Army*.

Through those same years, I appeared from time to time on television specials and in commercials. And, before long, I did my stint on nearly every talk show known to man. My most memorable guest appearances were with Bob Hope, Joey Bishop, Johnny Carson, and Steve Allen. On most occasions I rendered at least one song, often more, as when I appeared on "The Hollywood Palace" and "Kraft Music Hall." I made the rounds of the celebrity game shows, and I made regular appearances in such series as the "Danny Thomas Show," "Make Room for Granddaddy," "Movin' On," and "White Shadow." One of my singing tours, which took me to more cities and towns than I can or want to remember, was used to create an album of my songs entitled "Soul City." It was produced by Bobby Darin.

Sirhan Bishara Sirhan's trial began on January 7, 1969, seven months after the assassination. The case against the twenty-four-year-old immigrant from Jordan was overwhelming. DeWayne Wolfer, a professional criminologist, testified that a bullet taken from Bobby's body had been fired from the pistol I had wrenched from Sirhan's grasp that night. Numerous witnesses were able to identify Sirhan as the man they had seen shoot Bobby at close range. The Los Angeles police had a list of seventy people who were in the hotel kitchen that night at the moment of the shooting. Even Sirhan admitted he had fired the shots.

At the trial, I sat and looked at Sirhan and thought about how I had fought to save his life that night in the Ambassador. I was glad that he had been spared to face justice and that we had behaved like civilized people in the face of his barbarity. But the course of justice as I saw it in that courtroom troubled me. Some people giggled during various parts of the testimony and arguments, and that particularly upset me. Here was a man who had devastated a family and deprived a wonderful woman of her husband and eleven children of their father; how could anyone giggle?

Sirhan's lawyers concentrated their efforts, not on proving him innocent, but on saving his life, using as grounds Sirhan's "diminished mental capacity" at the time of the assassination.

It was all handled too matter-of-factly and, sometimes, light-heartedly. To my grieving eyes, it seemed a festival where everyone was having a good time — except me. Had they forgotten that our system of democracy was at stake? Had they forgotten the price Bobby had paid for attempting to make this country better?

John Kennedy, Martin Luther King, Jr., and Bobby had given their lives for the cause of freedom and justice. Yet, how quickly we were forgetting. I resolved not to forget.

One way in which my resolution took shape was in my refusal to capitalize on my relationship with Bobby. I was offered a lot of money to write my story about Bobby Kennedy, but I wouldn't do it. "I won't do that," I said. "I'm not going to make money off my dead friend." Rafer Johnson and I were talking one day during the trial and we both agreed not to capitalize on our friendship with Bobby.

With Sirhan's own confession at hand and with all the evidence against him, the jury found him guilty. On May 21, 1969, Judge Herbert V. Walker sentenced Sirhan Sirhan to the penalty of death, as imposed by the jury, at a time to be fixed, in the manner prescribed by law in San Quentin Penitentiary. On the evening of May 22, he was flown by helicopter from a pad near the Hall of Justice to Van Nuys Airport and thence by twin-engine Beechcraft to Hamilton Air Force Base. A six-car caravan took him from there to San Quentin. The sentence was changed to life imprisonment in 1972 after the California Supreme Court declared the state's death penalty unconstitutional.

The nation forgot about Sirhan more quickly than it might have otherwise, because on July 20 that year we all watched Neil Armstrong and Buzz Aldrin walking on the moon's surface. The two of them spent almost twenty-two hours there, in the Sea of Tranquility as the sector is called, exploring the vicinity near their lunar module and setting up several scientific experiments.

For such an historic event, it had humorous moments. The astronauts were so hard put to find anything photogenic at which to point their camera for the live audience of millions down below on earth that they were compelled to go about picking up assorted and unremarkable rocks. For sheer barrenness, the Sea of Tranquility had the Mojave Desert, east of Los Angeles, beat by a country mile.

My trip that year was a more modest affair than the moon walk. I went on a Bob Hope tour to Vietnam, Thailand, Korea, Japan, and Guam. It was a momentous time to be in that part of the world. American troop levels in Vietnam reached their peak — 541,500 — in March. And, on June 8, President Nixon announced the first plans to reduce that number. I was doubly eager to go because of all the impassioned speeches I had heard Bobby make about what was going on there.

We went to Da Nang and all over Vietnam. I saw more grievously wounded men, women and children than I care to remember. Seeing them made me question more than ever why we were there. And, as I listened to some of the soldiers and marines in the hospitals, I also had to question why we were trying to fight a "limited" war. As a football player, I knew what that could lead to. When I was with the Giants, we had an expression — "playing for nickels." I don't know where it came from, but it meant playing with serious determination.

The phrase would come into use on the practice field when the team would scrimmage — the offensive squad playing against the defensive squad. It often happened that a scrimmage — since it wasn't a "real" game — would devolve into a half-hearted affair. The players would get careless and irritable, and team morale would fall. Then the coach would tell us to get busy and play ball. In response, we'd shout back, "For nickels, coach?" If he nodded "yes," that meant we were free to tear each other's heads off — no holds barred. Strange to tell, when we played all-out like that, there were fewer injuries.

On one of the shows during that tour, I followed Ann-Margret on the program. Ann-Margret (Ann-Margret Olsson is her full name) was born in Sweden and originally "discovered" on the Ted Mack Amateur Hour. She is a superb performer and much better-looking than I am. That audience of GIs was crazy about her. My heart sank at the thought of trying to follow her! My style was different, however, and we weren't competing. I did a song entitled "Bad News," which has a soul sound. I did my best, and it was wonderful the way the troops responded. But I never wanted to follow Ann-Margret again!

During another of the Vietnam shows, mortar fire started coming in on top of us. "This is one time the show must not go on," Bob quipped. As we were running out of the building, I saw an old acquaintance from Penn State. "Come on, Rosey," he shouted. "Go with me."

So we jumped into his armored combat helicopter and took off. I looked back below to see Bob Hope and the others getting into one of the other big choppers. The next thing I knew, the one I was riding in was diving and firing. The roar of the multi-barreled machine guns in the chopper was deafening. Then I noticed streaks flying in our direction. "What are those?" I asked.

"Tracers," he replied matter-of-factly.

I never felt so scared in all my life!

But we got away from there and back to earth safely, and the troupe eventually got back to the States. When we arrived at the airport in California, Governor Ronald Reagan was there to greet us. "Rosey, come and meet the governor," one of my fellow entertainers urged. I was reluctant, at first, because his politics set him far apart from Bobby. I felt like it would be disloyal of me to shake his hand. But he was making some kind of presentation to us and so I went, out of respect for his office.

After I parted from Bernice I dated a number of women, but I was liking one in particular named Margie Hanson. She was a nurse working for a doctor who was an official of the American Medical Association. I was working on a campaign to get black pharmaceutical companies the chance to sell to white doctors. Margie's employer sent her to gather information about the outfit I was working for and about me, since I was the spokesman.

I loved her beautiful blue eyes and striking good looks the minute we met. But nothing happened between us instantly. Our relationship began casually and slowly. Once it got going, she would stop by the television studio or I would take her to some social event. Gradually, other women drifted away until Margie and I were an item. She helped me to keep my life organized and to pick out clothes that looked good on me. And she ran errands for me. Her ability to follow through and get things done impressed me.

Then, in May of 1970, we got married, by a rabbi. The rabbi helped us out because Margie was a Catholic and I was a Baptist (at least, that's what I said if anyone asked). We talked about it and realized there was no Christian clergyman we could agree on. The ceremony was held in the rabbi's home.

Neither of us was ready to get married. I hadn't made any changes in my attitude. We had a fair relationship, better than my other marriage. But I never stopped living the way I wanted to. If I wanted to go out with some other girl, I went. Just as we were on the brink of breaking up, however, Margie announced, "I'm pregnant, and I am going to have the child."

So I said, "Okay."

By the time Roosevelt Kennedy Grier was born in 1971, Margie and I were barely hanging on together. We did better for a while after he came, though. Both of us loved the child deeply from the start and we found a common task and interest that drew us back together.

Margie is a beautiful lady, stubborn, but a wonderful mother, and a good friend to her friends. She treated me fine. But my motivation still was to be independent. I didn't want anyone to have a firm grip on my arm. It was the same old Roosevelt Grier story. I took care of her and I took care of my son and my daughter, but I didn't like that responsibility. I was always running from it.

My roving eye and yen for beautiful women generally got me in trouble, and was certainly at the heart of the deterioration of my marriage. But, on one occasion it resulted in something more positive. One day I walked by a shop in Beverly Hills and saw a group of beautiful women inside.

"I'm going in that shop and see what's going on," I decided.

When I got inside, they were all doing needlepoint, so I walked around striking up conversations and acting as if I knew all about it by critiquing their work. Then I ran into Babs Schumacher whose husband, Willie, is the well-known jockey.

She caught on right away that I didn't have the faintest idea what was going on. "Rosey," she said, "if you are going to 'jive' with the ladies in here, you had better learn how to do needlepoint." So, she and some of the other girls in that shop taught me the craft.

After that, I made needlepoint my hobby. I found it especially relaxing when I took plane trips. And it was a handy device for striking up conversations with women.

After a while, some photographs of me doing needlepoint ran in the *New York Times* society section as "unusual hobbies" of athletes.

Shortly after that, I was asked to do a book, which was published in 1973 as *Rosey Grier's Needlepoint for Men*. I also designed a line of Rosey Grier Needlepoint Kits for Tina of California. Margie was eager to promote this hobby into a serious business. But my interest in it was not strong enough to carry me that far.

After a photo of me doing needlepoint was on the cover of the *Saturday Evening Post* and in the centerfold of *Look Magazine*, I got calls from my friends in athletics! "What are you doing, Rosey?" they asked. "You've lost your macho! Needlepoint is for sissies!"

But their opinions didn't bother me, especially after kids began to come up to me and say, "If it's all right for you to do needlepoint, it's all right for me to play the violin and not be a sissy."

In the early seventies, the violence of the war in Vietnam seemed to create a fallout of violence in the States. After the disclosure, late in 1969, of the My Lai Massacre of women and children by American troops, the already strong opposition to the war became even more vehement. Kent State University in Ohio was put on the map in May of 1970 when National Guardsmen fired into a group of student anti-war protestors, four of whom died of their wounds. In May of 1971, over 13,400 demonstrators were arrested in Washington, D.C., in a four-day period.

Adding fuel to the flames of protest was the publication of secret Pentagon papers, a study and analysis of the Vietnamese war. The *New York Times* and the *Washington Post* began simultaneous publication on June 13, 1971.

President Nixon responded adroitly to the anti-war pressure by gradually reducing the number of land troops in southeast Asia, but he stepped up air and naval bombardments. Meanwhile, Henry Kissinger was regularly in the news, working hard to achieve a settlement with the North Vietnamese. As the 1972 election approached, Nixon was able to defuse Democratic efforts to depict George McGovern as the candidate of peace by taking that role for himself. The result was an electoral landslide of a size not seen since Roosevelt squashed Landon in 1936: Nixon, 520; McGovern, 17 (the 1936 margin was 523-8).

It was during the 1972 campaign that George Wallace again set out in quest of the Democratic nomination. As one of the country's leading spokesmen of racism, he was not my favorite person. But when he was subjected to an assassination attempt in Laurel, Maryland, in May, 1972, I was grieved to the extent that I wept uncontrollably. Hate had surfaced violently again, and we were all diminished by it.

The seventies for me personally were foggy years. I wandered about, trying to cope with the sadness that lingered long and heavy after Bobby's death. It was difficult to put my heart into anything I did. Being an entertainer was paying the bills, but I was not doing all the things one needed to do to make it big in Hollywood.

My life had been an exciting passage on a ship someone else was steering. The years that football had given me were the pleasant and adventuresome part of that cruise. But, suddenly the ship had entered treacherous waters. At first, the adventure of the voyage in these treacherous waters was exciting and exhilarating. However, the ship was torpedoed at the height of the excitement and I found myself clinging to a bit of flotsam and being washed ashore on a desert island. As the seventies progressed, I sat on the shore and looked longingly out to sea.

24

GREAT EYES OF EXPECTATION

One day I picked up the newspaper and saw a headline about some gang kids who had accidentally killed a helpless three-year-old girl. It wiped me out. How my heart ached for the little girl's parents. I began to weep and say someone had to go out and stop such a thing from ever happening again. I called the police and social agencies to see what they were doing to stop the violence. Everyone I talked to seemed to be hard at work, but still, this horrible thing had happened. Something more was needed.

Not long after that, as I was brushing my teeth one morning, I looked in the mirror. "Why don't you go out and do something about it, Rosey?" I asked.

"Wow, man!" I argued. "How can I do something about it? I'm just a retired football player."

Somehow, my old excuse didn't hold water, and I went out looking for gang kids. For a year and a half, whenever I was on the street, I kept an eye out for "gang" kids. But I never saw any. Finally, it dawned on me one day. It happened when I was looking at a little girl, the young daughter of a friend of mine. She was beautiful, and a big part of that beauty was in her eyes. They were full of joyous expectation. Then I realized that I had seen the same great eyes of expectation in every neighborhood child from Watts to Beverly Hills. It dawned on me that all little kids look the same. I wasn't going to find gang members by walking down the street.

But I had seen those same eyes drained of the life and light and hope that made them so beautiful. It happened when they were abused, lied to, cheated, scared, and neglected.

I saw in the faces of young people all the things I desired for America — and for the whole world. I saw the smiles, the friendliness, the eagerness to trust. Gangs were made up of young people who had been robbed of those things — whose resentment had turned them into haters and fighters. I wanted to turn the gangs into teams of youngsters dedicated to hard work and wholesome play in the spirit of love.

The weight of the need of these children for time, attention, and love fell on my shoulders. I brought politicians and actors and actresses into the community to meet the kids. I began to take kids to meet some celebrities, to watch some of the football games, and anywhere else I could think of that would broaden their horizons.

Willie Naulls, a former player with the New York Knicks and the Boston Celtics, saw what I was doing and wanted to help. So he introduced me to the owner of the San Diego Chargers, businessman Eugene Kline, who gave me $100,000. "Rosey," he told me, "I like what you're doing. Helping you do it is a way I can return something to the community."

Brad and Bobby Wyman, two boys who had lost their father, were the first young people in the project that grew out of that grant. It eventually grew to include around 400 young people.

As I met and worked with more and more kids, I often heard these words: "Rosey, you got it made. You're a big guy!"

I'd smile and shake my head. "Being big is not where it's at. What counts is what's inside," I told them.

To encourage kids, I made a film entitled, *Courage To Be Me.* It was a short documentary about my life, and it's still being shown in many schools and on Public Broadcasting System stations around the country. It encouraged young people not to be afraid to be themselves. I also did a television special with Marlo Thomas and

Friends, which won an Emmy. On this special, I sang "It's All Right to Cry," a song which told boys it was all right to show emotion. An album from that special also is in many schools around the country.

Many young guys have mentioned having seen or heard one or another of those productions, even in recent years. "Rosey, you taught me it's okay to cry," they tell me.

After a while, however, Eugene Kline sold the Chargers, and my funding ended. Willie Naulls came to my rescue again and introduced me to the man who, in 1973, had succeeded Sam Yorty as mayor of Los Angeles, Tom Bradley. We found out we had something in common: Mayor Bradley was the son of a sharecropper and had grown up on a cotton plantation in Calvert, Texas. We swapped stories about life on the farm, and then got down to business.

"Why don't you work out of my office?" the mayor suggested. "I'll use part of a budget we have set aside for just this sort of thing. That should be enough to sustain the project and help it grow."

That was an offer I couldn't refuse. I became the mayor's assistant on youth and senior citizens. The project did grow and eventually evolved into Giant Step, a non-profit corporation.

But, as I worked so energetically to help youngsters get their lives in order, my own was still out of order. I continued to refuse to keep my commitment to Margie, and — since I also refused to lie to her about my misdeeds — our marriage was deteriorating fast.

During 1975 and 1976, I played the part of Moose on a prime-time NBC adventure series called "Movin' On." It starred Claude Akins as Sonny Pruitt and Frank Converse as Will Chandler, two gypsy truck drivers whose backgrounds differed drastically. Sonny was a burly veteran trucker who owned their giant rig and who liked to settle things with his fists. Will was a young law school graduate who was trying to learn more about himself by working as a trucker. They balanced each other as they traveled back and forth across the country in search of adventure and freight to haul.

President Ford, we found out, was a great fan of the show. One time, when we were doing a show in Atlanta, the President happened to be staying in the same hotel we were. A Secret Service agent approached Claude Akins with an invitation to come to the presidential suite to discuss the program. The President and Claude chatted for half an hour, after which Ford told Akins, "Now I can tell Betty I know more about 'Movin' On' than she does."

I joined the show during its second season. My partner was Benjy, played by Art Metrano, and we were two of the slickest con artists ever to cruise the highways in a big rig. The show was filmed on location in a different part of the country each week, so I was constantly gone from home. Those absences and my indifference to Margie's protests that we needed to build a family unit were the last straw for her.

I wanted a woman to love and care about me, to work with me — but not someone to whom I had to remain committed and for whom I had to be responsible. One day, I sat down for a talk with little Rosey. "Rosey," I said, "I'm going to leave you and your mom."

"Where are you going?" He looked puzzled.

"I'm going to stay someplace else. I'm going to get a divorce." I don't know if he knew what a divorce was or not.

"Dad, you shouldn't get no divorce."

"You don't understand, and I can't explain it to you."

"Tell me, Dad, tell me," he urged.

But I couldn't tell him, because I was crying. I don't know if I was crying for him or for me. Probably for both. The thought that my day would no longer begin with him running into the bedroom with his cheery greetings was intolerable. Gone, too, would be the tender moments when I slipped into his room at night (after coming home late) to check on him and to watch him a moment in peaceful sleep. I longed for such sleep for myself. Since the night of Bobby's assassination, I had hardly slept a night free of a recurring nightmare.

Finally I looked back at little Rosey. "I want to teach you something before I go," I said. "I want to teach you to pray. Would you like that?"

"Yes!" came his enthusiastic reply.

I taught him the only prayer I knew, the Lord's Prayer. Afterwards I started talking about God. "He's your Father in heaven," I explained. "But He's always close. He'll be with you even though I'm not. He's always taken good care of me, and He'll take care of you, too."

Rosey listened intently.

I moved out in 1975 and filed for divorce. After living in a motel for a while, I moved to Malibu Beach. Still feeling like a man stranded on a desert island, I now had unlimited opportunities to stare longingly out to sea. And, as I did, I couldn't give up the idea that a strong leader would come along to change the way things were going in this country.

"Rosey," the voice came over the phone, "this is Jimmy Carter. I'm calling you from Georgia to ask you to help me in the upcoming presidential race."

"I'm proud that you would ask, Governor," I replied. "Since Bobby's death, I've kept looking for someone to carry the fallen banner. And I've already helped several people about whom I felt hopeful. All of them had started strong, then dropped out of the race. So you'll understand when I say I'm reluctant to get involved again."

"Yes, sir," he replied. "I appreciate your position."

"But I keep hearing about you," I went on. "You seem to have a fine organization. I hear a lot of young people are campaigning for you. Is that right?"

"Yes, it is."

"I'm not promising to help you yet," I told him, "but if I do, I want you to do whatever you promise the people. If you say you are going to do something, try to do it. And I'll be happy."

"That's the sort of spirit I like to hear in a man, Rosey."

"I'm still not saying that I'm going to help you, but I do want to find out more about you."

"Fair enough."

I had learned not to support anyone without personal contact. I needed that face-to-face meeting before I could make up my mind about a man. So, the fact that Governor Carter himself had called me on the phone stood him in good stead with me.

The next week, I got on the phone and did my homework. I talked to friends in Georgia where, I learned, Carter had started his political career in 1962 by getting elected to a seat in the state legislature. Then, in 1970, he was elected governor. His home town, Plains, was thirty miles from my birthplace in Cuthbert. He knew what it was like to pick peanuts, so I knew he couldn't be all bad.

I asked Teddy Kennedy about him, and Teddy said Governor Carter was a decent man. I called up columnist Art Buchwald, and his staff said the governor was a nice man, a smart man. Some of Bobby's supporters told me they had sent money to the Carter campaign.

I also found out that he was a pious Baptist deacon who taught Sunday school. He was undoubtedly a better Baptist than I was, but, at least, it was something else we had in common. And when I heard he'd taken a stand for the integration of his church, and that, as a result of his efforts, a portrait of Martin Luther King, Jr., hung in the portrait gallery of the State Capitol building in Atlanta — the first such painting of a black person to hang there — the scales tipped fully in his favor.

So I began to go here and there to campaign for him. After a while I found myself spending a lot of my time stumping for him — though I never spent time at his side as I had with Bobby. When he was elected, I was proud to have helped him.

In 1976 I was also, in addition to campaigning for Jimmy Carter, working on plans for the first fund-raising program for Giant Step. However, in spite of being excited about the possibilities of helping inner-city youth, I would go back to my room and cry many nights because I was lonely and depressed. Then one day I talked to Bobby Kennedy's second oldest daughter, Courtney, and as I talked, I cried. Later, I was talking with Jackie and told her I had cried on Courtney's shoulder.

"You can call and cry on my shoulder any time you want to," she told me.

Jackie listened to me talk about Giant Step and said she would come out to help with the fund-raiser. My nephew, Robert Blackwell, loaned me $25,000, and I borrowed another $35,000 from other sources to raise the $60,000 we needed to stage this event in the Dorothy Chandler Pavilion, the place where the Academy Awards are held.

I called President Carter's staff to ask if he would be honorary chairman of the event. When they said yes, I told them two boys from the peanut fields of Georgia were making a mark for the things that counted most in America. They agreed, and Dr. Ruth Senay, a wonderful woman, agreed to be chairperson of the event.

Jackie came as the guest of honor, and we got worldwide press. Marlo Thomas, Aretha Franklin, Henry Mancini, Ben Vereen, Harry

Blackstone, Jackie Vernon, Ray Charles, Booker T and the MGs, Frankie Ortega, and Fred Travelina also came to help. Movie producer Jerry Schafer produced the show for us. We took in about $125,000 which netted $65,000 for Giant Step after I repaid the loans.

The idea behind Giant Step was "the Penny Concept." The fund-raiser started with my displaying a penny and Roberta Ernisee, my secretary at the time, asking the question, "A penny for your thoughts?" Then I explained that, for a mere penny's profit, people would squeeze the life out of old folks and devastate kids.

"But this penny can be used for good," I told her.

One day, not long after the fund-raiser, two men showed up in my city-hall office in Los Angeles and asked me if there was anything I would like President Carter to do for me since I had helped him get elected.

"Yes, there is something he can do for me," I said.

They asked, "What's that?"

"Do what he promised the people," I said.

They thought that was funny. They said, "You mean you don't want anything?"

"Not for myself," I told them. "I want him to do what he promised to do to help the people."

They said, "Well, give us your resume."

"I don't have a resume," I told them.

"Well, give us something," they said.

So I wrote on a piece of paper: "Roosevelt 'Rosey' Grier: Jack of all Careers, I Can Do It." I signed it and gave it to them.

And they said, "You — you're unusual. All those other people we visited, they wanted something."

In the years that followed that, Giant Step accomplished much. It secured $4.5 million in federal funds to build a housing project for senior citizens in San Bernardino, called The Beautiful Light Inn. It operated a school in Gardena for three years that trained a hundred kids a year and then helped 98 percent of them to find decent jobs. A joint effort between Giant Step and the United Auto Workers recruited kids to be trained similarly by the Job Corps.

I talked to a lot of people, kids in trouble, lawyers and businessmen, and handled a lot of details. In addition, I was earning my living as an actor, singer, and writer.

But none of that eased my loneliness. And, as time passed, the joy and satisfaction I derived from Giant Step began to disappear, too. I began to find out that I had no way to control the people I was supplying with money.

The Giant Step school had gotten a government grant and along with it a mandate to operate in certain other inner-city areas across the country. In these schools the students would learn to silk-screen trendy designs on T-shirts.

The grant was for $650,000, with a stipulation that I raise $100,000 — which I did by going to some New York athletic teams and to Coca Cola. In each of the Giant Step inner-city training centers, people were supposed to be training kids to go into business for themselves. But it wasn't working that way. The man sent by the government to implement the program lacked the know-how to make it work.

I had only one way to lodge my protest. That was to refuse to disburse the money.

"Why?" demanded the official supervising the project for the Department of Commerce agency that had made the grant. I had gotten his attention.

"I'm supposed to send money to people you pick to run the centers. That leaves me with all the accountability and no control. It's no good."

In the big argument which ensued, he threatened a congressional hearing if I didn't do what he said. I told him to go ahead, because he would lose.

Eventually, however, he and other officials at the department listened. We agreed to focus our efforts on the one site in Gardena. Then we worked together to find a replacement for the incompetent manager. They came up with two or three candidates who proved to be no more effective than the first man. Then I brought in Wally Choice from New Jersey. I'd known him a long time — from those days in the army — and trusted him.

Wally hired a consulting firm to help us think about our task. Under Wally, Giant Step Training School was set up to do the silk screening, lithography, printing, and various aspects of the training project. It took Wally about a year to get it going. Then he stepped down, and we hired Carl Johnson, a businessman from West Virginia and a member of the Giant Step board of directors, to take over. He developed it into an even finer operation.

That experience taught me a lot. Because we were using government funds, we were supposed to rent whatever equipment we needed for the schools. But, when we did our arithmetic, we figured that, by the time a project was over, the money we would spend renting equipment would be enough to buy that same equipment four or five times over. So we bought equipment instead of renting it. At the end of the project, we gave close to $300,000 worth of useful equipment to the government.

When we built the housing project in San Bernardino, it took three years to work through the hassles over sites and finances. One place found that we already had the money to finance the project and raised their price $200,000. I put my foot down! Just because it was government money didn't mean I didn't care about it. Government money is our money in the final analysis.

Owners of another location wouldn't let us build there. "Rosey Grier is going to bring all those black people into the community," was their reason for objecting.

In spite of these things, we were able to show the kids and the old folks that people did care about them. And we were able to show some young people that they could learn a skill enabling them to go out and get jobs. Some of them had never had a job before, but were able to start at good salaries.

Helping kids find a life when they thought there was nothing for them made me feel great. But I saw that as fast as I could pull twenty out of the soup, twenty more jumped in. I hired lawyers with my own money for some who had gotten into trouble, doing everything I could to help them get going. I worked myself into a frazzle getting all the people I knew to come and talk to the kids, to share with them, give to them, and love them. I was visiting schools and speaking, but it was not enough. In fact, sometimes it even seemed hopeless.

We helped many youngsters, but we lost some to violence. In fact, we lost a lot. Some who pretended to be on the "good team" were not.

I learned a lesson about these pretenders from a wise young man named Michael Tobin. "Rosey," he said, "if you stand by an anthill with honey on your feet, you're going to get ants."

"What are you trying to tell me?" I asked.

"If people find out you're willing to help, they'll come running to get whatever you have to offer. But among them are a lot of kids who have no intention of changing. They're just after the honey on your feet — if you get bitten in the process, that doesn't concern them."

Realizing that he was right, and that it was not possible to save all the kids we worked with, was a tremendous blow. All I wanted was to be able to stop the violence and get people to care for one another.

And that sad knowledge made my personal prison of loneliness and unhappiness close more tightly around me. I was missing something in my life. I had fame as a football player, a singer, and an actor. And I was doing my best to help kids in trouble. But I was not happy, joyful, peaceful or content. The more I thought about it, the sorrier I felt for myself. "I guess I'm never going to be happy," I began telling myself.

I watched other people holding hands, snuggling close in automobiles, smiling and dancing, having dinner together, and enjoying one another. Every time I found someone to do all these things with, however, she got to be a weight on my spirit.

The women I knew wanted me to be responsible for their happiness, but I didn't know how to be happy. How could I make anyone else happy? It was a responsibility too great to bear.

The pain was helping me to grow a little more. After awhile I learned that sex wasn't the source of happiness. When my dates brought their overnight kits along, I began to say no. "What are you bringing that for? You're not staying all night at my place," I announced to them flat out.

For the first time, I began to set some standards. Before, it had not mattered whether a woman was married or not. Now it did. When married women came on to me, I found myself lecturing them about helping their husbands be the kind of guys they wanted instead of running around with other men. Life seemed to make more sense that way. A lot of people thought I was weird, but I knew better. For one thing, when I started doing the right thing morally, I felt better — even a little bit happy.

I lived in Malibu several months after the divorce in 1975. Then I moved to an apartment complex called Oakwood in Burbank at the east end of the San Fernando Valley. There, a strange encounter with an Israeli awaited me.

25

NO PLACE
TO RUN

President Carter did not get off to a bad start. He was a populist in the jargon of politics. And he helped to raise the nation out of the doldrums of Vietnam and Watergate. To me, Richard Nixon symbolized the white backlash that had arisen and gained some measure of respectability in response to the likes of Malcolm X and Stokely Carmichael. In that sense it was only fitting that his administration perished as a result of inner corruption. The mighty one had fallen, the cynical, urbane and worldly Nixon — to be supplanted by a lowly hymn-singing populist from Georgia's hinterlands.

During 1977, his first year in office, Jimmy Carter did what he had promised. He pardoned the draft evaders from the Vietnam era. He sought and gained congressional approval to slim and tighten the federal bureaucracy, to lower income taxes, and to establish the Department of Energy. He halted the production of the B-1 bomber in favor of the cruise missile. The economy improved and unemployment fell. And he began a policy of making appointments to federal judicial posts and the like which favored black candidates, so that, by the end of his term, he had appointed more blacks to such posts than any other chief executive.

While he was busy in Washington, and Rosalynn was leading a delegation on a tour of Latin America, I was busy in Los Angeles.

Among other things, I was working on a project called Cities and Schools. It was a federally-sponsored project which put me together with a group of young men that included President Carter's second son, twenty-seven-year-old Chip — James Earl Carter III.

The project involved us in visiting corporations to solicit their support for our efforts to help poor kids learn. It was this aspect of the project which brought Chip Carter to Los Angeles with Bill Miliken. Bert Chamberlain and I met with him, along with several other people involved in the project in the Los Angeles area. Part of Chip's itinerary included an appointment with Armand Hammer, the well-known oil billionaire of Southern California. When they announced that only Chip and Bill would make that call, I protested, "If you all think you're going to leave this nigger sitting outside, I ain't playing. Either I'm going all the way in to hear what's going on, or I'm not going to be involved at all."

Since no self-respecting white person is allowed to say "nigger" (in public, in any event) any longer, it is a word which we black people can employ occasionally for its shock value. They got my message: namely, that they were treating me like a second-class citizen and I wasn't about to put up with it.

It was immediately decided that I should accompany Chip and Bill to this important meeting. Armand Hammer listened politely to our pitch, and he served up a bowl of imported Russian caviar. While Chip talked, I consumed the caviar.

"You ate up half the man's caviar," Chip and Bill chided me good-naturedly as we drove away from the house. "Do you know how expensive that stuff is?"

I defended myself by saying, "If the man couldn't afford to serve the caviar, he wouldn't have brought it out."

Early in 1978 I happened to be in Washington, and the Carters asked me to stay at the White House for the weekend. The President would be away, Chip explained. But they hoped I would partake of the executive hospitality anyway.

At first, I turned down the invitation. But they told me to think about it, and then let them know. My reluctance to accept the invitation was based on my hunch that Teddy was going to run against the President for the Democratic nomination in 1980. If he did, I wanted to be on his bandwagon, and, to me, that meant not allowing myself to get too close to the Carters. So I called Jackie Onassis. She said the chance to spend the night in the White House was an experience I shouldn't miss.

Little Rosey was with me that weekend, and I decided that Jackie was right. I called the Carters back and asked if I could bring my son, too. They said that would be fine, and the plans were made.

As it turned out, little Rosey wanted to spend more time with the children who were close to his age at Ethel Kennedy's. She continued to reside at Hickory Hill after Bobby's death. So, I effected a compromise. The first night he stayed at Ethel's and I slept in the Lincoln Bedroom. The next night, I brought Rosey over to spend the night with me, and we slept in the Queen's Room.

When we got to the gate, he said, "Daddy, is this our house?"

After I got him settled down, I called my mother to tell her where we were. I expected her to be excited, but all she said was, "Let me talk to little Rosey."

Then I called my sister Eva, and she didn't seem excited either. All she wanted was "to talk to that boy." I couldn't figure it out.

During the late summer of 1978 I went back to Linden to visit my mother. She had been ill with diabetes for some time — in and out of the hospital. She needed a walker to get around. When my lifelong friend, John Arthur Wilson, and I walked into her room, she looked past us both to see if anyone else was in our party. "Where's that grandson of mine?" she demanded.

"I'm sorry, Mama, I couldn't arrange to bring him along this time."

"Well, you bring him next time, y' hear?"

"Yes, Mama. Now, tell me, how are ya feeling?"

"I'm tired, Roosevelt, I gotta admit it."

We talked awhile longer and then I said it was time for us to leave. She looked at me, but she didn't have to say anything. I reached down and gave her a squeeze and a kiss.

Only a few years before this, I had been about to leave after a visit to see Mama at home, and she said, "Aren't you going to kiss me?"

I had stood there a minute, dumbfounded because she had never said that before. We were not demonstrative people. Then I went over and hugged and kissed her. After that, I never missed kissing her when we arrived for a visit and when we said goodbye. And that day in the hospital was no exception.

About two weeks after I returned to California, I picked up the ringing phone, "Hello?"

"Rosey, this is John Arthur."

"Hey, what's the long distance call for?"

"Ever since we went to see your Mama, I been thinkin'. I saw somethin' in her eyes, Rosey. I don't know if your Mama is going to be around much longer. You need to prepare yourself."

"Okay, man, thanks. How's your family?" As he talked, my mind went back over my visit to the hospital. I saw mama trying to smile and be happy, and I could see the struggle that I tried not to see then. John Arthur was right. I knew it and I began to feel empty. I didn't know what to do; I was helpless.

After John Arthur and I said goodbye, I left the apartment and went for a walk. As I passed the recreation room, a young couple stopped me. "Mr. Grier?" the young man asked.

"Yes?"

"Excuse us. My name is Yigdal Levi and this is my wife, Esther. [These names are fictitious.] I am an Israeli, and I understand you help young people."

"I do."

I invited them in to sit down on a nearby bench, and Yigdal told me his story: "I was in Las Vegas last year with my Israeli friend, Menachem Eshkol. Menachem broke into a room occupied by an older couple from Canada. He tied them up and came and got me. I didn't know what he was doing, so I went with him. When we went into the room, and I saw what was going on, I tried to talk him out of it. But he wouldn't listen. He was high on drugs. And I was afraid for that older couple if I left him alone with them. So, I did a stupid thing. I stayed until he finished. Later, we were arrested by the police."

"What happened after you were arrested?"

"We were allowed to put up bail of $25,000 each. But then Menachem jumped his bail and went back to Israel. I was afraid the authorities would punish me as the only culprit they had left. So, I left Nevada and have been hiding out here in Southern California for a year."

"You're a fugitive, then?"

"Yes, and now Esther is going to have a baby. I am desperate for help."

"How do you want me to help you?" I asked.

"Please, Mr. Grier, you have connections. I want you to help me get a new identification card with a new name. Then I could come out of hiding and stay here and take care of my wife."

I paused a moment and looked into Yigdal's eyes. Then I spoke. "The only way I can help you is to advise you to go back to Las Vegas and get the incident cleared up. You can't spend the rest of your life running, especially with a wife and a young child," I told him.

He didn't want to hear that at first. But a couple of weeks later, he came back and asked if I would help him do that. I called the district attorney at Las Vegas and told him I believed I could help him solve a case. He became instantly suspicious and threatened to have me arrested! It was impossible to get him to understand by talking to him, so I wrote him a letter. But the letter got no response at all.

Between then and the next episode of Yigdal's story, I got a call Friday night, October 20, from my sister Eva in Jersey. "Rosey, Mama has died."

In the moment I heard those horrible words, I thanked heaven for John Arthur's warning to me on the phone just weeks before this. Having some advance knowledge made it easier to remain strong.

I caught the next plane to New Jersey to be there for the funeral. My younger brother Rufus conducted the service. Then we buried Mama in the Rose Hills Cemetery in Linden, right next to Poppa. Just as it happened when we buried him, folks came from everywhere to pay their last respects to the woman who gave me birth. She was seventy-nine when she passed away.

After the funeral, I felt as if I were in a tunnel. I was numb for a long time. Her death struck like an earthquake in the family. We had no home base anymore. "Home" had been where Mama was. We would still get together from time to time at one of my sisters' homes in neighboring towns in New Jersey — but it wouldn't be the same without Mama.

In early November, I flew to Las Vegas to appear at a benefit for boxing champion, Joe Louis. The Brown Bomber had fallen on hard times after the IRS reduced him to penury by demanding $1.2 million in back taxes. He had been working as a greeter at Caesar's Palace in Las Vegas to help make ends meet — when he felt well enough to work.

The benefit — held Wednesday night, November 8, 1978 — was Frank Sinatra's idea and he was hosting it. The plan was to raise money for a foundation set up by Sinatra to take care of Joe's needs and living expenses. Frank invited people from all over the world — the super, super stars — to participate. It was an honor to be on the stage at this affair for the man who had been my hero as a kid. A lot of money was raised for the Joe Louis Foundation.

Frank Sinatra is a generous and benevolent man who has done a lot of things to help people for which he has received little or no recognition. (In fact, he doesn't even want recognition. I went over to thank him for what he was doing for Joe Louis, but he didn't want to hear any compliments.)

I told Frank about Yigdal Levi and his problems with the Las Vegas police, and he gave me the name of a newspaper reporter in the city "who might," he said, "be able to help."

When I followed up on Frank's suggestion, the reporter was indeed helpful. He arranged for Yigdal's attorney to meet with the D.A. — but the result of that meeting was that Yigdal would have to turn himself in before any deals could be discussed.

Yigdal and Esther's father came to see me when I got back to Burbank. Esther's father asked me, "'If things go against Yigdal, would you guarantee that the governor will grant a commutation?"

"You overestimate my standing with the governor of Nevada," I said. "But, even if I could, I wouldn't. For the sake of his wife, his child, and himself he has to go back and face the music. I have done everything I can to make sure all the facts are brought out. That's the best deal I — or anyone else — can offer!"

Then I turned to Yigdal, "Whatever happens, I'll stand with you in this, no matter how long it takes."

The next night, Yigdal came to see me alone and said, "I don't know what to do. Everyone is telling me all these things."

"The life that you live is your own. You have to make up your own mind about how to live it. No one is going to live it for you. You have to decide how to live and how to face your responsibilities." I was the last person in the world to talk about facing responsibilities, but that was what Yigdal needed to hear. My turn would come.

He was quiet for a while. Then he looked up at me and said, "I will turn myself in if you will go with me."

"You got a deal!" I replied. And we made a plan. Early the next week, I met him at the Burbank Airport and we flew together to Las Vegas.

We hailed a taxi, went straight to the courthouse and reported to the deputy district attorney who was handling Yigdal's case. The first order of business, however, was to give me the cook's tour of the courthouse and introduce me to everyone, especially those who wanted autographs. Yigdal had to sit around and wait for that. Finally the tour concluded and they got down to the business of booking him. After that, I went home to Burbank.

Later, the police gave Yigdal a lie detector test. Based on the fact that he passed it, and on other evidence, they dropped the charges and let him go. This young man who had been running for a year not only got his freedom but his bail money back! I was excited about that. That was one time of helping people that worked out.

A similar incident involved a young man I read about in a magazine who had been in prison nine years. Tim — as I'll call him — had been promised time off for helping the FBI break up a drug-smuggling conspiracy by a group called, "the Brotherhood." However, that promise had not been kept.

When I read about him, Tim was working on his doctorate but, in spite of his exemplary record, prison officials were unwilling to let him leave his maximum security cell block to attend classes at a nearby college. His life was in danger, they said.

I began to write letters for him. I wrote senators, mayors, and people I knew in Washington. After I had worked on the case a year and a half, I contacted Ted Kennedy's office. Through Senator Kennedy's efforts, Tim's sentence was finally reduced by the amount that he had been promised.

After another two years, he went up for parole and was turned down until 1988! Here was a guy who had gotten his college degree and a master's degree *magna cum laude* while in prison and was working on his doctorate. He had been rehabilitated if anyone had, but the authorities wouldn't let him out. I called governors, and kept working at it. After about six years, one Christmas Tim called me, and his voice was incredible. It had the biggest, deepest, most power- ful tone I had ever heard.

"Rosey," he said, "I'm free!"

Free, after fourteen years! Because his life was still in danger, he was given another name and identity by the government. He is work- ing on his second doctorate now, is married, and has a good family. He is a productive citizen, and I was happy to have played a small part in seeing that this man, who was facing a hopeless situation, got another chance.

But, in spite of heartening moments like the two I've just described, the general course of my life during the mid-seventies was downhill. Ever been on a roller coaster and wondered why you got on the dumb thing? That's what life was like to me.

I wanted to bring in a man to relieve me as president of Giant Step, but the board of directors wouldn't hear of it because he was white. Then I became involved with a project that seemed to be a good thing for kids, but it turned out to be a total scam.

Things kept turning sour, and I couldn't figure out why. Either I got hurt or someone else got hurt. My phone was ringing constantly with more bad news. I was lonely and afraid.

One night I went to a party at Valerie Harper's house. Everyone else was dancing and drinking and having a good time. I sat there and looked at them — a spectator. So I got up and started to leave.

Valerie stopped me, "'Where are you going, Rosey?"

"Home," I grunted.

"How come?"

"I'm just going, that's all."

Back in my apartment, I tried to play my guitar, but it didn't relieve my depression. I only grew sadder. I sang sad songs, cried and wallowed in melancholy, which didn't help a bit. I had gotten home from Valerie's about midnight. From then until six o'clock in the morning, I sat in front of the blank screen of a television set. I was in bad shape. I wouldn't even answer the phone.

The roller coaster had come all the way down from the highest point to the lowest. My father and mother were both dead. My brothers and sisters had their own lives. Besides, I didn't think they would understand my problems. I could think of no one to call, no real close friend. I had come to the place Poppa talked about when I was a kid. I had been "run home" by life. Eva's question in the peanut field — "What will happen when Mama and Poppa die?" — was finally going to be answered.

I was on my back with my feet up, in the same desperate position from which I had defended myself against Arthur's onslaughts when we were kids. Only now, it was 1978, and I was forty-five years old.

26

THE BIGGEST SURPRISE?

Not long after Valerie Harper's party and the miserable night that followed, there was a knock on my door. I peeked out, and Carl Johnson was standing there. I had known Carl for some time. It was he who succeeded Wally Choice as the director of Giant Step. And, when Giant Step started expanding out of the Los Angeles area, Carl had done much of the groundwork, flying all over the country with me. He was a fine man and an able worker, but I was in no mood to greet anyone. I ignored his knock, just as I had been ignoring the ringing of the phone much of the time of late.

But Carl kept knocking. After several minutes, he shouted, "Rosey! I know you're in there. Now you let me in!"

The noise made me worry about what the neighbors would think, so I got up and went to the door. "Huh?" I grunted my indifferent greeting.

"God sent me, Rosey," Carl smiled.

"God sent you?" I thought he had gone crazy. I started looking around for a stick or something in case I needed it. He walked through the door and into my living room.

"Do you ever read the Bible?" he asked.

"Read the Bible?"

"That's right."

Carl had sent me a Bible from a trip to Israel and had given me another one earlier. But I hadn't read them.

"Well, I don't understand the Bible," I said.

He asked me if I'd really studied it. And he started talking about God and Jesus. After a few minutes, I grew impatient with his talk. I went to the door, opened it, and held it open so he could leave. But Carl was undeterred. He finished what he had to say, and then he left.

Then I picked up one of the Bibles he'd given me and looked at it. I opened it, but nothing caught my eye. The Bible seemed worlds apart from what I was going through. Whoever heard of the Bible solving any problems? So I closed it and went back to feeling sorry for myself.

I had to fly to Chicago not long after that. I didn't want to go, but I had to earn a living.

The stewardess said, "You're Rosey Grier, aren't you?"

I was really depressed and didn't want to talk to anyone, but I said, "Yes, I am."

She said, "I've been watching a man on television, and I think you ought to watch him."

"What's he do?" I asked.

"He teaches."

"What does he teach?"

"The Bible," she replied cheerily.

"What is your name?"

"Ann Ludic."

"Well, Ann, you're the second person in the last four days to bring up this subject with me. I don't know what to make of it."

"You will!" she sparkled.

The Bible hadn't entered my mind for several years. The last time had been when I was lecturing one of the kids in Giant Step about doing right.

"Rosey," he asked me, "what is right?"

I opened my mouth, but, before I spoke, I realized I had nothing to say. So I said, "I don't know. I'm going to find out and let you know."

Before I could come up with an answer for him, he went out with a group of kids. They all got high on something and, for no reason, they beat him to death. I went to his funeral and wept with regret. If only I'd had an answer.

His question — "What's right?" — haunted me after that. It made me think about the Bible and God. Eventually I was asking myself, "Where did God come from?" I had wanted to call my mom and ask her, but I kept talking myself out of it. She wasn't educated. How would she know? But one day I called and asked her.

She said, "God is, was, and always will be."

That gave me pause. It was no answer, but it was the right answer.

Now, years later, two people within a short time had told me about the Bible, not knowing the kind of desperation that surrounded me. Their remarks had come out of nowhere, as far as I was concerned. I couldn't understand it.

Stewardess Ann Ludic came by my seat a little later and asked, "Why don't you give me your phone number?"

I didn't want to be bothered, but I was miserable, and she was cute. So I gave her my number.

Back in Los Angeles, I shut myself in my room. Turtle-like, I went deep inside myself, and I understood what bitter loneliness was all about. I dropped into a pit.

Then it seemed I heard an answer. "Why don't you kill yourself?"

"I couldn't do that," I objected.

Yet, at that moment, I understood why people kill themselves, even when they are afraid of death. Depression's iron grip thrusts them to the bottom of the pit of despair and tells them they have nowhere to turn, no one to trust, no peace. Suicide seems the only alternative.

Strangely, however, moments after that thought of suicide struck me, the memory-picture of the time I taught little Rosey the Lord's Prayer sprang to mind. Then I heard myself repeating, "Our Father, who art in heaven . . ." And, as I recited those words, my mind grasped their meaning for the first time in my life. It seemed as if God Himself was in that prayer, and that, if I said it long enough, I could get myself wrapped up in it like a safety net.

I said the Lord's Prayer over and over, crying all the time. I didn't know what else to do. I didn't know how to get going again, but it was working — it kept the depression at arm's length.

I started thinking that if I went to sleep, I would sink back into that pit and never get back. So I tried to wrap myself around the Lord's Prayer so that, even if I went to sleep, I would be safe. It's hard to put into words what I was feeling. But I tried to see how many ways I could get myself around that prayer, so it couldn't get away from me. My thoughts were totally centered on God, but all I knew about Him was the Lord's Prayer. I held onto it like a pole stretched out to a drowning man.

The next morning was Sunday, and the phone woke me up. A strange voice said, "Rosey Grier?"

"Yeah?"

"My name is Ken Ludic."

"Yeah?" I didn't know any Ken Ludic.

"My wife told me to call you."

"Huh?" I replied and woke up a little more. What wife would be having her husband call me? I didn't go out with married women.

"My wife's name is Ann Ludic. She's an airline stewardess," he said. "She asked me to call and wake you up."

Then I remembered the cute stewardess on the Chicago flight. "Okay, yeah, okay. I'm awake."

He said, "Get up and turn your television set on. It's eight-fifteen. This man whose program she wants you to watch is coming on."

So I got up and turned on the television.

He said, "Are you awake?"

"Yeah," I grunted.

"Are you sure you're awake? I want you to watch it. Make sure you watch it."

Then he said, "God bless you," and hung up! And I was left sitting, half awake, on my bed, with the television set blaring at me from across the room.

"This is dumb," I thought. "A guy calls me up. I don't know who he is, and he tells me to watch a program. I don't know what it is — and I'm sitting here like a dummy gonna watch it."

After a couple of commercials, orchestral music announced the beginning of the program. Then a choir was singing, "Evidence, evidence! Do they have enough evidence?"

Then a verse in the song asked, "If they were going to convict you of being a Christian, would they have enough evidence?" and, "What does your life show?"

What did my life show? I was a desperate, lonely, middle-aged man with hundreds of friends and acquaintances — none of whom could help me now.

After the choir had sung, the camera picked up this black man with a Bible in his hand, a nice-looking man who began talking about a verse in the Bible. He said that God loved the world so much that He gave His only Son, . . . *that whosoever believeth in him should not perish, but have everlasting life.* The speaker impressed me as a happy man whose life was "together" — unlike mine.

I picked up the Bible that I hadn't read in all these years and tried to find the verse he'd named — John 3:16. I had no clue as to where to find the book of John. I flipped from back to front and from front to back without any luck. Finally, I realized there must be a table of contents, and I looked and found it. And there, low on the page, I found the page reference for the Gospel According to St. John. I turned there and found John 3:16. I read it, and it said exactly what the man had read.

It said "everlasting life." I sat and thought how long everlasting was. I decided to call little Rosey. I thought he would like to hear this man, also.

I called Margie. Our divorce had been stormy and the subject of a lot of publicity. Consequently, she was never pleased to hear from me. "What do you want?" she asked icily.

"I really want you to let little Rosey watch this preacher on television. You can listen, too."

"I don't know, Rosey. What's the point? You never. . . ."

"Oh, please, Babe," I pled. "He's really going to want to hear this."

So she called little Rosey, and they began to watch Dr. Frederick K. C. Price that morning, just as I did. I don't know what the program meant to them, but it meant something to me. As Dr. Price moved from verse to verse, I began to see my need for God.

In spite of my Baptist pedigree, I recalled I knew nothing about God and Jesus and the Holy Spirit. I had been baptized when I was seven and I knew some gospel songs and hymns. But, as good as those things were, I had not made Jesus my friend. I had no relationship with God. What I did know about Him was religious and not personal. Suddenly I saw how badly I needed that personal dimension — a relationship.

As I listened to Fred Price teach the Bible, a thread of hope began to grow in my heart. His sermon was not a commentary on current events and the ills of society — I knew enough about those. Instead, he commented only on the text of the Bible — with abundant applications to my daily life.

The title of his program was "Ever-Increasing Faith" — and, as I continued to watch it, my meager faith became ever increasing. I made it from week to week by watching that program. If I was out of town, I would rush home Saturday night, call up Margie and little Rosey to make sure they were listening, too. Every other Sunday, I had Rosey with me, so he and I would watch together, and Margie would watch at her house.

One Saturday night, Rosey said, "Dad, can we go over there?"

"Over where?" I asked.

"You know — that man we've been watching on television. Can we go over there?"

"Oh, Rosey, I don't want to go over there."

"Why not, Dad?"

I didn't have a "why not." So I said, "Well, sometime we'll go over there."

"Tomorrow, Dad! Let's go tomorrow."

"Well, okay," I sighed.

At five-thirty the next morning, little Rosey woke up and said, "Dad, get up. Wake up, Dad. Let's go over there."

I looked at the clock and wondered if I were back in Giants' training camp in 1955. But, no, there was Rosey's glowing face. How could he glow like that at this hour? But it was the right time. We had heard you had to get there early to get a seat, and the Crenshaw district was a little distance from Burbank. So we got up, dressed, and went outside. A heavy early-morning fog lay on the valley floor. "It's too foggy to go to church," I thought to myself.

Rosey was reading my mind. "Dad," he said, "when we start somewhere, we don't turn back, do we?"

Little Rosey knew me well. It was the same as it had been when I was in the army driving around the countryside with Wally Choice. If I got lost going somewhere on a highway, I refused to turn back and retrace my steps. Instead, I always kept going in search of an alternate route.

I had made a virtue of my stubbornness by calling it persistence. Turning back from a goal after once setting out was a shameful thing — that's what I'd always told little Rosey. I could hear my own preaching — he had me pegged to the wall. The fog would not deter us.

When we arrived at Crenshaw Christian Center, cars were everywhere. So I parked in the red zone in front of the church.

A long line of people filled the sidewalk, waiting for the doors to open. It looked like a sold-out rock concert. We finally made it inside and, as first-time visitors, we got to sit in a special area. As we were being ushered to our seats, I noticed that everyone else was carrying a Bible. I hadn't been to church in about twenty years, but even then I didn't remember seeing that many Bibles. Little Rosey and I had not brought one.

They sang and took up "tithes and offerings." I knew what an offering was, but I had never heard of "tithes." *What could they be?* I wondered. I kept watching.

Finally, Dr. Price started speaking, but not from behind a pulpit. He walked as he spoke — across the platform, up and down the aisles. And, as he spoke, it was as if he were addressing me in counseling chambers after listening to me spill all my troubles.

He said that man is a spirit who lives in a flesh suit. And we need to regard our suits of flesh much as an astronaut regards the special clothing he needs to exist in space — essential, and yet not at the heart of his being.

Instead, at heart, man is a spiritual being, made by God in the image of God to rule over God's creation. And God placed His human creatures in the Garden of Eden to take care of it. They could, He told them, eat the fruit of any tree in the garden except one, a special tree called the tree of the knowledge of good and evil. If ever they ate that fruit, He added, they would die.

In the next scene, Satan, a creature of God who had fallen from heaven, came in the form of a beautiful and seductive serpent who called into doubt the things the Lord had told Adam and Eve. "What did God say?" he asked.

"We may eat the fruit of any tree in the garden," the woman answered, "except the tree in the middle of it. God told us not to eat the fruit of that tree or even touch it; if we do, we will die."

The serpent said, "Humph. God knows that once you eat of that tree, you will be like God yourselves."

So Eve ate the forbidden fruit and persuaded her husband to do the same thing. Then they lost the nature of God, which had been love and joy and happiness and peace, and took on the nature of Satan, which was rebelliousness against God. Their relationship with God was broken and they were expelled from the pleasant garden. The soil was cursed on man's account, and death entered their lives for the first time.

The destiny of Adam and Eve's children was to rob and kill, rape and pillage, and so on. Dr. Price said that Adam and Eve's descendants were born in a rebellious state, in an entirely different dimension from God. There was no way man could have a relationship with God because their natures were so different.

Yet God loved His creatures in spite of their rebellious ways. So, He provided a way for them to come back to Him, to get a new nature. He sent His Son, Jesus, to forgive man for making the wrong decision and to restore his relationship with God, to undo what Satan had done. When we take Jesus as our Savior from the consequences of a rebellious nature, then we become born again, Dr. Price explained.

My mind said, "Born again? Did he say born again? That's what born again is?"

Many questions I had been asking myself for years began to be answered that Sunday morning. I saw that it is possible to be involved in religion but not have a genuine relationship with God. I wanted to know this Jesus Dr. Price was talking about.

I became convinced that this was the missing element in my life. Through all my forty-six years I had tried to fill a hole in my life that God had put there and which only He could fill. But I had tried to fill it with people, with fun and pleasure, with good works, with money and power — all things that decay or get stolen or die.

I learned that John 3:16 means what it says — God gave His Son to get us back. But He never forces our love in return. No matter what our response or lack of it, His love is steady.

I had been saying, "Love me first and then, maybe, I'll love you back. . .if you don't ask too much."

I had thought that I could take the things that mattered — love and friendship — and give back the things that didn't matter — houses and cars and jewelry and clothes. No wonder I was in such a mess!

At the end of the service, Dr. Price asked anyone who wanted to accept Jesus and become a new person to raise his hand. A lot of thoughts came to my mind: "You're not going to raise your hand. All these people are going to be looking at you. You're a football player, a movie actor, a singer. You're somebody. By raising your hand, they're going to think you don't know anything. Don't raise your hand. You can do it later. This is your first time in this church, and you're going to raise your hand? Why don't you wait? You can do it later."

Up went my hand. The church was quiet. Tears began to flow down my face. They were tears of relief because I had at last found a hand to hold, the hand of God which would meet my need — the hand of a friend.

Then I saw that little Rosey had his hand up, too, and tears were running down his face. Afterwards, he and I and others who had raised their hands also were escorted to a counseling room. A counselor asked why little Rosey came along.

"He came to be with me," I explained.

But he said, "No, Dad. I came because I want to know Jesus, too."

Rosey was only seven, but he understood the choice he was making.

The two of us walked out of that church that morning as new creatures in Christ. When we got back to the car, I found a ticket tucked neatly under the windshield wiper. I didn't mind. I was too happy, and, anyway, I deserved it.

That was the beginning of a changed lifestyle for me. Little Rosey and I got Bibles and began to go to church. Soon we could find the Bible verses without looking in the table of contents. Instead of walking around with my head down and my face sad, my head was up, and I was smiling. Well, at least, more often than I had been. All my depression did not lift instantly — most, but not all.

After a few Sundays of regular church attendance, however, I got the biggest surprise of my life. I was standing out by the Oakwood Apartments clubhouse — looking at the mountains which encircle the San Fernando Valley. They were green and full of life. It was then I was startled to notice that my depression was gone. Happy, verdant scenes had, for a long time, evoked depression and self-pity in me. I had grown almost accustomed to it, like a sore tooth, but — now — it wasn't there!

I thought, "What's wrong?" I felt wonderful. I could not remember anything like this before. I had no problems, no pressure, nothing was bothering me, my mind was at ease, and my heart was at peace. Life was great! And it was because of God.

I had been chased home, but this time it was different. When I was a child, the defense of lying on my back with my feet up — ready for Arthur's pounce — had worked. But much worse than Arthur's pounce had threatened me in 1978 after Mama died, and my own defenses failed miserably. I thank God they did, because, when they failed, I finally discovered that I needed a relationship with God on His terms — one in which He, and not I, was Lord.

Once He was in charge, the battle against depression reached a decisive conclusion so effortlessly that I was unaware anything was happening until after it was over. The Bible says somewhere that "the battle is the Lord's." That's how it proved in my case. Jesus became my Lord and changed my life dramatically. I had an answer, at last, to Eva's question.

27

GOD HAS
A SENSE
OF HUMOR

One Saturday night, after we had been attending Crenshaw Christian Center for several months, little Rosey said, "Dad?"

"Yeah?"

"Could we take Mom to church with us tomorrow?"

"Oh, no," I thought. I didn't want to have anything to do with Margie. I had been before the judge. And he gave her the inside of the house, and me the outside! She had cost me plenty, and besides, the cumulative effect of two failed marriages had been enough to make me shy of women in general. It was a bachelor's life for me from here on out. "I don't think so, Rosey," I said.

"But, Dad, why not?"

I was smart enough to know that if I hurt my son, I hurt myself. And, no matter what my feelings about Margie might be, she was his mother. If I said anything against her, little Rosey would be hurt, and rightfully so. "Well, sometime," I said. "We'll take her sometime."

"Tomorrow, Dad. Tomorrow, huh?"

If I said no, he would ask, "Why not?" Then what was I going to say? So I called her, figuring that she would decline my invitation anyway. After all, my distaste for her company was more than matched by hers for mine.

"Babe," I said (the endearing address had persisted — somehow), "little Rosey and I were thinking, would you like to go to church with us?"

"Yes," she said, "I'd love to go."

"You would? Uh, well. . .we have to leave early."

"That's all right. I don't mind," she replied sweetly. "What time do you want me to be ready?"

"Six," I said.

"I'll be ready."

I didn't know what to make of it. She was being so nice.

The next morning, we picked Margie up at her place and went down to Crenshaw. This time, I found a legitimate parking space, and we got in line. We found seats near the front, and little Rosey sat between us. The service went along in its customary manner. But, after the service, Margie shocked me again. She raised her hand and went up for counseling. She accepted Jesus also, and began going with us to church every Sunday.

Several months later, I went home with Margie and little Rosey for lunch. As she walked down the hall away from me to put her things away, her figure caught my eye. When she re-emerged from her room and came walking back down the hall, I was struck again by the thought of how attractive she was. And, as she spoke to me, I felt none of the old irritation. In fact, her voice seemed almost as attractive as her face and figure.

"How about if I take you out to lunch sometime?" I blurted.

She looked at me cautiously, "Sometime."

"How about tomorrow?" I had learned something from my son.

"I suppose that would be okay," she smiled.

So I began to date my ex-wife. For the first time, I was dating a woman just for the pleasure of her company — without designs or ulterior motives. We had fun and enjoyed going places together. We laughed and had things to talk about. We had been together five years between 1970 and 1975, when we were married. But it had never been like this.

Not long after we began dating, we were sitting in a restaurant. I looked across the table at Margie. "I've been meaning to ask you something for some time now," I said.

"What's that?"

"That first Sunday I invited you to church with little Rosey and me, why did you accept so easily? I was sure you'd turn me down."

She laughed, "That's easy. I never saw anyone change the way you did in those months after you started watching Fred Price on television. And you only got better when you started going down there in person.

"You know me, Rosey, I'm a pragmatist. I wanted to know more about anything that made such a dramatic and wonderful change in you. It had to be real. And, in addition, I had the advantage of having watched Fred on television for a while before you extended the invitation. I already liked him. He's intelligent and well-spoken, and he doesn't mince words. Actually, by the time you called, I was eager to go. Your timing was perfect, my dear."

God has a sense of humor. As I grew in my faith, I began to feel differently about being a husband and father. A healing was going on in me and I became confident that, with God's help, I would no longer resent the responsibilities of matrimony. In fact, I believed I would relish them. And I began to pray for a beautiful woman who would love God and me and my son.

It was not long after I started praying like that when Margie invited me to lunch at her place that Sunday after church and caught my eye the way she did. Then I found that the Holy Spirit was teaching me to love and forgive, and, at the same time, He was loosening the straps of fear, bitterness, and emptiness that had wrapped themselves around my chest — like those straps I had imagined as a small boy that police put around prisoners when they arrested them. And all this was happening in the context of a growing romance with Margie.

For the first time I knew how it felt to be in love because I was falling in love with Margie. I liked the way she was. Everything she did pleased me, and our conversations were so easy and gratifying.

Through them I learned to feel good about giving and receiving love verbally.

As our courtship progressed, Margie's caution gave way slowly. Whenever she expressed that caution, as, for example, when I suggested a date and she said "maybe" or "sometime," I inevitably replied, "That's all right. Don't worry about it."

One day, this light-handed attitude of mine finally provoked a question from Margie. "How come you're so relaxed about this? When we went together before, you were insistent and wouldn't take 'no' for an answer. What gives?"

"I'm relaxed," I explained mischievously, "because I know you couldn't get anyone better than me."

Margie's eyes flashed, "What do you mean by that?"

"Just this, Babe. I'm a new creature in Christ, and that makes all the difference. I'm a brand new man — and you can't get any better than brand new."

"Okay, okay," she smiled. "I got it."

After we dated for about two years, Margie and I decided that we were ready to give marriage a serious try. This time, each of us had a foundation in our lives, Jesus Christ, Who gave us assurance that we could succeed in Him in spite of our former failure. Even so, marriage was a scary thing to contemplate. We approached it slowly and cautiously, and we sought counsel from our pastor, Fred Price. Little Rosey, of course, was pleased as could be — although, to his credit, he never nagged us to get remarried. He was trusting God, too.

When the time came, on June 8, 1981, I asked a good friend and federal court judge, David V. Kenyon, to perform the ceremony. (Fred later inquired why we didn't ask him to perform it. We explained that we had heard so much about the lengthy pre-marital counseling he required of any couple before he would perform a ceremony for them that we felt a little intimidated. "You should have said something," he told us. The sort of re-marriage we contemplated would probably have been given special consideration. But we didn't know that at the time.)

The ceremony was a quiet gathering in our home. Little Rosey was not there because we wanted it to be a surprise for him. Only a few of our friends attended it. But, as I looked deeply into Margie's baby-blue eyes and said, "I do," I did it with perfect peace and I meant it with all my heart.

But I have gotten way ahead of myself. Back in 1979, I began looking for preachers and teachers and other Christian leaders who had made a name for themselves. As I met them, I began asking myself, "Which one am I going to be like?" I was like a little kid in a candy store with a blank check. I had come to realize I didn't know anything about God and I was hungry to learn everything I could as fast as I could.

In a short time, however, I encountered the common problem of every serious student. The more I studied, the less I knew. But still it was wonderful getting to know the Lord.

I learned that every Christian has a calling, which is to represent the Kingdom of God on earth. But not everyone will agree to follow that calling.

I also began to get a perspective on the course of my life before my conversion. The Bible comments often on the futility of trying to accomplish anything apart from God. "Unless the Lord builds the house," the psalmist wrote, "they who build it labor in vain." (Ps. 127:1). That had been the case with all my strenuous efforts at the head of Giant Step. Yes, there were measurable and positive results of the Giant Step program according to strict federal standards. But I knew in my heart that it had left me sapped — feeling that nothing lasting or important had been accomplished.

My work with kids and old people had been "my thing," not God's. I was trying to earn love, instead of letting God's love flow through me to other people. I not only had the cart before the horse, I was trying to substitute the cart for the horse.

During the fall of 1979, I was booked on a lecture tour of various college campuses. With the zeal of a new convert, I could think of nothing to talk about on that tour except what God had come to mean to me. And I earnestly urged my listeners to consider the claims of Christ on their lives and to respond with repentance and faith. Amen, brother!

One day, my booking agent called me. "Rosey, what are you doing out there?!"

"What do you mean?"

"I'm getting complaints that you're delivering sermons instead of lectures. You're not winning any points, Rosey."

I said, "Do you mean to tell me that I have the answer to the world's problems, and they don't want to hear it? I spent forty-six years looking for this. Other people are in trouble like I was, and I have the answer. And they don't want it?"

"That's right," he said. "And they have a right not to want it, while you have no right to jam it down their throats under false pretenses."

He had a point, but I wasn't ready to hear it. Instead I checked out a book about Jesus and the intellect and began to try to find out how to answer the questions and objections that those college students had been putting to me out there on the lecture circuit. After trying to read it for a while, however, I said, "Lord, this is too much. I can't learn all this."

I felt depressed and I lay down for a nap. When I woke up, words came clearly in my mind. "No one told you to learn all that stuff. Just tell them about Jesus. You know the answer. You don't need to know what is *not* the answer. Just tell them about Jesus. Speak what He said."

I thought, "Wow, man. That's great. Just tell people about Jesus. If some don't want to hear about Jesus, I'll go to other people who do."

Jesus was hated and eventually crucified by people who didn't want to hear what He was saying. As His servant I should not expect to win any popularity contests for proclaiming His message.

All I had to do was the best I could. I began to study the Bible harder, in order to know for sure what Jesus said.

When I refused to stop telling what had happened to me, all my speaking dates were canceled. So, by the time Margie and I remarried in 1981, I was out of work. Bills were coming in, and condominium time caught up with us. We received notice that we had to have $5,000 down and $17,000 more in a little while. You want to know how much I had? Nothing. Margie was crying.

Just months before, I would have gone into a tailspin in the face of such circumstances. But not now. I said, "Hold it. Margie, you and little Rosey come here."

"The devil has brought this upon us, but God is now going to use it to teach us more about His love and power," I announced bravely.

Then I opened my Bible and read, "Build up your strength in union with the Lord and by means of His mighty power. Put on all the armor that God gives you, so that you will be able to stand up against the devil's evil tricks. . . .Do all this in prayer, asking for God's help. Pray on every occasion, as the Spirit leads. . . . keep alert and never give up" (Eph. 6:10,11,18).

I closed the book, motioned for us to join hands, and said, "That's what we're going to do, pray. Father, we need Your help now. We have these obligations and no way to meet them that we can see, but we trust You to provide what we need at the right time. You told us not to worry about food, clothing, housing, and the like. So, we give our worry over to You. Help us not to worry. In Jesus' name, Amen!"

Margie and little Rosey chimed, "Amen."

"It's up to Him now," I said. Margie dried her tears and went back to fixing lunch. I sat down to read the Bible, and little Rosey went to his room. The anxiety and turmoil were gone. A strange peace prevailed in our house.

About an hour later, the phone rang. It was a Christian group asking me to go on campus tours with their ministry. It did not entail a lot of money. It did not meet all our needs, but it was the beginning of God's answer to that prayer. In time, the complete answer came and the roof remained in place over our heads. That was the first big test of faith, and the Lord didn't let us down.

That first invitation to speak to college students about Jesus led to others. Soon I was reasonably busy traveling about and doing that — and loving it.

However, one night I was coming out of the Rock Church in Virginia Beach, Virginia, where I had spoken about my testimony and my work with college students. Bart Pierce, one of the associate pastors, stopped me. "Rosey," he asked, "you're going all over the country and speaking to kids about the Lord?"

"Yeah?" I replied curiously.

"But what about the kids in your neighborhood? Your people?"

"Hmmm, you've given me something to think about." And I thought, "Why did he have to say that?"

But he was right. God was speaking to me through Bart — calling me to see that Giant Step had not been entirely in vain after all. My reading of the Bible had already helped me to understand that God's hand had been on my life, working out a plan since before my birth. That childhood baptism had circumcised my heart, unbeknownst to me. And slowly, through the years that followed my watery burial, God's hand had weaned me from one idol after another. It was a mystery, and none of the time had been wasted, in spite of how I may have felt about it. Everything had been designed to prepare me to do the thing God was calling me to do.

The weight of caring I had felt for inner-city kids who are menaced on every side by drugs and violence was something that God placed on me. It was He Who cared for them, not I. That care had brought Giant Step to birth, after which it grew to become so great a burden that it helped to drive me to my knees where I belonged — and from where I could find God's power to build that house of refuge for my ghetto children.

I called Margie, "Babe, we have to go back and get those kids in the inner cities."

She didn't understand, but she was ready to help me do whatever I believed we needed to do. So Margie and I set up an organization in Los Angeles called "Are You Committed?" Again, Willie Naulls had a big hand in this. He helped us find our building and set up operations. Today the organization is headquartered on South Grand Street in Los Angeles, squarely within the district that was most affected by the Watts riot in 1965.

Our building serves as a center for ministry to the whole community. It contains both training and teaching facilities in which young people learn the Bible and a trade. The front section of the building is a clothing outlet (we are located on the edge of the Los Angeles garment district) where our trainees get first-hand experience in retail sales.

"Are You Committed?" also provides classroom instruction and hands-on training in the latest computer hardware and software. Its Job Bank seeks to place qualified youngsters in responsible positions in the business community. The "A.Y.C." Business Opportunity Resource Center contracts with a variety of professional groups and individuals who provide, free of charge to AYC referrals, the help they need to evaluate, plan, implement and run an independent business — thus working to awaken and sustain the entrepreneurial spirit in the inner city.

In recent years, "Are You Committed?" has also entered into a partnership with Southland Corporation whereby it operates a Seven-Eleven market in south Los Angeles, staffed by "Are You Committed?" personnel. This gives the kids we work with a chance to move up within the Southland Corporation, or to gain experience for other enterprises, both in the community and elsewhere.

An important basic ingredient of the AYC program is its remedial reading center. The teaching of reading in America has become a public scandal, well documented elsewhere (for example, in *Why Johnny Can't Read* by Rudolf Flesch, New York: Harper and Row, 1955). The result is that illiteracy and semi-literacy have become commonplace in a nation that once boasted one of the highest literacy rates in the world.

No one can hold down a decent job in American society without good reading skills. The AYC Reading Resource Center offers services that evaluate deficiencies and plans individualized programs to surmount them, employing tutoring, computer training, and study materials.

The motto of "Are You Committed?" is:

If you
give a man a fish,
you help him for a day.
If you
teach a man to fish,
you help him for a lifetime.

28

A NEW
OUTLOOK ON
POLITICS

In 1979, while Jesus was turning my life around, President Carter was deciding to run for office again. With my new outlook, I was concerned afresh about what he stood for and whether or not to campaign for him. My personal contact with him was limited to that phone conversation in 1975 when he called me to ask me to campaign for him.

Margie and I were watching the news on television one evening (I had taken to spending a fair amount of time at her place by late 1979). Some item came on which spelled more trouble for Carter's administration, I forget which. In 1979 he had enjoyed some notable successes, most notably the Israeli-Egyptian peace treaty and the SALT II Arms Limitation Agreement with the Soviets. But, otherwise, it was a bleak year, marked by the nuclear accident at Three-Mile Island in Pennsylvania, soaring inflation, congressional foot-dragging on the President's energy program, high interest rates, the falling out of orbit of the Skylab space station, and the overthrow of the Shah of Iran — to mention only a few.

By midsummer the President's standing in public opinion polls was dipping badly. On July 17, he called his cabinet officers together and asked that all of them submit their resignations. In October, he permitted the former Shah to enter the United States to receive medical treatment, but his kindness to an old ally backfired when the Iranians seized the embassy on November 4.

Carter's personal style as Chief Executive received notice, too. He eliminated a lot of the ceremony around the White House. No longer did trumpets announce the arrival of the presidential family at official receptions, nor did a color guard march in front of them. State dinners ended by eleven at night, much earlier than had been the case since anyone could remember.

The Carters' youngest child, Amy, who was eleven when I first visited the White House with little Rosey in 1978, attended the local public school. Sometimes she enlivened things in and around the mansion by bringing some of her schoolmates home to play.

These things bespoke a down-home style in my fellow Georgian that I respected and liked.

I told Margie I was going to call him. I had never tried to call and talk to him before. But now I wanted to encourage him.

"You're going to call the President?" Margie's voice was filled with disbelief.

"Yeah, I'm going to call the President," I said, taking up her challenge.

"Right!" she laughed.

So I called the White House and said, "This is Rosey Grier. May I speak to the President?"

The operator said, "Just a minute," and she switched me to someone else who said, "This is the White House."

I asked again to speak to the President, and the second person said, "I'm sorry, you can't just call up and speak to the President. His schedule does not permit him to take unscheduled calls."

"Okay, thanks," I said, and hung up.

Margie laughed at me and said, "You're going to call the President. Right?"

So I called again and went through the same routine, got the same answer, and hung up again. Then Margie really got on my case, "Yeah, right, you're going to call up the President!"

After thinking about it for a little while, I remembered the name of President Carter's secretary — Susan Clough. I called the White

House yet another time, but this time I asked for her. The switchboard transferred me to her secretary. When I gave her my name, she transferred me to Susan, who said, "How may I help you?"

I said, "This is Rosey Grier calling."

She said, "*The* Rosey Grier?"

"Wow!" I thought. "She knows me." I said, "Yes. And the reason I called is that I care about what is going on and I want to encourage President Carter."

"That's wonderful," she said. "I wish he could come here to the phone and hear you say that, but you understand how his schedule is. Perhaps you could write him a note."

"Well, would you tell him that I called and I want to talk to him."

She said she would, but she didn't ask for my phone number. And, since my number was unlisted, I supposed that was the end of that.

Two weeks later, the phone rang, and Margie answered it. I was watching her, and her face showed panic, which is rare in Margie who always remains cool.

"Who is it?" I asked.

She put the phone in my face and said, "The White House."

"Mr. Grier, this is Susan Clough calling you from the White House. The President will see you on December 21. Can you make it?"

I was struck speechless. This was the last thing I expected. But, I got hold of myself and tried to sound casual as I said, "Yes, I can make it."

After I hung up, Margie and I stared at each other a moment.

"Well, what did he want?" she demanded, breaking the silence.

"He wants to see me in two weeks. What am I going to tell him?"

"That's your problem. You called him."

"Yeah, I called him, but I wanted to talk to him on the phone, not face to face."

"Let's pray," she said, her tone shifting from teasing to serious.

We joined hands and prayed I would know just what to say. I managed to relax in faith after that prayer for one day. But the second day I started to get nervous again, worrying about what I would say. Nothing came to mind, and my distress grew.

I spoke to a group of American Indians a few days later, and I mentioned to them my upcoming meeting with Carter. They had something they wanted to say to him — they gave me a paper to take to him. But what I wanted to say was not on that paper.

After a while, I started listening to the bushes! God spoke to Moses from a bush, perhaps? . . .

Thirteen days after Susan Clough's phone call, I was at a hotel in Washington, still praying for an answer — without success. Finally, it was time for my appointment. I was sitting in the waiting room when some senators came out and spotted me. They talked awhile and asked what I was doing there. I put my hand over my mouth and mumbled something.

They said, "Well, if there is anything we can do to help you, let us know."

When I got into the room where the President was, however, a sense of awe came over me. The responsibility of being in the public eye came home to me. I thought I had known before, but this was reality.

Jimmy Carter came over to me, shook my hand, and said, "My dear friend."

I bent over and hugged him.

He seemed to like that. When I saw his smile, my nervousness about what I ought to say disappeared. I told him that I and a lot of people loved America and wanted to help him be the best president he could be.

He said, "I'm glad you're going to help me. I'm really glad."

President Carter asked what I was doing, and I told him I was speaking around the country. I asked if there was something I could tell the people. I figured, in light of the forthcoming election, he would want me to say something favorable about him.

But he said, "Tell the people to love one another. Tell them your way. Talk to the people the way you do."

That made me feel good.

The experience taught me that Jesus meant it when He told His disciples, "Do not worry ahead of time about what you are going to say; when the time comes, say whatever is then given to you. For the words you speak will not be yours; they will come from the Holy Spirit" (Mark 13:11). Again, my faith was growing. I trust the Lord, now, to help me know what to say and to give me wisdom. And I don't fret about it ahead of time, it isn't worth it.

I got to know the Carters better after that, and, when things were rough — as they often were in 1980 when inflation rose fifteen percent in six months and the hostage crisis dragged on — I called to offer them encouragement. The Soviets invaded Afghanistan at the end of 1979, and President Carter was compelled to urge the U.S. Olympic Committee to boycott the 1980 Summer Games in Moscow. I told his staff that, as an athlete, I understood and supported this hard decision, and I assured them that most athletes probably felt as I did.

It was not long after that when I was invited a second time to spend the night at the White House — when I came to town to attend a State Department event. This time I accepted immediately, and, this time, President Carter was going to be there during my visit. It was early in the year and the presidential primaries were looming on the close horizon.

When I came in from the State Department event, it was not late, so I told the agent who took me to my room I wanted to say hello to the President. He said he would check. A few minutes later, he returned, took me to the President's door and left. The President was talking on the phone when I tapped on the slightly ajar door and peaked my head through. He looked up and motioned for me to come in and sit down. He was barefoot, dressed in dungarees and a shirt. When he finished a few moments later, he asked, "Are you hungry?"

"Always," I chuckled.

"Me, too. C'mon, let's see what we can find to eat in the kitchen."

But when we got there, we smelled smoke. "Oh, oh," he murmured, as we walked into the kitchen. It was filled with smoke because somebody had left ham hocks on the stove over a low heat, and they were burning.

"You get on out of here," I said. "I'll take care of this."

"Don't get carried away, Rosey," he laughed. "This is not a life-threatening emergency. The exhaust fan switch is over there. Would you turn it on?"

"Okay," I acceded. The smoke was thick and I worried that a Secret Service man would come barging in when he heard the commotion.

President Carter turned off the fire under the skillet and, after flicking the exhaust switch, I grabbed a pot-holder from the counter, picked up the smoking pan and took it over to the sink.

After that, we raided the refrigerator and found some cookies. They were good, but I could tell the President would have preferred those ham hocks.

As I listened that night, I could see the President wanted to be on top of everything. He took seriously the adage of Harry Truman who put a sign on his desk which said, "The buck stops here." And I began to appreciate what a solemn and lonely task was his. For example, later, in April, 1980, he authorized an attempt to rescue the Iranian hostages by army rangers — over the objections of his Secretary of State, Cyrus Vance. Three of Colonel Charlie Beckwith's helicopters broke down in a sandstorm and the mission ended in failure. Vance resigned and President Carter named Senator Edmund Muskie of Maine to replace him.

President Carter was an excellent teacher. I learned much about the workings of politics from him. He explained clearly and simply how things get done, the meetings and people which are involved. As I listened to him describe how he had to grapple with Congress, I began to wonder how our nation manages to survive the ongoing power struggles between selfish people in influential positions. But I was glad that my understanding was growing. I trusted it would help me to make my decisions more wisely in the future.

The same week that I visited the White House, I tried to get in touch with Teddy Kennedy to find out what he was going to do. Some of his friends said he would run for President and others said that he wasn't going to. I wanted to hear it from his own mouth. I called his office, and they told me he was too busy to meet with me. Then I called Jackie, but she did not call me back. I did reach Ethel at Hickory Hill, and she explained that Teddy was awfully busy. "And everyone wants to talk to him," she said.

In August, 1979, polls had indicated that Democrats preferred Teddy over the President by a big margin. And, of course, I felt a strong attachment to Teddy and the family. Still, it was troubling not to be able to reach him for a talk. I need that personal contact to make important decisions. I told President Carter, back in 1976 during our phone conversation, that if he would sincerely try to do the things he was promising, I would stay with him. And I had since found a kindred spirit in the President who was not only a Georgian, but also a sincere Christian. Finally, I decided to go with him.

When newspaper stories saying that I was going to support President Carter began to appear, I got a call from my young friend, Courtney Kennedy. She asked me, "How could you support Carter over my uncle? My uncle will make a better President."

"Courtney," I replied, "I have no doubt that your uncle would make a fine President. But I have given my word and I have to keep it."

"But, Rosey," she asked, "what has Carter ever done for the blacks?"

"Sweetheart," I said, "no one can excel the Kennedy record for courageous support of my race in its struggle for equality. But it's not fair to imply that Carter doesn't care about us. I believe he has done the best he could."

What I didn't say was that the question of support for civil rights had — in the twelve years since her father's death — become a political shibboleth. It was used by everyone, and, consequently, had come to mean less and less.

Reporters began asking me why I supported Carter over Kennedy. I told them I liked both men very much and that it pained me to have to take sides. But, since I had to, I was standing with President Carter because he loved the Lord and was sincerely trying to carry out his campaign promises. In addition, I pointed to his unparalleled record of appointing blacks to government positions.

I campaigned hard, because I believed Jimmy Carter deserved a second term. A lot of Democrats shared my opinion, and support for his renomination grew stronger during the spring primaries.

The Republicans met in their national convention in Detroit, July 14-17. Ronald Reagan had swept the primaries and took the nomination on the first ballot. He selected George Bush, one of his opponents in the primaries, to be his running mate.

I attended the Democratic Convention which was held in New York, August 11-14. I, of course, was a Carter supporter and I was wearing a Carter badge which advertised my allegiance. When I saw some of the young Kennedys whom I had known since 1968, I greeted them affably, but their youth did not allow them to be charitable with me. They let me know what they thought of my advocacy of their uncle's opponent — in no uncertain terms.

It was painful — very painful, in fact. Playing football had taught me to be at peace, in a way, with my opponents. After a game, win or lose, I shook the other guy's hand and said, "See you next time."

Back at my hotel room, I knelt down and asked the Lord to help me. I wanted Him to show me if I had treated my old friends unfairly or had done something to earn their wrath. I was upset enough that I found it hard to sleep that night. But, finally, I did drift off, and, when I opened my eyes as daylight crept around the drapes and into my room, I believe God gave me an answer to my prayer. It seemed that He was speaking these words to my heart:

"I have allowed this to happen to free you from your idolatry. You must have no other gods before Me. I alone am the Lord."

Idolatry is a subtle thing. I had never seen mine before that moment. God sent Bobby, Ethel, Jackie, and the others as His gifts into my life. But I had focused my sight on the gift to the exclusion of the giver. And that, I found out, is something God will not tolerate. Jesus said, "You shall know the truth, and the truth will set you free." I was set free that morning. My hurt and rejection left, and I had a good time at the convention.

The President took the nomination on the first ballot and Walter Mondale was named again to be his running mate. As we left New York, the race was on. The Carter campaign stressed his achievements in the energy crisis and in helping to negotiate the peace between Egypt and Israel. Reagan, however, pointed repeatedly to inflation, still running at a crippling fifteen percent, and record unemployment. And he offered a convincing program of tax and spending cuts to cure these problems. The American people bought it, and President Carter carried only the states of Florida, Georgia, Hawaii, Maryland, Minnesota, Rhode Island, and West Virginia. Reagan won by a landslide.

I had grown to love Jimmy Carter, and his defeat in November came as a blow to me. I hurt for many days, but life went on, and my relationship with God was growing daily. I was learning to give thanks in every circumstance, especially those I didn't understand or found painful. As a consequence, depression didn't have a chance with me any longer.

The thing that threatened to depress me most in those days was the loss of my closeness with the Kennedys. Things were never the same after 1980. Perhaps that loss was inevitable, but it grieved me. I owe Bobby and the entire family an immeasurable debt of gratitude. They helped me grow up and to discover the wider world which had long been part of their wonderfully broad perspective.

29

FREE AT LAST!

I studied the Bible and watched the new administration during those first years President Reagan was in office. Then, one day, I got a call to go to Washington for a congressional hearing on the proposed constitutional amendment to allow prayer in public schools. Some of my old friends were there — Meadowlark Lemon, Lenny Moore, Tom Landry, Joe Gibbs, and Mark Mosley. Meadowlark, a former Harlem Globetrotter, is the "Clown Prince of Basketball." Joe Gibbs is the head coach of the Washington Redskins, and Mark is a field goal kicker for the 'Skins. Demond Wilson, who co-starred in the television series, "Sanford and Sons," and is now a preacher, was there.

After the hearing, we went to the White House to meet with President Reagan. I had not seen him in person since that time, back in the sixties, when I was with the Bob Hope troupe returning from the trip to Vietnam — and he, as Governor of California, had welcomed us back.

We all came by in a line to shake his hand, and, as I waited my turn, I noticed that nearly everybody was saying, "We're praying for you, Mr. President."

I thought to myself, "I'm not going to say that. Instead, I'm going to do it — right on the spot!"

So, when my turn came, I said, "Mr. President, I'd like to pray for you right now. Is that all right with you?"

"Rosey, I'd like that," he smiled.

I laid my hands on him and he bowed his head. The others gathered 'round and joined in — praying in agreement with us. And, as I stood there praying and with my hands resting on his shoulders, I sensed that Ronald Reagan knew the Lord.

Back in California, I urged people to write their congressmen and senators on the prayer issue. When it was voted down, I was stung to see that many of those who voted against the amendment were men I had supported and worked for in years past. And, when I asked why they had voted against it, they said the issue was political, not real — an excuse I regarded as particularly lame. That was the beginning of my disenchantment with the Democratic party.

In 1984, I did not participate in the Democratic primary. I might have, because Jesse Jackson was running, but he never called me. And I continued steadfast in my refusal to support anyone before I talked with him or her personally.

Although Jesse was not speaking on the issues of prayer, abortion, and morality — things which were now vitally important to me — I would have liked to have campaigned for him as the first black presidential candidate, and as a man who had impressed me favorably in what I had seen and heard of him.

But, after the primaries, when the Democrats decided on their platform and nominated former Vice-President Fritz Mondale and Congresswoman Geraldine Ferraro as candidates, I found President Reagan's candidacy becoming more attractive to me.

Not long after that, I found myself on an airplane sitting next to a leading Democratic fund raiser. When I told her I believed abortion was wrong and ought to be illegal, she became incensed. "I can't believe you'd say that. Without abortion, how can we reduce the number of babies being born to welfare recipients?"

I thought to myself, "Lady, you took your mask off when you said that." Her remark had all the charm of one of Hitler's harangues about the master race. The Great Society isn't working, and public assistance is getting out of hand. So the solution is to kill off the babies!

Abortion is an act of violence directed against the poor and under-privileged.

After that, my mind was made up. I called Margie, "Honey, we're changing political parties!" Without any public fanfare, we quietly switched our registration with the county registrar of voters from Democratic to Republican.

The next thing I knew, President Reagan called me from his ranch in Santa Barbara. "Rosey," he said, "I know you're on the 'other side,' but I remembered your prayer and I decided to call you anyway — to see if you would be willing to help me in this year's campaign."

"Mr. President," I replied, "I want you to be among the first to know that my wife and I have recently switched our registrations. We stand ready to help you in any way we can."

President Reagan understands what this country needs most — reconciliation. We need to forgive and embrace one another again. The mantles of Martin Luther King, Jr. and of John and Robert Kennedy — the mantles of racial equality and national brotherhood — were trampled underfoot in the streets of Watts and in the White backlash that swept Richard Nixon into power.

On both sides we need to stop lashing back. We need to lay aside our weapons and hear the call of God to each of us to come into His kingdom — where there is no room for arrogance and pride, and where the greatest one is the servant of all.

No need is greater than our need to be reconciled to God and, in turn, to one another. My life, with its history of broken marriages and failed commitments, is a parable of the kingdom. When I finally called on God to help me — beginning with my desperate recitations of the Lord's Prayer — He took the broken pieces of my life and made me whole. Then He took the broken pieces of my family and made it whole. Those are miracles of restoration and reconciliation that point us to God as the authentic source of supply for all our needs.

Centuries ago, Paul, the apostle of Christ, was arraigned before a king named Agrippa. As he addressed the charges that had been brought against him, he described the work God had given him to do: ". . .to open their eyes and turn them from the darkness to the light and from the power of Satan to God, so that through their faith in Me they will have their sins forgiven and receive their place among God's chosen people" (Acts 26:18).

My eyes were opened. I turned from darkness to light and from Satan's power to God's. And, through faith, my sins were forgiven and I received my place among God's chosen people. And now I serve God by helping others to experience the same thing. That is what the Church is supposed to be doing on earth. . .not forcing everybody to believe alike but showing God's love to everyone.

The Bible is not the white man's tool to keep the black man under control. It is the black man's passport to freedom, as well as the white man's. It is the means by which all of God's children — black and white, Jew and Gentile, Protestant and Catholic — will indeed join hands and sing, "Free at last! Free at last! Thank God Almighty, we are free at last!"

When President Reagan visited the Bittenberg cemetery in West Germany in which German soldiers — some of them members of the Waffen SS, a supremely racist group — were buried, outraged cries came from around the globe. Reagan's point in making the visit, alas, was missed. That point was not martyrdom, nor its rights or wrongs. The point was reconciliation.

In the absence of forgiveness, we inevitably foster hatred. And persecution and injustice thrive in an environment of resentment. The past is dead. Not one day that's past can be changed. Keeping hurts alive is the surest way to see them repeat themselves.

President Reagan was criticized for thinking that a career in acting could prepare him for the presidency. Now people criticize him for failing to perform as a polished actor in the presidency. But his ability to communicate his feelings is more important than eloquence or stirring phrases. I am thankful that we have such a man at the helm. It is God's blessing on our nation.

After I spoke at the 1984 Republican Convention in Dallas (August 20-23), a reporter asked why I had changed my party affiliation and decided to support Reagan. I recited my opposition to abortion and my advocacy of school prayer and the ways in which Reagan took positions on those questions which satisfied me, whereas the positions of the other candidates did not. And I spoke at length about my urgent desire to see our nation united — its divergent groups and races reconciled — under God.

That speech and interview constituted my Republican debut. After that, reporters wanted to know, "If Bobby Kennedy were still alive, would you still support him?"

I said, "Yes, if he believed what I believe and stood for what I can support."

"But aren't you a Kennedy man?"

"No, I'm God's man. I owe allegiance to no other."

Reporters consistently brushed that answer aside, refusing to take it seriously. "But what about all the blacks who are out of work?" they objected.

"Injustices against black people need to be set right. And, thanks to the civil rights movement, the laws are in place which stand in the way of institutional injustice. Now we have reached closer to the heart of the problem, the inherent wickedness of human nature.

"The answer to that wickedness cannot be found in legislative or judicial decisions. They can never break the chains of fear and hate that bind our lives. But God promised, long ago, that 'if My people, who are called by My name, shall humble themselves, and pray, and seek My face, and turn from their wicked ways; then will I hear from heaven, and will forgive their sin, and will heal their land.' (2 Chron. 7:14).

"The answer to wickedness lies not in the halls of Congress nor in the corridors of the White House. It sits, instead, atop a hill called Golgotha, and it stands at the entrance of an empty tomb."

An Afterword

Now I set aside my pen and rest. My story has been told — at least the first fifty-four years of it. How much I have to be thankful for! My parents and siblings, the years of growing up on Georgia's soil and New Jersey's pavement, Penn State, the Giants, the Rams, show biz. The joy and heartbreak of those few months with Bobby Kennedy and the shadowy years of gloom that followed until, at last, the light broke through. How I rejoice in that light. It has turned my sorrow to gladness and restored my family to me — and (the bigger trick) me to my family! It has helped me begin to understand all that came before its dawning. And, one day, I'll understand fully, just as I have been fully understood.

God bless you. I'd love to hear from you. My address is 3005 South Grand, Los Angeles, California 90007.

July 8, 1985

Dear Rosey:

I want to send my personal congratulations
and best wishes for the work you have
undertaken through "Are You Committed."

Under your leadership, this fine organization
is helping others to help themselves. You
are dedicated to enabling people obtain the
skills they need to make their way in life and
contribute to the community welfare. Your
method is private enterprise, your motivation
is Christian compassion. As President, I am
grateful to you.

Nancy wants me to thank you again for all
the work you have done against the abuse
of alcohol and drugs. God bless you.

Sincerely,

Ronald Reagan

Mr. Rosey Grier
"Are You Committed"
3005 South Grand Avenue
Los Angeles, California 90007